'Diligently researched . . . accurately po[rtrays] shape-shifting and flamboyant talent'

'This well researched biography shows slow motion car crashes played out against real artistic achievement'   *Q*

'An incredible amount of independent and interesting research . . . John Neil Munro has done an excellent job at portraying John Martyn's character'   *Spencer Cozens*

'Danny Thompson gives a good anecdote, and illuminating interviews with former bandmates flesh out the account of the sessions for Martyn's best-loved album *Solid Air*, its title track a lament for his improbable best friend Nick Drake'   *Time Out*

'Munro has done his homework, and done it well'   *Stornoway Gazette*

'Very readable and very thorough . . . meticulous research . . . hilarious and sometimes hair-raising anecdotes'   *Northern Echo*

'Perhaps the definitive biography of the musical maverick that is John Martyn'   *Dorset Echo*

'Munro does a service to music history as he explicates and makes arguments for some of Martyn's oft-neglected later endeavours . . . There is no doubt that Martyn is as woefully misunderstood as he is loved. By continuously retraining his focus upon Martyn's music, Munro is able to bring a much-needed level of critical depth to the forefront of his book'

www.music-box.online.com

SOME PEOPLE ARE CRAZY:
THE JOHN MARTYN STORY

John Neil Munro

Foreword by Ian Rankin

First published in 2007 by Polygon
This revised edition published in 2010 by Polygon,
an imprint of Birlinn Ltd

West Newington House
10 Newington Road
Edinburgh
EH9 1QS

www.polygonbooks.co.uk

9 8 7 6 5 4 3 2 1

Copyright © John Neil Munro, 2010
Foreword copyright © Ian Rankin, 2010

ISBN 978 1 84697 165 5

British Library Cataloguing-in-Publication Data
A catalogue record for this book is available on request
from the British Library.

Every effort has been made to trace the
copyright holders of the photographs in this book.
We would be grateful to know of any omissions.

Typeset by DataConnection
Printed and bound by
Clays Ltd, St Ives plc

Contents

This book is dedicated to Edinburgh 1977, Colin Ritchie, Michael Kay and Bruce Paton.

Foreword

A few years back I was invited to be the guest on BBC Radio Four's *Desert Island Discs*. I had to choose the eight records I couldn't live without. There were tracks by the Rolling Stones, Van Morrison and others. But at the end of the show, presenter Sue Lawley then asked, 'And if you could only have one of these records, Ian . . .?' Well, there was only one contender: 'Solid Air' by John Martyn.

The strange thing is, I'd travelled down to London that day for the recording, and had managed to find time for lunch with my literary agent. The sun was shining and we could hear gruff laughter from one of the pavement tables. When we left, I saw John Martyn seated there with a couple of friends – and I bottled it, lacking the courage to go up to him and say 'Guess why I'm here?'

I'd seen Martyn play live just once, around 1977 or '78 at the old Odeon in Edinburgh. A school pal called John Scott had loaned me *Solid Air* a couple of years before, and I'd become a fan. When I worked as a hi-fi reviewer in London, I would use the title track as my 'reference work', comparing turntables, amps and speakers by playing it. By then I'd bought a slew of other John Martyn albums. I loved everything about him – the voice that somehow blended gravel with butterscotch; the majestic guitar-playing; the tunes; the lyrics. From interviews, I knew he could be 'difficult' and that his health was suffering. Fans told stories and offered anecdotes. It was sometimes impossible to separate the legend from the truth. That's why it was such a pleasure to pick up John Neil Munro's *Some People Are Crazy* when it was first published in 2007. Munro is obviously a fan, but the book is no hagiography. The John Martyn who emerges is a complex figure with a huge appetite for life to go with his boundless musical talent. There's plenty of humour, too, to leaven the darker reminiscences.

And then I heard that John Martyn had died. I felt numb, but then was invited round to a friend's house for a night of celebration – our 'wake' for a man we'd admired. Three of us sat and listened to our favourite songs, adding memories of gigs, parties, record shops and girlfriends. John Martyn had soundtracked our lives for over thirty years. That music remains essential, but to get to know the man behind it – Johnny Too Bad – you really need this book. Tuck in.

Ian Rankin
Edinburgh
2010

Introduction to new edition

You can't mess with Father Time, can you? He's going to catch you, whether you run fast or slow.

John Martyn

Well, old Father Time finally caught up with John and he died on 29 January 2009. A bout of double pneumonia did for John but even after reading all the fulsome obituaries it still seemed unbelievable that he had really passed away this time. Throughout his life John was a magnet for misfortune and the list of ailments and calamities he survived was genuinely astounding: an exploding pancreas, a leg amputation, impalement on a fence post and a car crash with a cow were the most eye-catching, though during the research for this edition I discovered that he nearly died once from seizures and almost drowned after slamming his head into a rock while swimming underwater. Fist fights were a regular occurrence in John's adult life and he often claimed that he had been shot at and stabbed a few times. In his day John was also a heroin user, fiendish cocaine addict and habitual hash head.

And then there was the booze . . . John Martyn liked a drink in the same way as vampires are partial to sinking their teeth into the creamy white neck of a chaste young girl. John adored drinking and loved pubs, saying they were the only place that lost souls really felt they belonged. Over the years John must have drank colossal amounts of vodka, rum and cider. His friend, the great jazz saxophonist Andy Sheppard, still talks with incredulity of seeing Martyn down a full bottle of Bacardi in one swig as he prepared for a gig. Along with the drugs, the alcohol powered John to amazing artistic achievements in the 1970s but it also scarred him later in life. For over forty years, he played a dangerous game of chance with the demon alcohol. In January 2009 it hacked him down . . . no matter what it says on his death certificate.

*

The first time I saw John Martyn play live was in tiny smoke-filled club above the Edinburgh Playhouse in 1980. John was at the top of his game on that sultry summer's night, an effortlessly brilliant musician with an engaging stage manner that seemed to reinforce the musical vibe that he was a genuine, gentle peace-loving good guy who wouldn't even talk badly to, never mind harm, a fly. When I mentioned this to a friend who vaguely knew his first wife, the reply was quick and to the point . . . 'no he's not, he's a complete bastard!' This dichotomy between the mild music and the malevolent, wild artiste never left me and a few years back I decided to write a book to try and find out who the real John Martyn was.

I first spoke to John after visiting his hometown in Kilkenny in the summer of 2004. Unable to speak to him during that visit I left a note behind the bar in his local boozer explaining who I was and why I wanted to write his life story. A couple of weeks later my mobile phone rang . . . 'Hi, it's Johnny Martyn, where are you? . . . Stornoway? What the fuck are you doing in Stornoway? I thought you were in Thomastown! I was going to take you for a drink!' Once the confusion was cleared up, he agreed to help me and this book is the end result. Along the way I talked to acquaintances who genuinely adored John. His closest friend, Danny Thompson, summed it up best by telling *Q* in September 1989:

> I'd do anything for John Martyn: if he phoned me up and said 'I'm in the Pennines and my car's knackered', I'd be on my way. It was a blessing from heaven that we were able to rave together so much in the 1970s and live because we lost a lot of friends who raved only half as much. He's the biggest, softest teddy bear, a generous, warm, sensitive person and he spends a lot of the time covering it up.

By way of complete contrast, one former manager refused to speak to me and sounded genuinely fearful at the mention of John's name. Before he put the phone down he said:

> You must not come to me for praiseworthy things on John Martyn. I've experienced his darker side much too often. I'm not interested in adding to the myth of the man. I don't enjoy talking about John Martyn. If you cannot say something good about somebody, don't say anything. I find it hard to say anything meritorious about John Martyn.

That was the way it was with John. Some people loved him and talked fondly of a warm, generous and loving individual. Others genuinely loathed him and recalled tales of his violent temper, dark moods and drunken debacles.

Music critics were equally divided over Martyn's abilities. In the early 1980s, when John was hopelessly out of fashion, *NME* still proclaimed that his music was the very definition of cool. As Nick Kent commented in the paper on 29 November 1980, John's music at its height possesses that rarest of essences: real soul. Twenty years later, in December 2000, *Uncut* magazine's David Stubbs argued that John had made 'some of the most palpable, almost physically emotional, music ever recorded'. Other critics were less charitable and likened his singing to that of a horribly wounded bear. In *NME*, 9 October 1982, Julie Burchill – at her most acidic – dismissed John as someone who 'cooked up aural monosodium glutamate in a melting-pot mind fit for jingles'.

The child of a broken marriage, Martyn was born Iain David McGeachy[1] and was brought up in a Glasgow home that echoed to the sound of music. His dazzling ability as a guitarist soon won him acclaim playing alongside his mentor Hamish Imlach. After moving to London he became a fixture on the Soho folk scene, before hitching a ride with the

---

1. A couple of his close friends from school told me that back then he spelled his first name Ian. The registrar's scrawl on Martyn's birth certificate could read either way. But when I asked Martyn he replied 'I have two eyes and two i's.' So Iain it is.

formative label Island Records and releasing a string of the most influential and best loved albums of the 1970s. From *Bless the Weather* to *Grace and Danger*, Martyn forged a distinct sound, fusing acoustic and electric music, jazz, blues and reggae in a breathtaking, groundbreaking concoction. In an industry riddled with clones and copycats, no one sounded quite like him. Motivated by the soaring ecstasy of finding love and the sharp pain of losing it he crafted scores of beautiful songs. His herbally inspired live shows became the stuff of legend and he could sell out concert venues around the globe. He remains an influence on every fresh generation of rock stars – acts as diverse as U2, The Verve, China Crisis, Paolo Nutini, The Boy Who Trapped The Sun, Portishead and Beth Orton (who called him 'The Guv'nor') all cite John as a major inspiration.

But the music was only half the story. While he produced feather-light, gorgeous love songs, his own private life fell apart in a spectacular way and his two marriages were ripped asunder. Martyn's life became blighted by drug dependency and chronic alcoholism. He took to hanging out with gangsters and earned a reputation as a heavy individual not to be messed with. Rumours of violence were commonplace. As one of his close colleagues said: 'It's hearsay, but it's a *lot* of hearsay.'

The bass guitarist Dave Pegg told me how he had moments working with John when he looked in his eyes and was genuinely scared. John revelled in this notoriety, deliberately cultivating a bad-boy image and became a hell-raiser to rival the likes of Keith Moon and Oliver Reed. His fellow Scots singer-songwriter Eddi Reader talks of nights on the town with John but admits that she needed the strength of Hercules just to keep up with him.

A renowned womaniser, Martyn claimed to have fathered twelve children in and out of wedlock (others say three children is a more realistic count). Eventually the frenzied lifestyle sapped his creativity and his records became less consistent; overproduced and riddled with drum machines. Back in the 1980s using those devices might have seemed brave and experimental – now they just sound terribly dated. His public profile steadily diminished and as his musical reputation faded he became better known for his personal frail-ties. While his celebrity admirers Phil Collins, Eric Clapton, Paul Weller and

Dave Gilmour became global superstars, Martyn never even troubled the UK album chart top ten and eventually ended up bankrupt. But John had few regrets about the way things worked out – as he often said; he chose the route and the vehicle. When fame stared him in the face, John wilfully rejected it and opted instead for experimenting with all types of music, even hip hop.

Late on in life, Martyn lived in relative tranquillity with his long-term girlfriend in Ireland. But he remained a mess of contradictions. His music was a mirror-image of his personality – veering unsettlingly between the tender and the turbulent. The same man who could write a lyric as benign and beautiful as 'Curl around me like a fern in the spring' could also break the ribs of one of his managers during a vicious brawl. In a good mood he was the soul of any party and advocated the benefits of Buddhism and pacifism. John could also be an extremely generous man and an incurable romantic. On one of the occasions I met him, we drove through his teenage stomping ground in the South Side of Glasgow and passed one of the many Asian shops selling beautiful lengths of cloth for saris. John told the driver to stop and sent him into the shop to buy twenty pounds' worth of the material. Half an hour later he presented it to his slightly bemused Irish girlfriend in their hotel room. But on other occasions his temper flared and he became stubborn, arrogant, angry and resentful about the music industry he despised. Even he admitted that on those occasions he was a nasty person, best avoided.

He was aware of the paradox at the heart of his work, how a man who produced such loving gentle music could at the same time live such a self-destructive lifestyle. As he said in *Q* in May 1990:

All my songs have always been utter misery or lunatic belligerence. I actually think those two sides are a racial trait in the Scottish . . . I don't want to be able to control my moods. I probably am a little schizophrenic, exacerbated by all the raving over the years. I'm either John Wayne the bully or John the daddy and lover. But I have enough self-control and if I could control myself more, I think the music would be much less interesting. I'd probably be a great deal richer but I'd have had far less fun and I'd be making really dull music.

I hope this book will shine a little more light on where John Martyn came from and what factors motivated him along the way. The aim is to discover the roots and the consequences of both his musical brilliance and his chaotic lifestyle. During my research John spoke to me and also helped smooth the way so that others would also offer their views, but I cannot claim to have known John Martyn well. So wherever possible I've opted to rely on the oral testimonies of those that were present at the time rather than offer intrusive personal views. For example, I think most readers would prefer to learn Ralph McTell's opinions on the relative strengths of the main players on the London folk scene of the late 1960s rather than read any assessment of mine. I've also spoken to over forty people who either knew John well or helped create the sound of those classic albums. Some of those interviewed would only speak anonymously while other former associates reacted with a mix of fear and anger at the mention of Martyn's name. To paraphrase the words of one of his most famous songs, some people are crazy about him, but some people just could not stand to see his face.

Thanks to the following for taking time to answer my questions: John Martyn; Linda Dunning; Danny Thompson; Dr Kirk McGeachy; Spencer Cozens; Ralph McTell; Bridget St John; Andy Sheppard; Claire Hamill; Dave Pegg; Michael Chapman; Steve Tilston; Wizz Jones; Daisy Flowers; Dave Mattacks; Eddi Reader; Simon Climie; John Glover; Sandy Roberton; Martin Levan; Paul Wheeler; Robin Frederick; Tim Denley; Phill Brown; Brian Young; James MacPherson; Hans van den Berk; Steve 'Monk' Moncure; Susanne Mead; Robert Kirby; Alan Dunbar; AMN; Mo Barnes; Ann Sadler; Peter Wright; and Alec Milne; James McNair for access to unpublished interviews and John Mackinnon for help with photography. Thanks also for assistance to: Teresa Walsh; Calum Angus Macdonald; Scott McGowan; Stephen Manzor; Ann Macdonald; Gabrielle Drake; Cally at Bryter Music; Martin Kielty; Vivienne Nicoll; Eddie Mould, CMP Entertainment; Kate Pool, Society of Authors; Ken Goodwin of Shawlands Academy; Colin Braham; Dee Harrington; George MacCallum; David Clayton; Pippa Hall, Monkey Business PR;

Christine Waters; Mandy Moncure; Roy Corkill; Aileen McCulloch, *Carluke Gazette;* Robert Meek, *Hastings Observer;* staff at Stornoway Library; the National Library of Scotland; the Music Library, Edinburgh; 'Swedish Peter'; Neville Moir, Alison Rae and Sarah Morrison at Polygon.

For this new edition, particular credit goes to Donnie Barclay, Davie MacFarlane, Iain Hamilton, Michael and Mary Furlong.

All quotations are from interviews with the author, unless specified.

A deep dark hurt

There is a deep dark hurt within John Martyn, which stems from way back. He may well have had a happy childhood. I had a happy childhood but I was a deserted child from a broken home and we went without and had lots of things missing in our lives. No one goes on stage without seeking approval and admiration for their talent. John was especially like that, if not you just go and play your chops in some wee jazz band. John wanted more.

Ralph McTell

I know there is a lot of angst in John's music and I think that kind of comes from the fact that his mother sort of disowned him at an early age. I guess he must have had a hard time growing up without a mother figure.

Kirk McGeachy

The boy who would one day be known as John Martyn, grew up as Iain David McGeachy in the Queens Park district of Glasgow to the south of the River Clyde that bisects the city. He was brought up by his father and granny in the top two floors of a traditional sandstone tenement at number 10 Tantallon Road. It was a safe, idyllic setting for a youngster to grow up in. Turn right at his front door and two minutes' walk along the road you find Langside Primary where young Iain attended school. Turn left and across the road is the 148-acre Queens Park with its manicured lawns, tennis courts and boating pond, where he would spend many happy days playing with his schoolmates. And a couple of blocks away stands Shawlands Academy where he would become a star pupil between 1960 and 1965.

The McGeachy family had roots in Fife and the Kintyre area in the west of Scotland, where one of Iain's ancestors was known as the white witch of

Gigha. Fishermen on the tiny picturesque island off the coast of the Kintyre peninsula came to her for advice on the best places to catch herring. Iain's paternal grandparents, William and Janet, raised a family of seven in Edinburgh, where William owned a successful garage in the Gorgie district. The family lived just off the Royal Mile and Iain's father Tommy was schooled at Moray House Primary. Besides Tommy, there were three other brothers, Eddie, Ross and Robert along with three sisters, Janet, Agnes and Kitty. (At the time of writing the first edition of this biography, Agnes was the only surviving sibling and lived on Islay.) When William McGeachy developed chronic arthritis the family moved out of the city centre to Apple Tree Cottage in the suburban village of Newbridge. But when William died in the late 1940s, Janet moved the family west to Glasgow, buying the Tantallon Road property and converting the top floor into a boarding house, which provided valuable income.

Iain's early years were anything but conventional. His parents had a great love of classical music and both were professional light-opera singers; his mum was a trained soprano, his dad a tenor. They plied their trade in the variety theatres that dominated the post-war entertainment scene, belting out Gilbert and Sullivan songs while dressed in Victorian garb. (At one such show, young Iain was introduced to Roy Rogers and Trigger.) Iain's father, with his theatrical waxed moustache which made him look very much the part of an operatic singer, was also a mainstay at Burns' Suppers. Iain was born on 11 September 1948, in New Malden, Surrey, while his parents – formally named on his birth certificate as Thomas Paterson McGeachy and Beatrice Jewitt of 58 Beechcroft Avenue, New Malden – were on the road performing. They separated soon after; eventually divorcing when Iain was just five and his father took custody of the boy. Inevitably his upbringing was fractured and made even more complicated by the fact that his dad soon moved back north of the border, leaving his mother to live in the Home Counties, including a spell when she stayed on a houseboat in Kingston-upon-Thames. As he grew older, Iain would travel south to spend a large part of the summer holidays with his mother and stepfather. To make matters even more complicated,

Iain never really got on with his stepfather and he often stayed with his mother's sister and her husband in Hampton Court instead. One lasting effect of this split upbringing was on Iain's accent – throughout his adult life it fluctuated between Glaswegian and Cockney with unsettling ease.

The McGeachy household on Tantallon Road where his father and his granny Janet brought up Iain echoed to the sound of music. It wasn't uncommon for passers-by to hear Tommy's wonderful singing voice streaming from an open window as he practised for performances. Even the old man's pet canaries, which were kept in upstairs rooms, did their bit. When guests visited, Tommy would take them to see the birds; at the shake of a matchbox the birds would start singing in unison. Grandmother Janet was a fine piano player and all Iain's aunts and uncles weren't shy when it came to singing when they visited. There were also relations in the seaside town of Largs who were stage entertainers. It all helped to instil a sense of theatrics in young Iain. The house had thirteen rooms, many of which housed a piano and Victorian-style family sing-songs around the piano were a regular occurrence with all concerned launching with gusto into traditional Scots songs. Love of this music would stay with Iain throughout his adult life. Presbyterian psalms were also often heard in a household that respected religion without ever becoming obsessive about it. It was a cultured background for a precocious child. Iain could read by the age of four and a few years later he was apparently an admirer of the French Impressionists, badgering his dad for prints of Chagall paintings.

Iain's first cousin Kirk, from Anstruther in Fife, remembered visiting the house regularly and talked fondly of the happy atmosphere:

As you walked in there was a long hallway with a big sitting room and three bedrooms downstairs, and also a big kitchen which had a Raeburn stove with a pantry off to the side. We spent a lot of our time in that kitchen, sitting around a great big long table. At the far end of the hall was the stair up to the next level. And up that stair were all these wee bedrooms on either side of a corridor. Iain slept in one of the bedrooms downstairs. The sitting room had beautiful Victorian furniture, a piano and a pair of Ghurkha knives that my own father, Eddie, had brought back from India, hanging by the ornate fireplace. The room had great big bay windows with views out to Queens Park and lovely smells of scented geraniums. It was quite an imposing room.

Tantallon Road was very close to one of the gates of the park and on Sunday afternoons we would go over to the boating pond and sail our wee toy yachts and walk around the park. Shawlands at that time was not a rough sort of area; not totally well-to-do, but certainly not like some of the poorer areas of Glasgow at that time.

In fact it was a solid middle-class, almost genteel neighbourhood. The McGeachys shared the tenement with a pair of spinster sisters called The Winchesters; a Jewish brother and sister, Annie and Isaac Levinson; and a married Russian couple with communist leanings.

As a young man Tommy McGeachy had harboured ambitions to study divinity and had worked for the Scottish Bible Society, sending bibles to Africa. But when he was called up to serve with the navy in Italy during the Second World War, Tommy put his gifted vocal chords to use singing for the British Forces Network before taking up singing professionally after hostilities ceased. Inevitably, the war left a lasting impression on Iain's father; John Martyn later recalled how the horrors of combat and seeing his dead comrades seemed to drain Tommy's own confidence and ambition.

When he came back he could only think of having a good time. Didn't want to work. And as far as I can see he lost faith in the whole of society. He was a very sweet man but the war just destroyed his brain, took his illusions and his innocence away. (*Mojo*, October 1994)

After the war, John's father worked fitfully in a wholesale grocery business, but continued to sing in variety under the pseudonym of 'Russell Paterson – Scotland's Troubadour' (Paterson was his mother's maiden name). While performing was his main focus, he cared well for his son, teaching him to ride a bike and also taking him for long walks in the country at weekends, where young Iain learnt to shoot and freshwater-fish, an obsession that stayed with him throughout his life. One of his uncles would also take Iain out on his fishing boat, which nurtured an interest in bird watching. At the age of twelve he was made an honorary member of the British Ornithologists Club for sending them the rings of over 100 seagulls. Iain would also later attribute his not inconsiderable success in bedding women to his father's tuition!

John Martyn would later forcefully deny any ideas that, as a single child from a broken marriage, he led a dysfunctional or unhappy childhood. He maintained that those were happy days, telling *Sunday Herald* journalist Alan Taylor:

> It was great. I didn't have any brothers and sisters to wreck my train set or annoy me. I was very happy and I was brought up by my granny; and grannies are awfully good at bringing up wee boys.

Granny Janet was a fine substitute mum – a loving and stable influence on young Iain – bringing him up in a quasi-Victorian way; all mustard baths, hair washing with carbolic soap, and foot massages. Iain's lifelong friend Davie MacFarlane told me how he remembered Janet as a lovely person who used to make fine homemade lemonade and would also cook her own spaghetti bolognaise sauce – quite a novelty back in the early 1960s when most people only got it out of a can. Kirk McGeachy also spoke highly of Janet and the positive influence she had on young Iain.

> His granny Janet did Iain proud really. She was a wonderful lady. If anything came up that was sad and was going to cause a situation, she would always say, 'Oh, we won't talk about that!' She would just get on with life and look at the positives. She learned that because it must have been hard when she lost her husband and was left with her young family. My father was in his late twenties when that happened and he basically became the head of the family. Tommy and he went out and worked and provided for the family.

John Martyn talked fondly to me about the kindness shown to him by Granny Janet.

She was an amazing character – all she needed after a war and seven kids of her own was a wee man like me. Very few people would take on that responsibility these days. Without people like her the whole world would go to pot.

But like the rest of the family Janet had a taste for alcohol and used to tipple on the quiet in the kitchen – drinking out of eggcups with the bottle well hidden. Blissfully unaware that she was influencing a life of heavy drinking, Janet introduced young Iain to his first dram of whisky to help wake him up for his 4 a.m. milk round. A few years later and still way before the legal drinking age, Iain first experienced getting drunk:

> I was nine years old and it was at number two Hampton Court Way in high summer, the middle of August. My Uncle Ray, who loved me like a son, gave me two glasses of Bulmers cider. It set me on my arse. I'll never forget it – I was doing somersaults and I ended up falling down the stairs!

By his mid-teenage years Iain would be taking the rite of passage of many young Scots.

> We used to drink a half-bottle of fortified wine and smash the empty bottle against a wall, and then a bottle of McEwan's light ale. If one didn't get you, the other would!

By the time he had graduated to secondary school, Iain was a bright young pupil, excelling at English and Art, eager to learn and popular with class-mates. Tall and athletic, he was also into sport, but unlike most Glaswegian kids, football wasn't his preference. Although he remembered going to see the now defunct Third Lanark, he had disdain for football and his favourite sports were rugby and cricket. He told me:

> I used to play fly-half or flanker. I liked the position at the end of the scrum where you could nail the opposing scrum-half, that was my favourite posi-tion! I used to torment scrum-halfs. I was a good all-round cricketer too but

I was best in the field, a good catcher in the slips. I used to play in the Clydesdale cricket team. It was always very relaxing.

The love of cricket never really left him – later in life John Martyn played for village teams while living in England. As to just how good a rugby player he was at school, Davie MacFarlane comments:

During the rugby season we would both play in the school teams. He was an ok player but not *that* good . . . put it this way he never made the first fifteen for the school.

In the 1960s Shawlands Academy was a well respected school that allowed Iain to build upon his natural intelligence and prosper. (The fact that the school's most infamous former pupil is Moors Murderer Ian Brady is seldom mentioned these days.) It was a large school, split into Junior and Senior Secondary – with a roll of over 1,500 pupils, some travelling from the new South Side housing schemes. The pupils learned under a system that would now be considered austere. Boys and girls had separate gym areas and playgrounds; errant youngsters were kept under control by the use of the belt; and school uniform was mandatory. Anyone spotted not wearing school blazer and badge would be sent home. A quick trawl through old school magazines shows that Iain McGeachy won the Jubilee Memorial Prize in English and – as a pupil of class 3B1 – he represented the school in an inter-schools quiz on Scottish Television called *Round-up* in 1963. When – forty years later – I mentioned the *Top of the Form*-style show to John Martyn, he broke into spontaneous laughter, and claimed that they had won the competition. (In fact they lost narrowly by three points.)

I don't remember being beaten! Anyway I only got one question wrong – something about non-ferrous metals!

If they had asked him questions about beat poets or existentialists, young Iain wouldn't have let the school down. By his mid-teens he was starting to rebel. After a spell as a sharply dressed Mod – complete with Vespa scooter and a taste for Prince Buster and The Four Tops – the teenager was now getting more experimental. He told me:

I was fairly seriously into the guy who wrote *One Flew Over the Cuckoo's Nest*, Ken Kesey. My father gave it to me when I was fifteen – which was strange because my father was a very straight man. I liked *Naked Lunch* too, and all the junkies like Burroughs and Alexander Trocchi. It was hip to be a beatnik back then, not a hippie. My father, he allowed me everything, he was very cool. When I had my first smoke of ganja he said, 'What's that, son?' I said, 'That's hash, daddy.' He told me to heat it up properly!

Besides the beat writers, Iain also had more conventional tastes in literature: Robert Burns' poem 'To a Mountain Daisy' would remain a favourite throughout his life. But Kirk McGeachy recalls how Iain's dad came to worry that his son's increasingly offbeat interests would harm his academic career.

Iain was always very, very good at English and debating, and he read a lot. He passed Higher English with flying colours without hardly any studying. He had a very good brain on him, though his father was always a bit pissed off with him for not trying harder at his studies. There was certainly a period there where they thought he was a bit of a waster.

Iain would go down to London, especially in the summertime, and he would come back from the big city with fancy clothes like neat jeans and wonderfully colourful striped jerseys that really impressed me! I'm younger than him by a year and I kind of looked up to him because he was the older cousin. I was the town boy from Anstruther and he was the city boy, a pretty cool guy. I would say that overall he had a pretty good relationship with his dad. His father was a dapper, even-keeled, loving sort of chap who wouldn't really raise a finger to anyone. He liked a pint back then, but nothing to excess. Most of the time they got on very well; there were arguments when Iain was in his later years at Shawlands Academy and he wouldn't put his head into studying fully. But there was nothing major.

Davie MacFarlane remembers that Tommy McGeachy could be strict with his son and Davie got the impression that he could be quite physical towards Iain though that was probably due more to frustration over Iain's rebellious attitude than any badness. Certainly there was no lasting animosity from son to father. Donnie Barclay, who would later live with the young John Martyn in London, recalls:

> John was very protective of his father and his mother. His dad used to drink in the Corona Bar at Shawlands Cross all the time and the Masonic Club around the corner. Before we went to London we would go for pints with him – his father was a steady drinker back then, a social drinker, not the type of guy who would sit in the house. We were young guys but John always wanted to go to the bar with his dad when most teenagers would not be seen dead in public with their parents. In return, you could see that his father was proud of him.

Given his parents' musical abilities, there was a sense of inevitability that Iain would follow in their footsteps. In 1964, he came under the wing of a music teacher fondly nicknamed 'Boozy' who was keen on having a couple of lunchtime pints at the nearby Sammy Dow's pub. Iain's brief flirtation with violin lessons ended after mickey-taking from his mates in the school rugby side. A couple of weeks later though, Iain was won over to the guitar while watching TV. The initial inspiration came from seeing Joan Baez play the song 'Silver Dagger'. It was the first time he had heard finger-picking guitar playing and straight away he was a convert. Interest in the instrument turned to near obsession when he heard Davey Graham, the Leicester-born guitarist whose revolutionary guitar tunings effectively changed the way music was made and spawned a host of imitators. Graham first started playing guitar at the age of twelve and when only nineteen he had penned 'Anji' which was to become a benchmark for all young acoustic players. In the early 1960s he invented a new system of tuning – DADGAD – and following a trip to Tangiers he developed a unique mode of playing incorporating North African styles. Graham's 1964 Decca album *Folk, Blues and Beyond* and the 1966 Decca release *Midnight Man* would become prime influences for Iain. Like just about every young guitarist of that era, from Bert Jansch to Jimmy Page, Iain worshipped at the altar of Davey Graham. He loved Graham's mix of blues standards by artists like Gary Davis and radical takes on classic songs like 'Summertime'. Much of the young John Martyn's work – especially his first two albums – would owe a heavy debt to Davey Graham, though Martyn would soon move on and develop a style all his own. John told me:

A friend of mine called David MacFarlane, whose father was a conscientious objector – a terrible thing in those days – introduced me to all the protest music. His family were all lefties, I first heard Bob Dylan there. And then I heard Davey Graham and that was me gone. I loved Davey Graham's 'Anji'. That was the test piece – if you could play 'Anji' you were taken kind of seriously, you had the basics. Because you have to move the thumb and the forefinger at the same time as the other fingers. They're both going in opposite directions, quite tricky. Davey Graham is a genius and such a nice guy, without him there wouldn't be anyone like Bert Jansch, Renbourn or me. He's the first of the great modern acoustic players.

My first guitar was a right dodgy thing borrowed from a guy called Johnny Briggs in Glasgow, who played for the Paisley Pirates ice hockey team. He was older than we were and all us kids wanted to be like this guy Johnny Briggs! I started to like the music and I actually begged my father for a guitar. I still have the first guitar I bought – it was a Rolif acoustic made in Bulgaria. And a very fine guitar it is too. I was in love with the thing; I used to run home from school to practise.

Iain paid for the guitar with money from his newspaper and milk delivery rounds. He was now looking the part of the teenage rebel, having grown his hair long and taken the unusual decision of declining to wear socks. His near neighbour Mo Barnes remembers how he used to sit wearing a long leather coat, playing his guitar on the wall under her window.[1] His cousin Kirk – who went on to play guitar and sing with the Canadian folk band Orealis and sadly passed away in 2006 – told me how word quickly spread about young Iain's musical talents.

1. The idea of young Iain playing his guitar out on the street under his neighbour's window may seem fanciful but I suspect it is true and probably came from his infatuation with Davey Graham. A clip of Graham playing 'Cry Me A River' outdoors in a 1959 BBC documentary directed by Ken Russell was almost certainly an influence on Iain and can still be seen on YouTube.

Fairly early on I remember Uncle Tommy telling my dad that Iain had this amazing musical ability. As I got a bit older I began to realise and say to myself, 'This boy can really play'. In his early teens he would play stuff like Duane Eddy or The Shadows along with songs like 'Ghost Rider In The Sky' and 'Blue Moon' on his record player. But a few years later he started getting into the blues. One of his prize possessions back then was a boxed set of LPs of American blues legends like Leadbelly and Blind Boy Fuller. He would just get totally into a trance listening to and learning this kind of stuff. I used to love going through to Glasgow to visit back then. He would play me all the new stuff he'd been learning and I'd record it on my reel-to-reel recorder. He was a major influence on me musically. He taught me to play 'Anji' and introduced me to all sorts of new music and techniques. He handed down all the old songbooks he'd finished with (many of them old Oak publications). He was a generous, loving guy and we got on very well. He was also quite a hippie back then; I remember one summer, he went to Morocco and he came back with a box full of marzipan-type sweets and his dad thought it was some sort of hash!

As his interest in music grew, Iain still managed to excel at school. One classmate, who preferred to remain anonymous, recalls:

He was very bright and seemed to have a fantastic general knowledge. He was outstanding at English and this was recognised by our English teacher 'Wild Bill', who had a fearsome reputation for breaking kids' wrists with the belt, though in reality he hardly ever used it. Anyway, he tolerated McGeachy's mischievous behaviour and he obviously recognised Iain's talent. I can remember McGeachy sitting in class making flies for fishing and being allowed to do it – while the rest of us would get bollockings for even dropping a pencil! I can also remember him getting up to various pranks in the Latin class to irritate the teachers. But really he wasn't a bad pupil – just a typical, fidgety, slightly hypersensitive lad.

Davie MacFarlane remembers how Iain was growing into a good-looking albeit chubby-faced lad with a reputation for being something of a brainbox – though that predictably turned some pupils against him.

I remember him writing a composition once about poaching and we were all gobsmacked by this wonderful descriptive writing of the moon and the water etc. But because he was so smart he was sometimes given a hard time by some of his schoolmates. I wouldn't call it bullying but there was a bit of name-calling, things like 'Keechie McGeachy'.[2] But I think that was more caused by envy on the part of other kids because he was so bright.

When the rugby season was over, we would spend our Saturday afternoons going into town and buying records by people like Ray Charles, Son House, Leadbelly and Big Bill Broonzy. He used to come around to my house; my dad used to be into people like Pete Seeger and Matt McGinn and we would listen to those records but we were more into people like Davey Graham and Bert Jansch – Iain idolised these guys.

Aside from Graham and Jansch, Iain was also listening to John Renbourn and Roy Harper – acoustic players who were already starting to make a mark on the London folk scene while Iain was still in school. Jansch's debut album was a particular favourite and Iain also took a liking to the Edinburgh guitarist's image as a rebel with a taste for the underground scene and a liking for smoking grass. Other early idols were even more exotic. Visitors to the Tantallon Road house were soon listening to obscure artists like the blind New Orleans guitarist Snooks Eaglin and Chess Records imports. Iain was a young man with mature tastes – the acoustic blues of Robert Johnson, Blind Lemon Jefferson, Bukka White and the political singer Pete Seeger.

*

Looking back on his early years, John Martyn was always adamant that they were happy days. Occasionally when full of drink he would cry out that he was 'a child of a broken home' but always the words were said in jest. Iain David McGeachy undoubtedly did have a happy childhood and was never short of love and affection. But those who know him are

2. It may sound harmless to the non-Scot but the nickname 'Keechie' was far from complimentary. The *Scottish Vernacular Dictionary* defines the word as 'rubbish, detritus and crap, excreta – human or otherwise'!

convinced that the unusual circumstances of his upbringing had a serious effect on the way his life and career developed. One close friend from Shawlands Academy thought that his mother's absence had a real impact on Iain, but it was a subject that was seldom mentioned. 'He never really spoke about his mother to me but I do think it had a big effect on him . . . she just got up one day and basically left him behind.' Iain's first serious girlfriend, Linda Dunning, remembers how Iain missed the presence of his mum and was self-conscious of the fact that he was not the same as other classmates who saw their mother on a daily basis.

> I believe that Iain had essentially a good childhood, being raised by his father and granny. I loved his father dearly; he was a wonderful man and did a great job bringing up Iain. If Iain was a child now, where divorce is commonplace, it may not have had such an effect. In those days no one was divorced. He did visit his mum on holidays, and looked forward to those times very much. But I remember him telling me about his aunt who lived at his home for a while. When it was school sports day he would ask his aunt to attend and pretend she was his mum, because he did not want the other kids to know that his mum lived in England.

Equally telling is Kirk McGeachy's answer to the question of where the deep hurt evident in John Martyn's later music comes from.

> I know there is a lot of angst in John's music and I think that kind of comes from the fact that his mother sort of disowned him at an early age. I guess he must have had a hard time growing up without a mother figure. John is quite a proud guy and he probably wouldn't like people to think that it got him down.

Some would argue that – in a roundabout way – coming from a broken home actually spurred Iain on to great things and made him even more eager to succeed in life. Ralph McTell, who became one of the best known names to emanate from the London folk club scene, told me how Iain's family background was far from unique among the batch of great singer-songwriters who emerged during the 1960s.

There is a deep dark hurt within John Martyn, which stems from way back. He may well have had a happy childhood. I had a happy childhood but I was a deserted child from a broken home and we went without and had lots of things missing in our lives. No one goes on stage without seeking approval and admiration for their talent. John was especially like that, if not you just go and play your chops in some wee jazz band. John wanted more. If you do a quick survey of musicians you will be astonished about how many of them come from broken homes. People like Wizz Jones, Bert Jansch, Roy Harper, John Renbourn and myself – all from broken homes. When you have a hurt like John has, you can either become all reclusive or you can come out fighting – John does the latter.

'I never took lessons from anybody!'

Hamish [Imlach] was very kind to me – he was my guide and mentor . . . an incredibly generous man, wild in spirit but just totally socialist with a wonderful sense of humour. I miss him terribly.

John Martyn

[Iain] was very intelligent, artistic and unusual. We listened to Bob Dylan, Donovan, the Rolling Stones, but I was always aware that he had musical interests that were beyond my level. He liked Joan Baez and Joni Mitchell and he would talk a lot about Davey Graham and Big Bill Broonzy.

Linda Dunning

Music may have been an obsession for Iain but, as with any teenager, there were other more pressing hormonal demands. His cousin Kirk recalls that even in his early teens Iain was blessed with good looks and always in demand with girls.

I remember when I was about sixteen, Iain and I would get dolled up and head out on the town on a Saturday night with our respective girlfriends. Sometimes we'd end up getting home pretty late, sitting on the big kitchen table in Tantallon Road comparing our evenings and having a few laughs. He was a good-looking boy even then.

Decked out in bell-bottom jeans and an army surplus jacket, or long fur coat along with the trademark sandals, or old tennis shoes without socks, Iain stuck out from the crowd at the regular Saturday night dances at the local Whitecraigs Tennis Club.

At one such dance in November 1964, he met and fell in love with the girl who was to be his sweetheart for the next four years, until he left Glasgow and headed south to London. Back in 1964, Linda Dunning was a pupil at the slightly more upmarket, fee-paying Hutchesons Grammar School. Five feet four, with fringed, long, dark blonde hair, Linda and her classmates made regular weekend trips to the tennis club to dance to local bands like Dean Ford and the Gaylords. (Who would later gain success when they changed their name to Marmalade.) Much to the horror of their school principal, many of the Hutchie girls ended up romancing with the boys from the less salubrious Shawlands Academy. In fact Linda was suspended from school at one point when the principal saw her walking hand in hand with Iain. Linda, who now works in real estate in Detroit, Michigan, recalls how Iain always stood out as being just a little bit cooler than the rest.

> He had long curly hair, was baby-faced and was very cute. He was very clever, but he was a real rebel. If I remember correctly when I first met him he was on probation for some minor offence. We pretty much fell in love right away, and vowed to spend our lives together. We even decided to have four children and had names picked out. It was really a very sweet and simple time in our lives. He did like poetry but when we were together he did not spend much time reading – we were teenagers with hopping hormones!

Linda became a source of inspiration for the young musician and many of the songs that would emerge on his first albums can be traced back to those teenage years. Iain would meet Linda after school and the pair spent many happy hours together in the Queens Park while Iain strummed away on his acoustic guitar. Weekends were usually reserved for hanging out with friends at the Embassy café, the local Wimpy bar or at the two cinemas in the area – The Waverley and The Embassy. The highpoint though was always the tennis club dance, which attracted gangs of youths loaded up on booze and invariably looking for trouble. Linda remembers that Iain was not shy in defending the honour of her or a friend.

There were often fights at these dances. Gangs would show up looking for trouble and Iain would jump in to defend, whatever the issue was. It was typical in those times that the boys would show up with a 'bevvy' [drunk]. He was extremely possessive and would get very jealous and we would argue if he thought some other guy liked me. He would usually escort me home on the last bus from Shawlands to Newton Mearns where I lived, and then would have to walk home. He did get picked up by the police a few times on the walk home, not because he was doing anything, but probably because of the way he looked. My parents did not like him because of the way he looked, especially if the friends or neighbours made negative comments.

When Iain came to collect Linda for a night out, the neighbours' curtains started twitching.

According to my mother, the neighbours in our nice estate in Newton Mearns used to watch from their windows to see what get-up I was wearing when I was going out with Iain. I was usually wearing bell-bottom jeans, kaftans and a long, flowing black cape with a purple satin lining. Some of these things I would design and make myself. We had reefer jackets, and some army surplus gear, and a healthy collection of Ban the Bomb badges. For special occasions, like dances, I would wear mini, mini-skirts and long boots. Iain would even surprise me and wear a suit to these dances. One lady who was new to the area even commented at a Tupperware party that 'one of those hippies lived in the estate'!

In a later interview with *Zigzag* magazine in April/May 1974, John Martyn would make mention of occasional violent incidents during his teenage years. He recalls having to:

Kick a few heads in or get looked upon as a pansy . . . You don't have any choice up there, either you're violent or you're a weed. And I haven't got the capacity for being trodden on. I'm a natural born coward just like everybody else, but I don't like being taken advantage of. I'm probably still the same now. But at the time it was just either eat or be eaten . . . There were fights in school all the time and knives were bandied about.

However, there's probably an element here of John exaggerating for a southern audience. True, Glasgow then, as now, had a reputation as a mean city with high levels of gang-related crime and Martyn's friends recall how Iain often had to run the gauntlet of abuse from local hard men who took objection to his pretty boy looks and who really seemed to hate youths who dared to wear their hair long. The city's main thoroughfare Sauchiehall Street even had the nickname back then of 'Murder Mile' which would hardly have filled young Iain with confidence as he prepared to head into the city centre on a Friday night. But his assertion that he came from 'a very stroppy part of town' doesn't ring true. It's safe to say that life on Glasgow's South Side in the 1960s wasn't all knife fights and gang culture. One suspects few gang members would say, as Martyn did, that their earliest musical memory was their mum playing Debussy's 'La Cathédrale Engloutie'! His contemporaries say that knives were never carried at school. One classmate told me:

> It is normal for the Glasgow hard man image to follow people around but Iain was never really that type of guy. There was the odd scrap – but he was more likely to run like hell or cross the road from a real fight. I'm sure when he went to London it did him no harm to cultivate the hard man reputation. The alternative image – of a former Academy boy with a blazer – was hardly the correct image in the rebellious 1960s.

As he became more confident on the guitar, Iain began to hang out with like-minded individuals including Josh McCrae, a guitarist who eventually recorded a song called 'Messin' About On The River'. McCrae inadvertently had a hand in Iain's stage debut in 1966 – a concert which would be his one and only major gig under his own name. The venue was a charity concert at the Langside Borough Halls, just two blocks from Iain's family home. When McCrae – who was meant to be the star attraction – got drunk in a local pub, Iain was the only one who could fill the spot. He was eventually persuaded to take the stage for a set, which lasted about thirty minutes, to warm applause from the audience. Memories of the concert are sketchy but John remembered that he did perform 'Fairy Tale Lullaby', the only song he had written by then. A few months later he was paid £11 for a gig at The Black Bull pub in Dollar, but by then Iain McGeachy was performing under the name of John Martyn. Changing one's name at such a young age is certainly an unusual step and psychiatrists might argue that it signifies an attempt to escape from an unhappy childhood, disown one's parentage, or even show an early confirmation of ruthless ambition. In John Martyn's case the truth is less convoluted. Sandy Glennon, a friend back in the 1960s who would later act as John's agent, simply thought that Iain David McGeachy sounded too Scottish and was more appropriate for a traditional folk artist. Glennon, who had run the Excelsior Club in London's Charing Cross Road, opted for the surname Martyn in honour of their favourite guitar maker. John told me:

> In those days there was no traditional scene as such. You had to be American-sounding. I was more influenced by American music than Scottish music but the name Martyn was his idea – it had to have the 'y' in it, to sound posh.

Linda Dunning remembers Iain being very excited about having a stage name and that it made him feel like he had hit the big time long before he actually did. She also points out that both his parents were performers with stage names, so in that sense it was not an unusual thing for Iain to consider. Linda secretly feared that the name change was a sign that she was losing Iain. She would soon have her worst fears confirmed.

Around this time, a friend of Iain's father from the local Masonic lodge, Billy Synott, who had a love of folk music and socialist politics, spotted Iain's nascent talent. Synott actually made guitars and was an early influence on Martyn, helping him to adopt a bluesier style of playing. Synott was friendly with the traditional folk singer and raconteur Hamish Imlach and soon introduced the two men. Weighing in at around three hundred pounds, the much loved Imlach was already a sizeable presence on the

Scottish scene – eventually going on to record three dozen albums which blended boozy ribald tunes with more serious left-wing content and anti-nuclear protest songs. Imlach's initial notoriety came from leading a group of musicians and bevvy merchants known as the Broomhill Bums. Young talents like Josh McCrae and Archie Fisher became fixtures at Hamish's big West End home, holding a party in the converted stables that lasted – off and on – for around nineteen months. The moonshine sessions became so legendary that even visiting American musicians like Sonny Terry and Brownie McGhee visited the stables while on tour in Scotland. (John recalled how the two men wouldn't speak to each other on stage and how they had separate dressing rooms.) Imlach's crew used to contribute money to help bring people like Reverend Gary Davis and Tom Paxton over to play in Scotland. John remembered how at those concerts rogues would sell pound-deals of 'hash' to punters, which turned out to be a deadly mix of henna, chalk and black boot polish.

Imlach and Martyn became close friends. The young novice was soon carrying Imlach's guitar to gigs and playing a short set for handy cash on the same bill as Imlach and other influential players in the folk revival of the 1960s such as Archie Fisher and Josh McCrae. Imlach may have had a well earned reputation as a heavy drinker, but he was no fool. With no formal training, he was self-taught on guitar, picking up songs and techniques from the likes of Brownie McGhee along the way. Born in Calcutta, Imlach played his first professional gigs in the early 1960s and helped to start the influential Glasgow Folk Club (founded by Ewan McVicar and Drew Moyes) in the city's Trongate. Imlach became the resident singer there on Saturday nights and during the afternoons he earned good money – thirty shillings a lesson – giving tuition to young guitarists. As he explained in his autobiography:

We were kept going by giving lessons in the secret art of guitar playing to the younger generation. In Edinburgh, Archie [Fisher] was teaching Owen Hand, Robin Williamson and Bert Jansch. In Glasgow, I was giving lessons to John Martyn and the boxer Jim Watt!

John had a different take on his friendship with Imlach. He told me that he never had any trust in teachers, fearing that he would end up inevitably playing in their style. And he never bought a chord book or learned to read music to help his education. He preferred to watch the players' fingers on stage and if necessary to talk to them after the show for advice. John explained:

> I never took lessons from anybody! I used to watch the hands but I never took lessons as such . . . I used to go to Hamish's house on Sundays for Spaghetti Bolognese, which was like a ritual thing. They kind of adopted me, really.

John also shared Imlach's socialist outlook and took part in the CND marches to London at that time.

Imlach encouraged Martyn to expand his playing into blues, ragtime, country, traditional Gaelic tunes and gentle Dylanesque songs. In an interview with *Zigzag* magazine in 1974, John recalled:

> At that time I'd been chucked out of art school for being nasty and silly, and I didn't have much money – I was earning my money playing darts in those days, making about two quid a day.

Hamish Imlach had undoubted musical talents but his interests in life invariably centred on having a good time. His autobiography is soaked in tales of heavy boozing sessions, dirty jokes and 'cairry-oots'. This was a man who lived by the motto 'I would hate to die with a heart attack and have a good liver, kidneys and brain. When I die I want everything to be knackered!' And this was the man who in many ways shaped the career and outlook on life of the kid who would become John Martyn. It could be argued that it's a maxim that John adopted himself. (Throughout his career, Martyn would be inexorably drawn to individuals whose insecurities led to excesses and addictions.) The tradesman-apprentice relationship lasted for about eighteen months but they were to remain friends right up to Imlach's death in 1996. When Imlach's autobiography was first published, pride of place on the sleeve notes went to Martyn, who asserted that without the encouragement and patience of the big man quite a few careers, including his own and Billy Connolly's, might never have got off the ground.

Linda Dunning confirms that Imlach played a pivotal role in John Martyn's early musical development.

Hamish was quite a jolly, gregarious guy and he took Iain with him on lots of gigs. We spent one New Year's Eve at the Imlachs' home in Motherwell. Many of the known Scottish musicians were there, including Billy Connolly. Hamish's wife and kids were there and prior to that night I was not even aware that he was married. His lifestyle on the road was not that of a married man with a family. It was obvious his wife and family adored him and likewise he adored them, but he still had his other women. He made a marvellous huge pot of lamb curry that night and served it at 4 a.m. He was definitely a mentor to Iain in those early days. Because he was so highly regarded in the world of folk music, he later introduced Iain in the many clubs and pubs around the UK.

Donnie Barclay also saw up close the influence that Imlach had on Iain. Donnie was working as an apprentice panel beater when he first met Iain in a pub on Pollockshaws Road called the Kind Man. The pair had a shared interest in music and darts and soon gained a reputation as local hustlers on the darts board. Iain in particular was a very good player and excelled in games where drinks were at stake. The 'doubles for doubles' games helped finance many a drinking session for Iain and Donnie, who recalls:

The first night I spoke to Iain he invited me back to his granny's house to listen to some of the great LP's he had borrowed from Hamish – lots of obscure blues, contemporary American folk and stuff by Jansch, Renbourn and Graham. Iain's bedroom was very spartan, with a very basic record player, and hadn't been decorated in ages although compared to my wee council house bedroom it was massive. I am a guitarist myself but listening to Iain play I soon realised he was special and it was a real privilege to be there at the start of the career of a true original. Every time I went to his house he played me a new song that he had written.

Donnie became a trusted confidante of the young singer-songwriter, travelling with him around the country and backing him 100% when trouble arose. And right from the off, there was always going to be trouble when Iain/ John was around. A lot of the established folkies were jealous of how easy Iain made it look and would talk about him behind his back. Hamish Imlach though, was different and was a lot more supportive of the young tyro. Donnie explains:

Hamish was one of the best entertainers you could ever meet and I think he knew at once that Iain had a great talent and wanted to develop it. He used to drive us to folk clubs around the UK and it was Hamish who usually got Iain on the bill for those gigs. Hamish drove a small mini car which was maybe not the ideal car for someone of his stature. I would meet him and Iain in the Montrose Bar in Glasgow and we would just head off to do these gigs in places like the north of England. Sometimes though Iain and I would just travel to gigs on a bus.

We were invariably skint and in those days you could only get into a gig for nothing if you were playing so usually I ended up telling the organisers that I was his fiddle player but that I had left the fiddle on the bus. But I ended up getting worried that they might produce a fiddle from somewhere that I couldn't play so Iain told me to say that I was his Serengi player. I said to him 'what the fuck is a Serengi' and he told me it was a multi-stringed Indian instrument. But then I asked what would happen if someone produced a Serengi for me to play and Iain replied 'well then I'll take you to the toilets and jump on your fucking hand so you won't be able to play it!'

*

Besides his growing reputation on the UK folk circuit, Iain was also gaining a formidable name in his home city. Glasgow in the mid-1960s was fast earning a reputation as a lively, 'happening' city. There were a number of clubs and pubs specialising in live rock and pop music though the archaic licensing hours often caused problems. Pubs shut at 10.30 p.m. although some parts of the city allowed extra drinking time, sparking hurried sojourns from one pub to another at closing time. Sunday drinking was even more problematic. The venues for John Martyn's early concerts were invariably smoky bohemian Glasgow folk clubs, which only came to life long after dusk fell. Prominent among them was Clive's Incredible Folk Club on Sauchiehall Street (next to an Odeon cinema and on the fifth floor of a building now known as the Savoy Centre). It was started in 1966 by Ian Ferguson, a friend of London-born banjoist Clive Palmer who later rose to prominence as one-third of The Incredible String Band. One of the first all-night clubs in the city, with opening hours from 10 p.m. on Saturday night to 6 a.m. on the Sabbath, it only lasted a few months before the inevitable closure by the police. The long hours meant that there were plenty of opportunities for guest spots between The Incredible String Band sets – aside from the band set, Robin Williamson, Clive Palmer and Mike Heron would all do solo sets – which gave opportunities to the likes of Martyn, Archie Fisher and Bert Jansch.

During its few months of life Clive's boasted a loyal clientele, including young John Martyn who went there after seeing his girlfriend home before the midnight curfew on Saturday nights. Martyn was by now a skilful guitarist for his age and was already rejecting the Beatles-led beat boom of the early 1960s in favour of the less lucrative but infinitely cooler emergent folk revival. In Martyn's own words he picked up everything there, in a room crammed with music-minded people and the air thick with the smell of marijuana. On the opening night five hundred people had to be turned away from Clive's. Local stalwarts like Hamish Imlach, Billy Connolly, Alex Campbell and Josh McCrae were often on the bill as were more exotic acts like New York singer-songwriter Arlo Guthrie. Clive Palmer became a close friend to John, introducing him to an alternative to the parochial anti-English folk music played by many local musicians. Martyn and Palmer lived together on a couple of occasions. The first time was at Clive's flat in Coronation Buildings, Edinburgh, where, unable to afford any heating, they lived in a tent pitched in the living room. The menu was equally basic as both men were busking for a living at the time. John told *Classic Rock* magazine how the pair once lived off a prized ram, which they had managed to procure from a cattle show. After dragging it home the pair lived royally on ram chops for weeks to come.

Years later, the two musicians shared an electricity-free shed in the wilds of the Cumbrian moorlands, living off water from a nearby stream and playing guitar endlessly to keep warm. John got on well with all three members of The Incredible String Band, who all admired his playing style. They helped him get support slots – paying three pounds a time – at other Scottish venues, and advised him to try for a gig at Cousins, the London club, which was fast gaining a reputation as a hotbed for young talent.

Billy Connolly, in the Incredible String Band compendium *Be Glad*, remembers Clive's as more of a happening place than a real folk club. Without any stairs leading in, access could only be gained by lift, four ravers at a time. The lack of stairs meant that if you wanted to go outside for a fight you had to wait for the lift. Connolly says:

> It was illegal, it was a real sweatbox, and it was brilliant. It was just the most outstanding club I was ever in. It was like a shooting star – it flourished and we were lucky to see it – and then it was gone.

However brilliant it was as a venue, it was also an undeniable potential deathtrap and it was no surprise when the authorities shut it down as a fire risk after a couple of months.

John's growing band of fans could console themselves by going to see him at the other main venue in the city – the Glasgow Folk Song Club. Situated upstairs at 45 Montrose Street near George Square in the Trongate district, the Folk Song Club was another inauspicious-looking place which would later gain near mythological status as a venue which allowed the talents of youngsters like Billy Connolly, Alex and Les Harvey, and John Martyn to flourish alongside the more traditional Scottish folk musicians. The club dated back to 1959 but by the mid-1960s it was run by Drew Moyes with the help of Tam Kearney and had blossomed into a real mecca for local enthusiasts, no doubt attracted by the fact it was open till 3 a.m. on Saturday and Sunday mornings. Aside from the performance area there was a coffee bar, reference library and recording/rehearsal space. Linda Dunning remembers how she and John spent lots of time hanging about there.

> It was very spartan, the lighting wasn't great, and there was only a small stage, with rows of chairs set up in front. The big draw was The Incredible String Band and the place was packed when they were on. Iain and I were in awe of them; they were such incredible musicians and their music was magical. I still have all of their albums. Over time, Iain really earned their respect as he progressed as a musician and ultimately became friends with them.
>
> One summer I was going to London with Iain and we drove down with Clive Palmer. The two of them showed up at my house in Newton Mearns in an old Morris Minor. I got in the back seat surrounded by guitars and banjos, much to the horror of my mother, who has somewhat of a Hyacinth Bucket quality about her. Apparently she had to be comforted by the neighbours.

One of the singers at the Folk Centre, Iain Hamilton told me how the young Iain McGeachy, just as in the tennis club dance days, was ever eager to jump in and defend friends when a drunk attracted by the late-licence started trouble. Hamilton had a set of bongo drums and occasionally got paid 50p when he backed Iain on songs like 'Rolling Home' and 'Fairy Tale Lullaby' though they weren't the most sartorially elegant pairing. Usually Hamilton would wear a poncho, jeans and homemade sandals to gigs while Martyn wore a white cotton kaftan and trousers with no shoes!

Another regular at the Folk Song Club was Alan Dunbar, a young junior manager who stood out from the usual denims-and-T-shirt clientele because he chose to wear a suit. Alan, who now works for an American aerospace company based in Birmingham, recalls seeing lots of memorable shows at the Glasgow venue. Concerts by the likes of Sandy Denny, Doris Troy (playing the autoharp) and Davey Graham stick in his memory.

> You also got regular local performers who popped in and out, and got on the stage and did a couple of numbers. Often it was great but sometimes it was rubbish! To be honest though there was a lot of dross turned up to play;

quite often if it hadn't been wet outside I'd have just gone home. The club wasn't licensed, but I am sure I had a drink in there on more than one occasion. I know I sometimes went into the office or backstage room off the stage at the front door and managed to get a drink from Drew Moyes. People did sneak drink in with them too. There was usually a good atmosphere. Being near a university there was always a student crowd hanging about. There were the usual folkies of the time plus a fairly mixed bag of people who liked folk music and found that this was the only place they could get to see it at weekends. I went there almost every Saturday night and I never saw any trouble in the place any time I visited. One of the great things about the club was that they sold bacon, sausage and fried-egg rolls at around 12.30 a.m. They had a little kitchen-type thing at the back of the room with a counter and you went and ordered and queued there for the food. It really hit the spot at that time in the morning.

Alan remembers being impressed by the young John Martyn's appearances there:

My first impression of him was that he was quite an arrogant, good-looking type of guy with blondish hair. He was a women puller and very sure of himself and his ability. The arrogance he projected of course could have just been his stage style. Around that time a lot of guys used a very nasal-sounding, English-sounding voice to enunciate the lyrics. He did this up to a point but he had a more transatlantic style. On the Folk Centre's small stage he looked good and had a good act; he was a fine guitar player – his finger style was good and his selection of material worked well for him. I never heard him play the 'Anji'-type stuff but he had a range of numbers that he played that worked well for him, like the song 'Cocaine' and some other blues standards. I'm not sure if he sang much of his own material – although I guess from what I remember of his first two albums there was an element of familiar-sounding stuff in there. I spoke to him on a few occasions and he was a nice guy, very helpful when questioned about his music. He showed me a couple of little bluesy runs on guitar that I still cannot master to this day! I can't say that he hit the booze any more than I or anyone else there was doing. The lifestyle that he was starting to lead was taking something out of him even in those early days though. He was young but not too fresh-faced from the life and the hours he was keeping. On the one occasion I saw him with too much to drink in him it did not seem to affect his guitar playing one bit. He and Hamish seemed to be close friends, with Iain playing the role of accompanist to Hamish, who strutted about the stage, but then Iain did the odd song himself or solo. On one occasion Iain did most of the work but I think Hamish was a bit too drunk that night. They always seemed to have good-looking women with them.

Soho

He had the face of a wicked angel – clear skin, boyish charm and bright-eyed. He had very little regard for trying to appeal to people, his charm and charisma was enough for him.

Ralph McTell

It was the crest of the wave; it was fashionable to play acoustic guitar and John was a real prime mover. People came from far and wide to Soho just because that was where it was all happening.

Wizz Jones on the Les Cousins era

Venues like the Glasgow Folk Song Club and Clive's may have helped spice up the Scottish music scene but John soon realised that the real action lay four hundred miles to the south. Having seen fellow musicians like Bert Jansch cross the border and attain success, John knew that London was the place to be. In fact he relished the move down south – comparing London favourably to the violent streets of Glasgow which he described as a difficult place to live. And of course he had the advantage over other musicians travelling to the capital from the provinces, in that he was already a regular visitor to London. Because of his parents' divorce, visiting his mum in London during the summer holidays had become an annual occurrence. London's cultured suburbs in high summer were just about as far removed from urban industrial Glasgow as you could imagine. For Martyn, these Whitsun days when the Hampton Court Fair was in full swing, were simply

A gas, London was like a dream to me . . . even the Southern line, the green trains and the journey from Waterloo to Surbiton . . . It always seemed more civilised to be in England. (*Zigzag*, April/May 1974)

His mother hailed from a Jewish-Belgian family and like her erstwhile husband she was an admirer of Debussy and the classical guitarist Segovia. She was a talented singer and pianist, performing under the stage name of Betty Benson. Linda Dunning met her on trips to England and she remembers that mother and son got on well together. She also reveals that – no matter what countless articles have stated – John Martyn was not an only child.[1]

> The interaction between Iain and his mum was great. They were both highly intelligent and would engage in all kinds of conversations that probably went over my head. The first summer we dated he went down on his own to visit her in Bradford-on-Avon in Wiltshire, where she and her second husband ran an old inn. Later she divorced him and moved back to Surrey where she lived in a luxury apartment in Surbiton. That was where I first met her. Her husband then was called John Collins and he was the caretaker of the apartments. They had a baby at that time, David John Collins, and Iain was very excited to have a baby brother. Iain's mum was an attractive and very vivacious woman with a great sense of humour, who liked the occasional gin and tonic. She was a kind of high-class Elsie Tanner, she said what she thought, and really was way ahead of her time. She had lots of friends, and her mum and sister Ivy lived close by. She was wonderful to me and I thought the world of her.

By the age of seventeen, John Martyn was dressing in faded denims and copying the hobo image of Woody Guthrie. He became a common sight, wandering around the capital's folk clubs, carrying his guitar case or even an old sack, which contained his guitar, spare strings, a change of clothing and a couple of favourite paperbacks. His friends remember him, seemingly impervious to the cold, hitching to gigs dressed in just a T-shirt, jeans and baseball boots. John would also carry with him a practice amp, foot pedals and leads from venue to venue, where he would hustle for bookings. Sometimes he would sleep rough in Trafalgar Square, before getting moved on by the local cops. Martyn would always say later in life that he had no game plan to become a recording artist, but speaking to some of his early

1. Besides his half-brother, Martyn also had a half-sister, Jules.

friends I got the impression that he was actually very ambitious and image-conscious. He would sometimes rub down and stain a new guitar to make it look more authentic and occasionally carried a notebook to jot down song ideas. He was also ferociously dedicated to his music, practicing for hours until his fingers were bloody and calling around to the houses of friends at all hours to play them a new song he had written. Donnie Barclay recalls how John would use a product called Liquid Nails to help his guitar picking and used a new set of strings at almost every gig. 'He liked to give the impression that he had just strolled in off the street, but he was actually a perfectionist when it came to his music.'

John had left Shawlands Academy with good qualifications and before making the move south he had a short spell on a building site and also worked for a few months as an office boy for a company on Bath Street, Glasgow, that sold bulk supplies of petrol. There was also a very brief spell working as a delivery boy for a company that imported fortified wines (somewhat ironic given his later weakness for the stuff) and also a fleeting brush with the world of journalism. Davie MacFarlane recalls:

> My father used to work for William Hill the bookies and he had a lot of contacts with people in newspapers. Iain had expressed this desire to get into journalism and my dad helped to get him an interview for a job as a reporter at the *Glasgow Herald*. He didn't get the job and we later heard that they liked him but they thought he maybe could have dressed a bit better for the interview – he had turned up dressed in denims!

Despite these diversions, music was always going to be his career choice. John told me of his parents' reaction to his preference and how they never really rated him as a singer.

> They were rather jealous of me! The idea of being recorded – that was a big thing at the time – and I managed that when I was nineteen. I think it put their noses slightly out of joint. Also they didn't fully approve of my repertoire, they were really into variety.

Around this time, inspired by his hero Davey Graham, he travelled alone to Morocco to visit the holy city of Fez.

> I thought if it was good enough for Davey Graham then it would be good enough for me. I followed the hash trail, thinking it might rub off on me.

Exactly when he started gigging in the capital is uncertain. But a fellow Glaswegian, Alec Milne, recalls seeing John play at Bunjies Folk Cellar during a visit to London in October 1966. Alex remembers:

> All the stuff he played was from the first album he would record, *London Conversation*, and his trademark was performing barefoot, as on the cover of that album. John stood out from all the other artists that played that night because of his distinctive style – two-finger picking – and that voice!

Performing barefoot, with his long curly hair and angelic good looks, he soon attracted attention and consolidated a strong reputation on the folk circuit. Onstage he was a bundle of speedy energy, rocking back and forth while he thrashed away on his guitar. Between songs he would hold the audience with endless raps on any subject imaginable. On one trip to London, he visited the Cousins club in Soho and was inspired by seeing Davey Graham play live, sitting just a few feet from his hero and studying his every move. Within a matter of months, he would be playing blues guitar alongside Graham at the venue.

Situated under an illegal gambling hall and a top-notch Greek restaurant, Cousins officially opened as a music venue on Friday, 16 April 1965. It rapidly earned a reputation as *the* place to play in London during the 1960s, but it could be a challenging venue. In his autobiography, Hamish Imlach recalled all-night sessions there as being tough gigs 'full of drunks and junkies waiting for the chemist in Piccadilly to open at dawn so they can get their daily prescription'. Like numerous other young singer-song-writers, John Martyn owed much to Cousins and he grew to love the club, later selecting it as the friendliest and most relaxing of all the small venues he played. A former skiffle club and strip joint, it was situated right in the heart of Soho and became the focal point for the burgeoning folk scene (though other forms of music such as jazz, blues and avant-garde were often heard there too). It may have been small and remarkably uncomfortable, having only one electrical socket and offering bad coffee and stale sandwiches for fare, but its influence was massive. A typical night was split into an early session from 7.30 p.m. to 11.00 p.m. and then the much mythologised 'all-nighter' from midnight to 7 a.m. The temptation to sit in and listen all night before emerging bleary-eyed into the dawn was to prove irresistible for many and it soon became known as the 'cheapest hotel in London'.

Those learning their craft at Cousins included American tyros like Jackson C. Frank, Tom Paxton and Paul Simon. They were paid just a fiver for a set of songs, plus a plate of moussaka if they were lucky. Among the home-grown stars in the making to appear there were Al Stewart, Roy Harper, Richard Digance and Ralph McTell. The Farnborough-born McTell had changed his name from Ralph May and, following some time spent busking, by 1967 had embarked on a recording career with the seminal label Transatlantic Records. In time he would gain great fame, most notably with the number one and Ivor Novello award-winning 'Streets Of London' but talking to me he recalled with some relish the halcyon days of Cousins and the impact the young Scot had on the Soho scene.

It was in a basement at 49 Greek Street, below a restaurant called The Dionysus which was run by a guy called Andreas Matheou (anglicised to Andy Matthews or Andy the Greek) and his father. The restaurant served the best moussaka you will ever taste in your life by the way! The father had given the downstairs part to Andy to run as Cousins. It was supposed to be known as Les Cousins – as in the French pronunciation. But for a long time we all thought it was run by an English guy called Les Cousins!

Greek Street was part of the warren of little streets that had all the jazz clubs, blues clubs, cafés, delicatessens and strip clubs that made up Soho.

You entered the club by a very narrow staircase at the side of the restaurant. Old Mr Matheou would usually be sitting by the door, as young Andy would invariably be away getting stoned somewhere – often with John Martyn as I recall! Inside, the club was absolutely tiny. Legally it could hold about twenty-five people but I imagine there would be around 125 crammed in there some nights. The stage was on the left as you walked into the room and there were no more than three rows of seats in front of you because of the narrowness of the room. The toilets were at the far end of the room. Lots of people would come in, allegedly for the all-nighter, and just sleep there – it was somewhere for them to crash in the middle of London. Up the road there was a very trendy club called Le Kilt, which was full of foreign students and kids with money. Across the road there were a couple of pubs – The Pillars of Hercules and The Carlisle where you could get a quick drink. The Cousins wasn't legally licensed though the odd bottle of Carlsberg was known to be hidden away. But it wasn't a heavy drinking scene or indeed a really heavy dope-smoking scene, though of course that went on as well.

I used to run the all-nighter on the Saturday. To be honest with you, the place had such cachet that it didn't much matter whether you played before or after midnight. Generally though, the bigger names appeared in the second set, after midnight. The all-nighters were a way for people who wanted to make a name for themselves to get up on stage and say they played there in the same club as the great acts – The Incredible String Band, John Renbourn and Bert Jansch. Occasionally, Donovan or Cat Stevens would play Cousins, once even Jimi Hendrix played there. I think there were a lot of second-raters who were happy to put up with appalling conditions for very little or no money – it became a place to be seen to have played. There were more acknowledged clubs and folk venues, but none of them could get away with the all-night thing because they were mostly in pubs.

I've read Al Stewart in interviews say that he thought it was a very competitive scene, but I never really thought that it was. In my humble opinion the whole movement of that time threw up one true great poet-musician, and that would be Bert Jansch without any shadow of a doubt. He was the first poet; he was the first innovative guitarist that put music and words in one package. Prior to that, we had Davey Graham who of course is the granddaddy for us all. He is a superb instrumentalist and innovative guitar player but he didn't write songs. Bert did and – history will be my judge – Bert remains the greatest of all the talents around at that time. He was the reclusive, dark, mysterious one – an incredibly attractive, windswept, interesting Scottish guy who appeared not to bother about anything – he didn't even have his own guitar, and for a long time he had to borrow one. Al Stewart had this intellectual argumentative way of looking at everything, with a very clear penetrative voice and a hugely successful debut album. He was never one to hide in the background; he was confident and a clever lyricist. John Renbourn was the art college one, a lovely man with tremendous self-deprecating wit. He was a dazzling guitar player.

And then Johnny Martyn came down from Scotland. He was perky, full of vim, vigour and brash confidence for such a young man. He was so much younger than we were, and when you are twenty-five or twenty-six, a nineteen-year-old is very much your junior. Five years beyond me were people like Davey Graham and Wizz Jones, and they seemed to be on another planet. Johnny dressed in his own style in blue jeans with bare feet or plimsolls with no socks. John had a very strong self-image; he was always just one step ahead of us. People did notice what he wore; I remember him wearing a suit with diamanté brooches and stuff. He wore a suit, T-shirt and plimsolls before anyone else did.

His lightning-fast guitar technique dazzled rather than moved you. The hotchpotch of stuff he was playing was enormously boyish and sexy; he made a great noise and had a great rhythmic punch to his playing that very few others did. He was totally charming and I loved watching him. John played a very cheap Yamaha guitar and made it sound like the most expensive instrument imaginable.

The young prodigy from Glasgow was soon feeling right at home in the middle of Soho. For all his bohemian affectations in Glasgow, he had in fact led a fairly sheltered existence there. Given his future problems with alcohol, it will surprise many people to learn that the young John Martyn had no time for excessive drinking. Donnie Barclay says 'To to be honest we didn't drink that much back then as it was considered uncool to be a lush – if you came home drunk it freaked everyone out.' Linda Dunning never saw Martyn drink excessively or even get drunk in all their four years together. But when she travelled south to visit John she began to notice changes in him. He was now hanging out with a different crowd who had different ways of enjoying life. Linda says:

Hash got passed around at the clubs, especially in London, like it was sweeties. Everyone thought they were so cool. I made an issue on one or two occasions when we were in a place where people were using, because I wanted to be nowhere near it. I guess I wasn't cool and I made a scene. So naturally we did have arguments and fall out. But Iain never used drugs in my presence. I think music was his drug in those early days. What he did when I was back home in Scotland, I have no idea. He would make a point of calling me every night though to tell me that he loved me. I am sure he also wanted to make sure I was home (as in, not out with anyone else). If we went to the pub, he would order a half of lager and I would have a Babycham!

Martyn was now in the centre of a hedonistic scene full of liberated young ladies, strip clubs and like-minded kids who may have stayed with their parents in the London suburbs during the week but nonetheless flocked to Soho at weekends. And of course there were other attractions – speed and grass fuelled the all-night sessions. The white blues guitarist Michael Chapman was a good friend of Martyn in the early days and confirms:

John was a boozer and a stoner in his youth . . . mostly he was a stoner, but then we all were. Getting stoned was cheaper and also we were the *avant-garde*. That's what we did to prove that we were different to other people. John was just this curly-haired child. He just appeared from nowhere with this fairly devastating presentation and was brilliant from the word go. He was different from the rest of us musically. I was into vintage Gibsons in those days, while others were into vintage Martins; it was the done thing to have a fairly expensive American guitar in those days. You could pick up a decent Gibson for seventy quid but John always had this sort of forty-quid Yamaha that we all sneered at. He used to use a pencil and a rubber band as a capo. He had found out that with the pencil he could slide it up and down and so change keys during songs and go up in semitones or whatever.

Chapman recalls the first time he came across John hitching a ride from Bournemouth to London.

> I saw John bobbing down the road carrying his guitar. It's the middle of winter – fucking freezing – so he asks for a lift up to London. Now, I had this old van and the heating was struggling because it was so cold. I noticed he had a T-shirt on and baseball boots and he seemed completely resistant to the cold. I seemed to chauffeur John about quite a bit. Another time, me and my band were playing at Lancaster University at a weekend festival and then we had to go down to London to collect ferry tickets to go to Europe the day after. John came along with his 'give us a lift, squire' routine! So he gets into the back of the van and immediately falls fast asleep. Never says a word until we are just outside London when he stands bolt upright in the back of the van and shouts, 'My name is Colonel Nasty and this is my dog Biter!' in a terribly colonial accent – and then went straight back to sleep again!

Newly anointed by *Time* magazine as 'Swinging London' in the summer of 1967, the capital was – with the possible exception of San Francisco – the place to be for an aspiring musician. The emerging rock scene has been well documented but the folkies weren't far behind when it came to exciting talent. The folk scene had already spawned a genuine superstar in Donovan and The Incredible String Band – managed by Joe Boyd – were about to release their second album. Bert Jansch and John Renbourn were already big names on the London scene, both on the verge of joining the folk supergroup Pentangle. The renowned guitarist Wizz Jones remembers:

> The Les Cousins era was great. In those days alcohol wasn't such a big thing on the music scene. Cousins wasn't licensed; people were quite happy to go there and drink coffee and then sleep on the floor in their sleeping-bags during the all-nighters. Nowadays it's more geared to alcohol; if you go to a gig, there has to be a bar.

Martyn spent the summer of 1967 hanging out with friends like the Florida-born Robin Frederick whose song 'Sandy Grey' – written about time spent in Aix-en-Provence with the young songwriter Nick Drake – would appear on John's first album. Robin recalls how she and John spent the hot summer days living off tea and toast and listening to The Incredible String Band and The Beatles' *Sergeant Pepper's* album.

> John picked up the sitar and taught himself to play it almost effortlessly. His singing voice was gorgeous and he looked angelic. He was making his first album and seemed very happy about it all. It was a chaotic, creative time. I don't think there was much thought of the future.

Another close friend and influence on the young Martyn was Londoner Paul Wheeler, a teenage guitarist and student at Ravensbourne Art College who in 1968 would win a scholarship to Cambridge University to study English. Wheeler and Martyn first met at the bar during an Incredible String Band gig at the Kingston Folk Club. Both men shared a love for the band and Wheeler recalls being impressed by John – finding him open-minded and quick-thinking though rather clumsy, spilling large amounts of beer on the club floor. Paul and John would go on to share a residency at Cousins and Wheeler would eventually play guitar on Martyn's second album and also introduce Martyn to another Cambridge student, the phenomenally talented and equally introspective Nick Drake. Wheeler himself was a skilful player and Martyn cited him and another little known guitarist and singer, Les Brown, as influences around this time. Wheeler remembers:

> John was always interested in ideas – books and paintings and whatever. He usually had perceptive and amusing comments to make on them. We once went to see an exhibition at the Royal Academy and there were some painters and decorators on a staircase. John told them they would be able to say now that they had a painting at the Royal Academy. On another occasion he thought a woman was wearing something stupid when we passed her on a street, and John just stopped her and told her so. It was so disarming that the woman just laughed rather than got angry at him.

Required reading for the London hip set was the weekly music paper *Melody Maker*, even if it did make the odd factual error – on one occasion hailing the hot new Irish blues guitarist 'Rory Gulliver'. The first mention of Martyn in the paper came in the 15 April edition of 1967, which had The Monkees on the front cover and a main feature asking 'Who says Jimi Hendrix can't sing?' Buried away on the Folk Forum page, edited by Karl Dallas, was a mention of John Martin [sic] appearing alongside Steve Spurling at the Kingston Folk Barge on 13 April. Moored on the Thames, the floating candle-lit barge was in a near derelict state with a capacity of only around fifty but it was the springboard for many young performers. John Renbourn, Al Stewart, Jackson C Frank and a young student at the local Kingston Art College named Sandy Denny were among those who plied their trade on the barge.

Guitarist and aspiring songwriter Tim Denley was a regular at the Barge, playing with his friend Gerry Richardson in an acoustic duo named Candy Island. Tim remembers the old venue fondly but still shudders at the thought of its dilapidated state.

> It was previously a working river barge and was both truly disgusting and a fine venue in equal measure. It had to be pumped out regularly; it was cold, damp and was probably never cleaned. The gangplanks were very wobbly – really, Health & Safety would have had a field day inspecting it. The owner was very fond of cheap sherry but it was a great place to play as you could just turn up if there wasn't a big name on that night. No other venue in the area attracted so many players and it was nearly always full. Listening to John there was a truly eye-opening experience – his style was unmatched and completely unique. He was experimenting with open tunings and I remember being fascinated watching him.

Tim got to know Martyn fairly well and remembers visiting his bedsit, where John would hold court amid the sweet smell of weed.

> He was just enjoying the fringes of fame, and living life as it comes. He came across as very gentle, maybe even shy, but he always seemed to have this beaming smile.

Some time later Tim met Martyn on Shaftesbury Avenue when the young Scot had just purchased his first Gibson Les Paul Gold Top guitar.

> He was full of excitement and dropped to his knees there on the pavement and opened up the lid of the case. We both stared reverently at the content. I didn't know much about electric guitars in those days but this beauty just shone out of the box.

John Martyn would appear at the Barge on four more occasions that spring, but there are precious few mentions of him in *Melody Maker* for the remainder of 1967. Audiences for those Barge shows usually only numbered a dozen, but after one performance an excited onlooker called Theo Johnson approached Martyn, saying, 'I'll make you a star – would you like a recording contract?' Martyn called his bluff by replying, 'Go ahead then!' John gave Johnson his mum's telephone number – he lived in a house nearby without a phone – and promptly forgot about the encounter. Shortly afterwards, his mother was banging on his bedroom door saying Island Records wanted to speak to him.

Vinyl excursions

Of that first album I thought, 'You'd only been playing for eight months when you made it so you didn't do badly' . . . The lyrics though were acute, viciously accurate, and very personal.

John Martyn

John was the kind of bloke who would steal all the oxygen and he had quite a dangerous side to him. He was always full on, there was no off switch with John.

Steve Tilston

In 1959 Chris Blackwell, the only son of a wealthy palm-oil plantation owner, formed Island Records, with a view to exporting Caribbean music to the UK. For its first few years, Island was unrecognisable from the influential label we now all know and love – indeed, back then they released crude ballads and rugby songs to subsidise the Jamaican music and help pay the rent on their Basing Street headquarters in London. Theo Johnson had cut a couple of those bawdy discs for a set fee of £100 and having come across John at the Folk Barge he decided to exploit his contacts by taking a demo of Martyn singing the whimsical 'Fairy Tale Lullaby' to Island's offices. Blackwell loved Martyn's vocals and his style of playing. Pretty soon afterwards John Martyn – at the ripe old age of nine-teen and much to his own surprise – was offered a contract and promptly signed to the label. Subsequently the 'fact' that John was Island's first white artist became part of the Martyn myth until it was thoroughly debunked by a 1996 article in *Record Collector*. In fact, while Martyn was still attending Shawlands Academy, Island had already signed up the

Spencer Davis Group and the Glasgow singer Alex Harvey, though both saw their releases sold through the Fontana label. *Record Collector* also pointed out that the white West Indian Harold McNair, a future collaborator of Martyn's, had an album released on Island in 1965. Various other obscure white-skinned artists, including the splendidly named Wynder K Frogg, had albums released by Island before John arrived on the scene.

Theo Johnson's part in the Martyn story didn't last much longer. True, he did produce his first album for Island, and three weeks after John and Island linked up he did offer to manage the youngster, however, the contract, which would give Johnson 45 per cent of everything for the next ten years, was rejected. Yet Johnson did play a key role in setting the ball in motion and Martyn later admitted that this 'little, fat, mad hustler of the finest kind' – whose favourite tipple was supposedly methylated spirits and red wine – had set him on the road to fame. Theo Johnson was also on the same bill as Martyn in July 1968 at a human rights concert at Central Hall, Westminster, alongside Julie Felix, Fairport Convention and Al Stewart. But thereafter the trail goes cold.

John stayed at Theo's London flat in Richmond for a short while where, according to Hamish Imlach, the two exiled Scots would help themselves to Theo's deluxe whisky and replace it with cold tea. Robin Frederick also stayed at the flat and remembers Johnson temporarily disappearing – allegedly with the small advance given by Island for Martyn's first album. It was a flat that attracted all sorts of individuals. Robin says:

> There was a sort of ebb and flow of people in and out of the flat, giving it the feel of an extended family. I remember a couple of Swedish girls crashing there and an Italian poet named Angelo whom nobody seemed to actually know.

Two other blues/folk musicians of note – Johnny Silvo and Diz Disley – lived in an adjoining apartment, adding to the communal feel of the area. Another visitor to the flat was the guitarist Bridget St John, a languages student at Sheffield University who would go on to record a string of critically acclaimed albums. Robin Frederick introduced Bridget to John

Martyn and they remained close friends until Martyn's death. John helped Bridget expand her musical horizons, introducing her to open tunings and other unconventional guitar sounds. She recalls:

> I think the first time I met John he was a little out of it – but our relationship was not about getting high. I have always thought of John as my musical brother. He was very likeable and also had this immense musical talent which made him even more appealing.

Theo Johnson's flat was never going to be a permanent residence so John soon moved to his first real independent home – at 21 Whittingstall Road in Parsons Green, London. Donnie Barclay flitted down to London a couple of months after John and moved into the home along with two girls who had worked at the Glasgow Folk Centre, Mary Kerr and Ann McKerlie, and two rather well-to-do Canadian guitarists, architecture student Andy Wade and John Gibson who used to get tuition from John Williams the classical guitarist. Donnie remembers the flat having a turnover of visitors . . . Sandy Denny, Al Stewart and Roy Harper were regulars and the ongoing party was lubricated by endless dope-smoking, though nothing harder was taken and booze was still considered not cool. Donnie recalls an element of friction and rivalry between Martyn and Harper with John resenting what he considered to be Harper's superior air – Harper was significantly older than John and presumably more worldly-wise. Also Harper's wacky hash-head persona was never going to go down well with John: one gets the impression that he wanted that role all to himself. (Indeed back in Glasgow, Iain McGeachy was known for his offbeat humour; occasionally he would spend the day walking around with a cane, wearing a pair of dark glasses and with Davie MacFarlane's gun-trained Labrador as a 'guide'. Apparently the young star was constantly being guided across the road by concerned pedestrians.)

Donnie Barclay recalls:

> John was keen to learn from the guys he met but he also liked to be treated with respect. John either liked you or he didn't, there was no middle ground

with him and I think that is part of the reason there is such a divide between people who love him and others who don't. In the early days, a lot of people didn't treat him with respect. I would overhear people slag him off. A lot of it was down to jealousy because he was very much the new kid on the block. But John remembered these people and he never forgave them, he would never speak to them again.

But more generally, he was very possessive about relationships. I think that was the biggest weakness in his personality and it lasted throughout his life. He could not deal with rejection. And that didn't just mean with the women in his life. He didn't like his male pals getting too friendly with people who would visit the house. About a year after moving into Parson's Green he found another flat at 20a Beaufort Road in Surbiton and he just told me that we were moving, without even discussing it! When I told him I was staying where I was he was really hurt but I think he just forgot that I had a mind of my own. As it happened I ended up staying at the new flat anyway. Ironically when he moved out of the Parson's Green flat, Roy Harper moved in.

In the true sense of the word, John was never a hard man but like myself he could resort to the Glasgow vernacular when required. We were on the tube on our way to Cousins one day when a gang of skinheads got on board. I had long hair and a greatcoat while John had his blond ringlets and was wearing the flowery Afghan coat which is on the cover of the *Stormbringer* album. They started giving us the usual abuse and we both went straight across to them and launched into a tirade of menacing Glasgow threats. I don't think they understood one word but they got the message and backed down! When they got off the train they started making threats from the safety of the platform and John just stared them in the eye and blew them a kiss! Shit you should have seen their faces . . . I often think what might have happened if the bluff hadn't worked. No John Martyn story for a start!

*

John Martyn's first vinyl excursion was done on the cheap and in rapid time. The endearingly innocent *London Conversation* took only two and a half hours to record in mono in a Putney bedroom on a Revox tape machine and cost just £158 to make. Released in October 1967, it had Martyn's name on the writing credits of nine of the twelve tracks, most of which had their roots in his Glasgow writing. In later years Martyn was to belittle – if not disown – his debut, calling parts of it embarrassing. But considering he was barely nineteen and had only been performing seriously for a matter of months, it is a remarkably mature effort. The emphasis was on fairly formulaic songs, which would have even gone down well with the traditional woolly-jersey and pipe-smoking folk fraternity. There's little to suggest that within a couple of years Martyn would be tearing down the walls of conventional folk music. But already he was placing himself firmly in the contemporary rather than traditional folk movement.

The *London Conversation* album is an intriguing snapshot of Martyn as a fresh-faced teenager, before the heavy boozing and drug abuse kicked in; a smiling innocent before cynicism took hold in the 1970s. The simple sweet songs differ from his later work in that they're delivered in a crystal-clear voice and you can actually decipher the words without the aid of a lyric sheet. 'Fairy Tale Lullaby' – the song that first caught Chris Blackwell's attention – may be a touch naïve at times but it and Robin Frederick's 'Sandy Grey', a cryptic tribute to her time spent with Nick Drake, are very much products of the flower power era. The inclusion of the traditional blues number 'Cocain' [sic] was intriguing. Martyn was never shy of telling the world he was a 'natural drug taker' and even as a teenager he experimented with the devil's dandruff. Later in his career he would occasionally snort a line of heroin during press interviews.

The Davey Graham and Bert Jansch influences shine through on 'Run Honey Run' while the dodgy sitar soaked 'Rolling Home' was an experi-ment with Indian-flavoured music that Martyn never repeated. Even for 1967 the use of sitar seemed a bit passé. Around that time, The Incredible String Band were using exotic instruments like the gimbri, Arabian oud and bamboo flute on their albums. The Les Cousins club occasionally held 'Music of India' nights with sitar and tabla-players, including J Bharatia who had played on The Beatles' *Sergeant Pepper's*. A respectful cover version of Dylan's 'Don't Think Twice It's Alright' wraps up proceedings effectively.

The album, which has a cover photo of a barefoot John atop the roof of Chris Blackwell's Cromwell Road flat, soon sold almost 4,000 copies;

not at all bad for an unknown Glaswegian strummer. (It has never been deleted, and continues to sell well.)

The LP sleeve notes are of a sweetly hippie flavour, with John hoping that the listener would learn a bit about him and a whole lot about themselves, because 'that's the whole scene'. Lyrically it was innocent, insightful, and invariably centred on the mysteries of love, an obsession that stayed with him throughout his career. Many years later, John reflected that the lyrics contained seeds of later deviance, telling *Q* magazine in 1990:

> Of that first album I thought, 'You'd only been playing for eight months when you made it so you didn't do badly', but the voice on that album literally wasn't considered. The lyrics though were acute, viciously accurate, and very personal. It was like the confessions of a seventeen-year-old rebel . . . The songs were like a diary and an element of fantasy came in on songs.

Having earned a recording contract he seemed keen on making the LP a success. John told the writer Chris Nickson that at the time he was very enthusiastic about his career, even complaining to Island that he couldn't find the album in some record stores. He was convinced that his bolshie attitude impressed Chris Blackwell and helped forge a close friendship between them. Blackwell for his part should be credited for imbuing his label with the standards set by jazz labels like Blue Note where it was considered more important to work with the artist's career over a long period of time rather than fret over poor initial record sales.

Martyn's career was up and running, part of a new movement alongside contemporary folkies like Al Stewart, Mike Chapman, Roy Harper and Ralph McTell. His name began to appear regularly in the pages of *Melody Maker*. Although he undoubtedly appeared there earlier in his career, the first mention of John headlining at Cousins came with an appearance there in the early slot on 9 February 1968. On the same night, another little known singer Robert Plant, with his Band of Joy, was playing across Soho at the Marquee, supporting Edwin Starr! By March, Martyn was playing a regular prestigious support slot of his own with Pentangle at their residency at The Horseshoe, Tottenham Court Road. Other regular performers who shared a bill with John at this time were Stefan Grossman, Ron Geesin, Mike Cooper, Paul Wheeler, Clive Palmer and Gordon Giltrap. Cementing his new-found appeal John appeared on the BBC radio programme *Night Ride* in July 1968.

Island was sufficiently encouraged by the debut album's sales figures to agree to finance another effort as soon as possible. Again though, the budget was tight. Martyn's second album *The Tumbler* was recorded in one afternoon – at a cost of just £200. Island's publicity in the music press amounted to the faintly embarrassing advert – 'Tumble, Fumble, Rumble and Stumble – but above all listen to *The Tumbler*. John Martyn *is* The Tumbler.' Released in December 1968, the record was still rooted in the gentle inoffensive folk so prevalent at the time, but by now John was ready to experiment and accommodate some of the more leftfield influences on the London scene. The time between albums had been spent soaking up the varied strands of the local music scene, checking out his boyhood heroes Jansch and Graham, and meeting a host of older, more experienced musicians. When the new album emerged, it came laced with the lilting jazz flute and saxophone playing of Harold McNair. John could already hold an audience with his dazzling acoustic solos, but in McNair he met for the first time a cultured, refined jazz musician who would provide inspiration to try new types of music and open him up to new ways of playing.

He did a lot for me just by example. We were never really close friends or anything, just good acquaintances. We played well together. He was definitely the best flute player I've ever heard. Nobody swung like him. (*Zigzag*, April/May 1974)

The beauty of their playing together was given an added piquancy by the fact that McNair was already in the grip of a cancer that was to claim his life just a couple of years after the album's release. Quiet and unassuming, McNair was a white Trinidadian who had arrived in the UK in 1966 and for the next couple of years had a Saturday-night residency at the Bull's Head pub in Barnes Bridge. Musical excursions with Donovan and Mike Carr helped bolster his reputation and he was voted best flautist in *Melody Maker*'s Jazz Poll of 1969, ahead of Tubby Hayes. Among his many admirers was Rolling Stones manager, Andrew Loog Oldham, who came across McNair – nicknamed 'Little Jesus' – while they both worked at Ronnie Scott's Soho jazz club. McNair, according to Oldham, was super-cool with a style to match that of Miles Davis. Near the end of his life, McNair recorded an all-star jazz-rock album *The Fence*, with the likes of Rick Grech, Danny Thompson and Keith Tippett. In December 1970, a benefit concert in aid of Harold took place at Ronnie Scott's, featuring Julie Felix and The Scaffold. The £700 raised helped to send Harold to the Canary Isles for respite from his cancer but he died at his home in Maida Vale in March 1971. His place in the John Martyn story was small but significant; he was in the right place at the right time and his ability on the flute tied in neatly with Martyn's own burgeoning ability as a musician. Perhaps if McNair had lived he would have become a long-term musical partner to Martyn, in much the same way as Danny Thompson or Spencer Cozens did. Instead, McNair's death was to be the first of a series of tragedies that would affect John greatly and shape the direction his life and music took.

Though still essentially folk roots, McNair's involvement in *The Tumbler* led to a jazzier feel on some songs. The pair's interplay on tracks like 'Fly On Home' (co-written with Paul Wheeler) and the ever-so-slightly trippy 'The Gardeners' is impressive. Martyn's liking for the blues is also evident in songs like 'Going Down To Memphis' and 'Winding Boy'. The song 'Dusty' harked back to John's dreamy Whitsun days in Hampton Court and the first wide-eyed sojourns to Soho, and would eventually appear on the Island label sampler *You Can All Join In*. But there's also still more than a trace of the vaguely irritating, hippy-dippy vibe on songs like 'Fishing Blues' and 'Sing A Song Of Summer' – the latter being a rapid ride around some rather naïve and nonsensical lyrics. The album's nadir is undoubtedly 'Knuckledy Crunch And Slipp Ledee-slee Song' which, besides having possibly the most annoying title ever, manages to ruin a superb introductory verse with one of the most intrusive and incongruous choruses ever recorded on vinyl. The second album ends with 'Seven Black Roses', a showcase for Martyn's guitar virtuosity. It soon became a crowd-pleaser especially at concerts on the continent but, as with most of the songs from that era, it soon disappeared from the set list. Martyn cryptically explained that 'giving people what they want isn't always good for them. And it isn't what's good for you!' It was an early example of his determination to refuse to play to record-company rules or to pander to what his fans expected or demanded. Critical reaction to the new LP was generally favourable – Tony Wilson of *Melody Maker* thought it was less derivative of Jansch and The Incredible String Band, with plenty of variety, singling out 'the science-fiction feel' of 'The Gardener' for special praise.

Another alumnus of the Cousins scene, Al Stewart, produced *The Tumbler*. Martyn was good friends with Stewart, but seemed unimpressed by his fellow folkie's contribution, later saying that he wouldn't have been so silly to ask Stewart to help out! Chris Blackwell probably arranged Stewart's involvement but even Stewart himself later said that his role had been minimal.

> We were recording it right on the cusp of mono and stereo. I presented it to Island in mono, whereupon they said, 'But it's supposed to be in stereo.' So they just stamped STEREO on it anyway and to this day I don't think anyone has noticed! There was an engineer with me in the studio but I don't suppose my actual production called for very much because I didn't know anything about recording at the time. It was really simply a case of helping John through the process and saying, 'That's great' or 'That wasn't too good, let's try it again.' I've always felt that to say I produced the album was a slight exaggeration! (*Al Stewart: The True Life Adventures of a Folk Rock Troubadour*, Neville Judd, Helter Skelter, 2002)

The delegation of power to a producer he could fully trust was to prove a difficult move for John on many future albums.

Though he was still playing mainly in small folk clubs, he was already feeling restricted and growing restless over the lack of creative potential on the folk scene. He disliked the atmosphere in some folk clubs where only one in three of the audience would actually listen to him and the others just wanted a drink and a chat with some background music. The dearth of decent folk venues would eventually see him take to the college circuit. In truth, although always associated with folk music, Martyn had at best an ambivalent relationship with the traditional music scene, which was rooted in small clubs populated by well-meaning, if occasionally slightly woolly, individuals. He always had a liking for traditional Scots music, even the more garish elements – he was brought up watching the likes of Andy Stewart, Calum Kennedy and Jimmy Shand on TV – and he always had a great deal of admiration for mainstream folkies like Archie Fisher and Hamish Imlach, but he never had much time for the nationalist element attached to much Scots folk music and often talked disparagingly about the boring cliques who all dressed in corduroy and stuck a finger in one ear while singing. In any case, his songs were evolving away from the 'all-join-in', easy-to-sing chorus numbers and his interest in developing acoustic music with jazz improvisation or electric experimentation would soon distance him from the traditionalists. Pretty soon there would be complaints from the woolly-jersey brigade when he dared to use an amplifier at gigs.

The Liverpool-born singer Steve Tilston, who got to know John well during the Cousins era, witnessed how the young Scot's effervescent character often rubbed people up the wrong way.

> I remember there were some older folk singers who regarded him as a bit of an upstart. There was the odd occasion when he was told to just give it a break. John could really turn on the charm, but the trouble with him back then was that he had such verbal diarrhoea. He would come out with stuff that was seriously embroidered. It could be really entertaining – he had a great sense of humour – but not all the older folk got it. To people like me who were younger than him, we just thought he was a very funny guy, a very attractive, larger-than-life character. In a way it was a moth-and-light bulb scenario; you didn't want to be in his company too much because John was the kind of bloke who would steal all the oxygen and he had quite a dangerous side to him. He was always full on, there was no off switch with John.

His striking musical ability and constant quest to expand his musical repertoire soon meant that John had even less in common with what he considered to be his simpering singer-songwriter contemporaries. Michael Chapman, who had started on the Cornish folk circuit before going on to record for EMI Harvest, told me:

> John worked in the folk scene, but like me he was never really a folkie. We played there because that was where you could play acoustic guitars. He hung out with jazz musicians who were at the different end of the spectrum to the folkies. Also he hung out with Rabbit Bundrick, the keyboard player, who was miles away from the folk scene.

Martyn was never one to hold back with his views on fellow musicians who didn't reach his own high standards. Speaking to *Q* magazine in 1990 he let rip with both barrels:

> When I started, it was the era of the singer-songwriter, when people would say, 'Oh, what a lovely line!' when they listened to songs. I still appreciate that in others but for myself, I prefer the noise. I could have been a – perish the thought – Cat Stevens or a Paul Simon or something like that, but the idea of going out and singing the same thing the same way every night always horrified me. I was actually very shy and retiring and ever so sweet and gentle until I was twenty, and then I just got the heave with Donovan and Cat Stevens and all that terribly nice, rolling-up-joints-and-sitting-on-toadstools-watching-the-sunlight-dapple-its-way-through-the-dingly-dell-of-life's-rich-pattern stuff. Back then, everybody expected you to be like that. It'd be: 'Oh, this is the guy who wrote "Sing A Song Of Summer", he must be a really nice guy.' I'm not really that nice and I very consciously turned away from all that . . . It was a rebel stand.

Beverley

Stay away from him – he's a Glaswegian!

Joe Boyd to Beverley Kutner

When I first met him he was absolutely besotted by Beverley, talking about her all the while. In a way it was kind of a step up for him because she already was a bit of a name.

Steve Tilston

By the winter of 1968, people were beginning to recognise the name John Martyn. Just recently returned from a stint at the Glasgow Folk Centre where he had once been resident, he found *Melody Maker* naming him as one of the shining lights of the new folk scene. Fellow musicians were also beginning to take an interest in his work. Both Alex Campbell and Sandy Denny each wanted to cover 'Fairy Tale Lullaby' on their upcoming albums. Also around this time, a young unknown singer called Elton John recorded a couple of new Martyn songs, including 'Stormbringer', at London's DJM Studios. Martyn's friend from back in the Richmond days, Bridget St John, soon covered the wistful love song 'Back To Stay' on her 1969 album, *Songs for the Gentle Man* and John also played on the record.

While his musical reputation grew, so did John's notoriety for living a fast-paced lifestyle. Contemporaries recall John limbering up for Cousins gigs by polishing off half a bottle of vodka and liberal amounts of dope before going on stage. Steve Tilston remembers meeting John on occasion in Soho and ending up the worse for wear.

We would both end up pretty juiced. He was one of the first people I met to drink vodka and orange juice; he got me onto it that one memorable night. I remember him saying that the vitamin C in the orange juice neutered the effect of the alcohol . . . I still left the pub with rubber legs!

Speaking back in 2006, Ralph McTell was amazed that his old friend had survived all the subsequent hell-raising.

John can't help it, he's a bit insecure. His heart must be as big as an ox, to have done what he has done to himself over the years and to be still alive. There is no doubt he should be dead. Drink was a central part of the culture of that period. I don't know why. It was never in the American culture. The guys who came over from the States during that time could not believe the amount of booze we consumed.

And of course it wasn't just booze. By John's own admission, he was fast turning into a total freak, downing every illegal stimulant available and trying to emulate the Timothy Leary acid tests with friends like the American singer-songwriter Jackson C. Frank.

Frank, who lived on a Thames barge and was once the boyfriend of the young Fairport Convention singer Sandy Denny, played a crucial role in the Martyn story when he introduced John to a young female singer, Beverley Kutner, at the Chelsea Art College. (The year usually cited for this meeting is 1969; but it's more likely to have been 1968. By January and February of 1969 John and Beverley were sharing the bill at Cousins.) Martyn had gone along to the college to play – for a fee of £11 – on the same bill as Frank and Beverley who had known each other for four years. When all three artists had played their sets, after some pestering, Frank introduced her to John. Beverley asked for John's address and some days later she arrived at the house, gave him a big kiss and asked to be taken out for a meal. Ever the gent, John obliged and their romance began. He remembered his first impression of her as 'This very sexual lady, with a big hooter and great big brown eyes . . . and I thought I'd like to fuck that'

(*Supersnazz*, October 1973). He was to write far more eloquently in the future of a woman who would inspire some of Martyn's most beautiful and intimate love songs. But any romantic notions were complicated by the fact that Martyn was at the time engaged to Linda Dunning. He returned to Scotland and broke off the relationship. In an interview with *Supersnazz* magazine, John recalled that the relationship was already on the brink of falling apart, describing Linda as a very straight young lady: 'God bless her, and I just left her behind, I grew a bit faster than she did. So I came back (to London) a free person.'

Linda agrees with her ex-beau's assessment of how their love affair was in terminal decline.

It is pretty accurate. He had grown way ahead of me. After all, he was entrenched in the music scene and all that went with it, including the drugs, and I was finishing my degree at Queen's College, Glasgow, with every intention of following a career as a Home Economics teacher. We were to get married in June 1969. I had realised there was someone else. I found what I thought were songs that he had written and in fact they were letters. I believe that they weren't letters from Beverley; I believe they were from the girlfriend of another folk musician. I remember John sat me down one day and told me he had met this musician girl – Beverley – and he needed to have this thing with her and he thought that he could live with her until we got married in June! One time he told me she was so cool because she breastfed her baby on the London Underground – apparently that really impressed him. She had this free spirit that really impressed him. I was so naïve to his world. We just grew in different directions. Our relationship ended and naturally I was heartbroken, but it was one of those things that would ultimately have happened anyway because of our different lifestyles and my refusal to have anything to do with drugs. Needless to say, after we split up I was not following his career with Beverley, so I never heard the song 'Would You Believe Me?' which he wrote about me, until recently.

He is correct in saying that I was 'straight'. I refused to have any part of the drug scene, never used or tried anything, and I still haven't to this day. It was something that I had no use for in my life, and I did not want to be around the drug scene. Iain never used in my presence, which he managed because latterly our time together was limited to my college breaks when I would go down to London, or his occasional visits to Glasgow. I was pretty naïve about his life, at that time, so ultimately our relationship would never have survived.

A heartbroken Linda found a consoling shoulder to cry on when she visited Martyn's mum during a trip to London over Christmas 1968.

His Mum was wonderful. I will never forget her. She told me to forget about him, that I was too good for him. She calmed me down, I think it took a slap and a shot of whisky, and then she told me about the many groupies who were already coming around to her house looking for John. I guess it went along with the profession. They would come around bearing gifts, like rose petal jam and other cool little hippie-type things.

During her previous visits to the London home, Linda had gradually been moving her possessions south, including engagement presents and kitchen items. The kitchenware included pie funnels that her late grandpa used to make steak and kidney pies. When Linda tearfully said goodbye, John's mum emotionally replied with the immortal line: 'Take your pie funnels and go.' Linda took her advice and for almost forty years she had neither spoken to nor seen John Martyn, until they were reunited after she contributed to this book.

After John died in 2009, Linda wrote to me with some intriguing thoughts on how the old Iain that she knew and loved in Glasgow had changed after his move to London.

When I came down to London for college breaks he really had 'become' John Martyn. There was very little left of the Iain McGeachy who had left Glasgow. Iain always had this burning desire to stand out in the crowd and be that bizarre person who attracted attention. Even before he was a musician he was like this. But he was always extremely possessive. He didn't like the idea of me teaching all day when he would be singing in pubs and clubs till all hours. In other words he wanted me to be another of his groupies though I was to be the one who ultimately stayed at home and raised his kids. I thought of this when I heard Beverly speak once on TV; she essentially gave up her career to be Mrs Martyn and raise their children. At that time she was a very established musician in her own right.

*

Meeting Beverley Kutner wasn't just the start of a tempestuous, decade-long relationship, more immediately it led to a fortunate new career opportunity for John. In 1969 when the couple married, Beverley was a promising artist in her own right, having appeared at the Monterey pop festival. The first big write-up for the girl simply billed as 'Beverley' came in November 1967, when she told Tony Wilson of *Melody Maker* that appearing at Monterey was 'the greatest get-together and friendliest scene that I have ever experienced'. Rather presciently she also told Wilson: 'I don't want to be a star. I think other people wanted me to be a star rather than me. All I really want to do is sing and play and make music, perhaps work with others and form a group . . . you cannot do much on your own.' Having moved to London, aged just 15, from her native Coventry to study drama, she instead drifted into the Soho folk scene, learning guitar from an early boyfriend, Bert Jansch. In 1966 she opted out of folk to play with a blues trio, The Levee Breakers, who made one record with Beatles' producer George Martin. She then tried her hand at pop, cutting a couple of singles for the Deram label, before providing backup vocals and touring with Simon and Garfunkel (Beverley dated Paul Simon for a short time). Steve Tilston saw at first hand how fortunate John was to meet Beverley:

> When I first met him he was absolutely besotted by Beverley, talking about her all the while. In a way it was kind of a step up for him because she already was a bit of a name, there was certain kudos for him in moving into that bracket. In a way he ended up being like the cuckoo in the nest.

Ralph McTell recalls the impact Beverley had on the London scene:

I remember Johnny Joyce of The Levee Breakers saying he'd found this girl and that she was dynamite. When I heard a recording of her I had never heard anything like it. She knew all these blues and rags – we thought we were the only ones who knew them. She had a repertoire of astonishing depth and breadth and she sang with a confidence that was quite extraordinary for one so young. She was sexy and pretty and The Levee Breakers were hugely successful and traded very much on her. They did a single for Polydor, 'Babe I'm Leaving You', and then she kind of drifted into the slightly nihilistic, poetic scene of squats and guitars and intense love affairs with those strolling players, of whom Bert Jansch was one. She's pictured on the cover of his second album, *It Don't Bother Me*, sitting on the floor with Bert looking over his shoulder.

In 1968, Beverley missed out on the chance of a support act on Donovan's million-dollar US tour because of work permit problems and she eventually signed up with Joe Boyd's Witchseason company. A handsome and cultured Bostonian, Boyd played a crucial role in the growth of British folk rock after arriving in the UK in November 1965 to run the London office of the Elektra record label. But he later decided to start his own company, and, by the turn of the decade, Witchseason's roster of artists, all on a stipend of around £20 a week, read like a dope fiend's dream. Nick Drake, Fotheringay, John and Beverley Martyn, Fairport Convention and The Incredible String Band all worked out of the company's HQ at 83 Charlotte Street, London. Boyd offered artists a unique package of record production, concert promotion and management. Compared to other record industry organisations of the time, Witchseason, which was named after the Donovan hit 'Season Of The Witch', had an enlightened approach to looking after musicians. Instead of shoddy contracts, Witchseason artists were well looked after in an environment more akin to a family than a business (though in John's case the deal was not especially lucrative – in many interviews around this time he seems to be in a state of perpetual penury). Hooking up with Boyd also meant continuity for John as Witchseason had an arrangement where all their artists' work would be released through the Island label in Britain and – in John and Bev's case – Warner Brothers in the USA. In the UK, Island was by now established as a small company with an enlightened long-term view to developing their artists' careers. The emphasis was on Island being a communal-type unit – with Chris Blackwell as father figure.

A couple of weeks into the relationship, Bev and John were already beginning to pen songs together and play live shows as a duo. Initially, John found it quite tricky collaborating with another person rather than playing solo: by his own admission, he tended to want to dominate proceedings. Joe Boyd already had plans for a solo project for Bev, where her new partner would provide back-up guitar on the sessions, but he soon proposed that they record the album as a duet. With Warner Brothers willing to finance the project, he decided to move the recording to Woodstock in upstate New York. In the summer of 1969, Boyd accompanied the Martyns and Wesley, Bev's son from a previous relationship, to the USA where he also set up a tour of the States for the Incredible String Band. The Martyns stayed for a while in New York at the notorious Chelsea Hotel in 98-degree heat before moving upstate.

The move to America meant a change of emphasis for John Martyn's career and brought him to wider attention. Whereas before much of his time had been taken up with ingesting large amounts of drugs, now things were to become just a little bit more serious and big-time. Thanks to Boyd's connections, the album would feature heavyweight US players like bassist Harvey Brooks of Electric Flag and Mothers of Invention drummer Billy Mundi. Musical director and arranger for the project was Paul Harris, who lived locally and also played piano on the sessions. Although Harris had produced major artists such as The Doors and Crosby, Stills and Nash, it was actually Joe Boyd who helmed the Martyns' sessions. John loved working with musicians who brought a real sense of authority and purpose to the recordings. But the real delight for him was that Levon Helm, drummer with The Band, also worked on the sessions. The hugely influential Canadian group were just about to headline the 1969 Isle of Wight festival and were at the peak of their powers. Their seminal first two albums had a profound effect on just about every serious performer around that time, and Martyn was already a huge fan. John and Bev's next two albums, *Stormbringer* and *The Road to Ruin*, both tried with only patchy success to emulate The Band. Rather embarrassingly, John would later admit that he actually mistook Garth Hudson's Hammond organ sound for electric guitar on early listens to The Band's album *Music from Big Pink*. John was soon calling the stellar session musicians his friends. He found Levon to be 'friendly, sweet and decent'. Bizarrely, he also later said that Levon was the first person to ever give him a watermelon – a fruit he had never seen before! John and Levon became lifelong friends. John laughed enthusiastically at the memory of times with his old friend.

> The thing I loved about Levon and still do is that he has an awful sense of humour and his continual irreverence, he's a mad beatnik. He was just fucking real. I remember he once said to a bodybuilder called Fabio: 'Ya legs is awl swollen up – what's up, ya gawt gout?'

With John and Beverley having married at Hampstead registry office on 22 April 1969, the trip to America was effectively a recording session and honeymoon combined. Joe Boyd rented the couple a house for three months on Country Lane, Woodstock, belonging to local folkies Happy and Artie Traum, just weeks before the most famous rock festival of all time was staged. Woodstock, 1969, has a certain ring to it. It was the centre of the hippie universe, the air thick with hash smoke and sentiments rooted in peace and love. The Martyns had Bob Dylan, whose manager, Albert Grossman, lived locally, staying up the road and they occasionally called in to see him for a cup of tea. When they played on the bill of a local charity gig for the Hudson River Sloop alongside the Traums, Dylan was among the audience. John recalls: 'I played at a gig in Woodstock Theatre, sang a couple of things with Beverley and afterwards Dylan came up and said I played lovely guitar. I always remember him wearing white socks and black loafers and black shades. I was gobsmacked.' Beverley Martyn has slightly less rosy memories of the night, telling the writer Lee Barry how she ended up with a black eye from John after he disapproved of Dylan flirting with her.

John remembers another music legend who used Woodstock for rest and recreation.

Jimi Hendrix owned a house literally over the road. He used to fly in every Thursday in a purple helicopter. I used to just meet him when we were walking down the road; he was very quiet, used to tell me how much he loved the animals. He was a good lad but unfortunately I never played with him or saw him play live. The whole trip was wonderful, we were treated very well. Woodstock was so rural, you could walk out of the house and see trout leaping and terrapins in the river, chipmunks, groundhogs and skunks.

Local Vietnam veteran Steve 'Monk' Moncure became a close friend of the Martyns during their stay, ferrying them to New York City for recording sessions and remembers John being on his best behaviour: 'He would spend all his free time walking in the country. Not once that summer did I see him drunk or chase other women. John was trying extremely hard to be the epitome of a good dad.' Monk says the Martyns received a telegram from Island on the day of the Woodstock festival asking them to approach Dylan at the festival to try and get them on the bill of the upcoming Isle of Wight gig. 'I called the state trooper and he told me to forget it, there was a 26-mile backup on the freeway.' So John and Bev missed out on the greatest concert of all time – just 57 miles south of their temporary home.

In retrospect, the Woodstock jaunt sounds like the recipe for one three-month-long party, but Joe Boyd's business head prevailed and the whole album was wrapped up in eight days at A&R studios, New York – six days for recording and two for mixing. John hated New York City, but found the upstate adventures much more agreeable. Boyd brought discipline to the studio, although, as with Al Stewart's work on *The Tumbler*, Martyn would later play down just exactly how big a role Boyd had. Indeed, there seems to have been a deal of friction between the two men. Martyn later talked of how he felt that Boyd never really liked him even though he valued his musicianship. In 1974, Martyn told *Zigzag* magazine that he always had personality differences with the man . . . Joe Boyd approached the whole thing in a very straightforward way. He wanted the other musicians to know the chords and the changes before they went into the studio to save money on rehearsals and stuff . . . In Joe's case it was more of a discipline thing. He used to just say: 'Well, that won't do.' We used to have disagreements. He doesn't have as free an approach, as I'd like to see. But really I enjoyed making that album a lot.

The passage of time did little to ease tensions between the two men. John's bitterness towards Joe Boyd remained as palpable as ever, occasionally talking darkly of Boyd's effect on his career. Beverley told *Mojo* magazine in May 2001 that Joe Boyd had initially warned her away from Martyn with the timeless words 'Stay away from him – he's Glaswegian!' She claims that Boyd had initially tried to push her into a relationship with Nick Drake, but she found the reclusive singer too shy and settled for John instead. When approached to contribute to this book, Boyd politely declined, explaining that John was 'never top of my hit parade – as a musician or as a person'. Where John is concerned, Boyd sticks by the old maxim that if you cannot say something good about someone, best not to say anything at all. In his own excellent book on the 1960s, *White Bicycles*, Boyd does comment – with a nice touch of understatement – that John was 'a complicated character'. John was apparently extremely jealous of Boyd and the friction between the two men came to a head in New York when the young Scot threatened Boyd with a knife.

Martyn saw *Stormbringer* as one of his finest hours – a straight-from-the-heart album with a surprising degree of bite that finally nailed the lie of him being a twee folkie. His phrase at the time was that it was 'funky folk'. By May 1970, announcements of John's gigs were starting to appear outside the strict confines of *Melody Maker*'s Folk Forum. Certainly the use of drums, piano and Paul Harris's string arrangements and harpsichord playing alongside acoustic guitars was a daring departure from modern folk conventions. John especially enjoyed working with Harris and was eager to do so again. *Melody Maker* thought the new LP was a 'beautiful creation', stating that the Martyns were well ahead of their time. The magazine named it their folk LP of the month, calling it 'a relaxing agent that works like a drug'. But three decades later, *Stormbringer*, with its lovely cover shot of the doting couple on Hampstead Heath at sunset, all sounds a bit laboured and rooted in the era of kaftans and bells. Part of the problem is the fairly rigid division between John and Beverley, whose three songs are pretty enough but whether they merit inclusion is debatable. Certainly by the seventh minute of the perfectly pleasant 'Sweet Honesty' it sounds like a song running out of ideas. The real departures come from Mr Martyn – especially on the title track, with its foreboding chorus and sparse piano, and on both 'John The Baptist' and the final track 'Would You Believe Me?' Ironically, given the presence of his new wife, John had written the song as final comment on his break-up with Linda Dunning. Those songs show an artist maturing lyrically – forgetting the silly Summer of Love ditties, instead preferring to chart the ebb and flow of relationships. Indeed, he said that the intensity of his love for Beverley overrode any self-consciousness he may have held regarding detailing personal devotions on vinyl. Such was the strength and importance of their love that the music just fell out of him naturally.

When the Martyns returned to Britain the fact that they had recorded with such big-name musicians made a big impression on their contemporaries. Steve Tilston was living in Loughborough at the time and booked John to appear at a local hall soon after the triumphant return from the USA.

We were all really envious of him. He and Andy Matthews drove up in a big American limousine; John called it the blotting-paper car because it took most of his fee! There were only about 15 people in the audience, I cooked this big curry after the show and John was talking about his time in America. He was saying how great it was and we were thinking: 'God, he's actually played with those people!' What most impressed me was that he had met The Everly Brothers. He was going on about how they were real grizzled old men!

Tilston adds:

> The first album John did, you wouldn't find any indication on that record
> of the brilliance to come. It was very derivative. It's not on a par with say
> Nick's first album or Bert's or John Renbourn, is it? But I remember the first
> time I saw him play he did 'Would You Believe Me?' That now was different
> from a lot of the stuff that was doing the rounds at the time. Everyone else
> was locked into the Bert Jansch, Davey Graham mould. It was obvious that
> John was producing something quite fresh, something a little bit different.
> All his other early stuff you could see the reference points, where he got the
> licks from Bert and Davey. By then he was listening to people like The Band,
> as we all were. These new influences were seeping into his music.

Musical differences

Led Zeppelin just make a noise.

John Martyn

He wasn't content just to be a guitar player, playing with me . . . I let him take over.

Beverley Martyn

The critical acclaim offered to *Stormbringer* seemed to reinforce the perception of John and Beverley being the new golden couple of the folk revival. Certainly they were very much in love at the time, but closer inspection of them as a musical pairing showed that tensions were already beginning to surface. In a joint interview with *Melody Maker* in December 1970, the couple seemed less than ideally suited for each other – John on edge and garrulous, Beverley unassuming and rarely using two words where one would do. Indeed, the anonymous author of the article notes how few contributions Beverley makes to the interview, leaving it to her husband to moan about living in London and talk enthusiastically about moving back to Scotland after February 1971, when Beverley was due to give birth. The move home to Scotland never took place of course, but John was eager to move anywhere as long as it got him out of London. His initial enthusiasm for the city back in 1967 had long since disappeared and from the turn of the decade he was looking for a way out. He told *Melody Maker*: 'There are more people here [in Hampstead] than anywhere else, but it's the loneliest place in London.' He now thought that the capital was a breeding ground for 'constant paranoia', though that was probably as much caused by his generous intake of illegal drugs. The couple admitted to having quite distinct musical tastes and influences, and to using harmonies differently – though John's assertion that his wife was 'a lot more into pop . . . she isn't into unstructured things as much as I am' was greeted by a stony silence from Bev. At home, too, things were getting difficult. Monk Moncure, who had been invited by the Martyns to stay with them at their home on Pilgrims Place, near Hampstead Heath, over the winter of 1969 was witness to one of the many disputes that were putting strains on the marriage. 'It was a major freaking row – not physical, just major yelling and screaming at each other. I honestly thought it could have been a marriage-breaking row.'

Tellingly, despite the Martyns' union on record and in marriage, John continued to play the vast majority of his concerts as a solo artist. By February 1970, the couple had only played three gigs together. Beverley would later claim that this was due to John's chauvinistic attitude, denigrating her musical abilities and forcing her to stay at home and play the role of subservient wife while he went out on the road to earn cash to pay the bills. But even John seemed to go off the radar for long spells – by the end of 1970 he was only doing two gigs a week. And although the music press contained lots of interviews with the likes of McTell, Harper and Stewart, there was next to no mention of John. That changed at last with a showcase concert with backing musicians at the Queen Elizabeth Hall in London on 21 February 1970. The gig was hardly an unqualified success, which the couple attributed to a lack of empathy with the back-up musicians. Also on the bill that night was the Martyns' close friend, Nick Drake, who played a short set staring at his feet.

But whatever their differences, Beverley was undoubtedly helping John to expand his musical horizons, introducing him to bebop and other jazz forms. By now, John was also starting to stray from the acoustic guitar and preferring to play electric on songs such as 'The Ocean'. Martyn now wanted to introduce sustain at the press of a button to the musical mix. The Chicano horn players in the group Neu Nadir, who were also part of the Joe Boyd stable, had introduced him to the roaring sax sound of Pharaoh Sanders.

John's initiation came around 3 a.m. in a rehearsal studio in the village of Chilham, Kent. John was rehearsing with drummer Mike Kowalski and one-time Beach Boys guitarist Ed Carter. Stoned, he said hearing Sanders' 1969 album *Karma* for the first time was like being struck by a bolt of lightning or a veil being drawn away from in front of his eyes. In *Mojo* in August 2000 he told journalist James McNair that it was the record that changed his life: 'His tone blew my mind and he gave me a glimpse through a keyhole that I didn't even know existed. He was the first musician to convince me that you didn't have to show off to be good.' John had never heard someone play with such emotion and wanted to duplicate the sound, especially the use of sustain. For a while, John gamely experimented with the horn or saxophone as his instrument of choice for the new departure. But complaints from his neighbours and the fact that learning was too time-consuming meant that he eventually ditched the idea of playing sax or horn on a regular basis. Instead, after hearing Terry Riley's album *A Rainbow in Curved Air*, he concentrated on beefing up the sound of the acoustic guitar with gadgets – most notably the American device known as the Maestro Echoplex, which was to become his sonic signature. (Though on *Bless the Weather*, the distinctive electric sound was achieved by using a WEM Copicat.)

Mastering the Echoplex fully took the best part of five years, but it was to add another dimension to his sound – both in the studio and onstage. Learning to use it is nearly as difficult as understanding how it actually works. I've come across numerous explanations for this fiendish device, all of which leave me baffled so perhaps it's best to leave it to the man himself.

Roughly speaking, it goes like this: the note comes out of the guitar's mic and is fed into the fuzz box that I use. Then it goes into a combination of volume and wah-wah pedal. It comes out of there and goes into the Echoplex that repeats the note . . . So I can still play between these two moments . . . It is something very elastic. (*Atem*, March 1978)

The machine's ability to record sound-on-sound, where nothing is erased from the loop of tape and the player can build up layer upon layer of sounds, became the principal attraction to Martyn. He gradually came to find that the Echoplex could be used most effectively in this latter mode, and he changed the emphasis of the machine from his original intention of increasing sustain to a new function where, as he had described it, 'you can chop rhythms in between beats'.

John was delighted with the end result and the fact that listeners initially refused to believe that the wall of sound was the result of his playing alone. To listeners, the sound one man achieved from one acoustic guitar and a few gadgets was quite mesmerising. John knew the sound was unlike anything on the musical scene at the time. *Melody Maker*'s Andrew Means was amazed at seeing John with Echoplex and Al Stewart providing rhythm at a Les Cousins gig in February 1971: 'I can find nothing readily available to compare with his [John's] guitar . . . he has developed one of the most incredible sounds I have ever heard.' But if John was being drawn to electric music, he had little time for the heavy sounds coming to dominate the music scene, telling Jeremy Gilbert in *Melody Maker*, 28 February 1970, that 'Led Zeppelin just make a noise . . . To me, Jimmy Page is just an ego-trip guitarist producing smeth music [a combination of smack and methamphetamine].' Martyn preferred his electric music a little more subtle, with The Band regularly cited as a guiding light. Listening to them convinced him that electric instrumentation didn't necessarily have to mean hard rock and instead could be used in soft-textured, gentle, pastel sounds. The slow shift in his music towards an electric sound was summed up playfully by John (*Let It Rock*, December 1973): 'It's like your teeth rotting or hair growing – it starts imperceptibly and keeps on going!'

The uneasy relationship with Joe Boyd continued with the recording of *The Road to Ruin* – John and Beverley's second and final stab at vinyl togetherness. It was made in Chelsea at Sound Techniques studio – a former dairy that is now the site of a designer shoe shop – with John Wood again as engineer and Boyd producing. The same team in the same London studio had conjured up Nick Drake's seminal debut, *Five Leaves Left*, in 1969. But the Martyns' effort failed to live up to that daunting precedent.

Problems started during the recording – John remembers that when Joe Boyd was there, he spent his time reading financial newspapers during the sessions. He seemed to have other things on his mind and the Martyns weren't happy that the sessions stretched out for six months. The spontaneity of their earlier recording was replaced by delay. Boyd at times had to return to America on business between sessions (John always argued that Boyd would have been happier being a banker or owning a baseball team). The Martyns ended up trudging back and forth from the studios – sometimes overdubbing work done weeks previously. The disagreements with Boyd and the delays got so bad that John eventually took to missing sessions. All in all, it wasn't the happiest of times and John wasn't pleased with the finished product, telling friends that he listened to the album a couple of times and would never bother again. He told *Supersnazz* magazine: '*Road to Ruin* doesn't come into the running at all for me, there's a couple of nice songs on it, but . . . I listened to it three or so times after I made it and I'll never listen to it again.' The album came with a cover engraving by Max Ernst and a cryptic message from the couple that the music therein had nothing to do with dying or anything like that. It was an 'adolescent's view of mortality' – we are all doomed, so let's enjoy life in the meantime. It was preceded by full-page ads in the music press and *Melody Maker* thought it was one of the best folk albums of 1970, saying it had a more decisive and compelling edge than its predecessor.

The new album featured another cast of notable session musicians. Paul Harris flew over from America and Joe Boyd also brought in Mike Kowalski and Wells Kelly of the band Orleans on drums. Fairport Convention's Dave Pegg and Alan Spenner – who formerly played with Joe Cocker – were also in on the sessions. The horn sounds on the album reflected John's increasing interest in African music and his close friendship with Dudu Pukwana – alto horn player for another Witchseason outfit, Brotherhood of Breath. John learnt a lot from Dudu, who also led his own bands, Spear and Assagai, describing him as a kindred spirit who loved drinking. British jazz stalwarts Lyn Dobson and Ray Warleigh also guested on the record. By now, John was listening to all sorts of new music at concerts and on vinyl. Weather

Report, who emerged onto the jazz scene in the early 1970s, were to become perennial favorites, though he admits that it took a couple of stoned sessions before he finally understood their beautiful music.

But despite the musician's best efforts, *Road to Ruin* remains a lacklustre affair, with John and Bev failing to gel and their attempts at harmonies on one of the better tracks, Paul Wheeler's 'Give Us A Ring' are far from convincing. (John would later gift his wedding ring to Paul as thanks for writing the song. Wheeler still has the ring to this day.) Only the title track and the feather-light 'Parcels' hints at the greatness to come for John. It's a set of inconsequential songs, though the much maligned Mrs Martyn does at least offer a bit of jaunty bite when she takes vocal centre stage on tracks such as 'Primrose Hill'. The record-buying public seemed unimpressed and the album sales were disheartening. The powers-that-be seemed to pin the blame on Beverley with Island's A&R man, Muff Winwood, arguing that Beverley was no longer wanted because she sang flat. The couple retired to lick their wounds for a while. John was posted missing from the music press for a couple of months, taking time off from the concert circuit and concentrating on moving his family from London to their new home in Hastings. The couple had been living a flash lifestyle in Hampstead and smoking far too much hash. As John told the reporter Andy Childs: 'I just got into the whole suburban-creative person intelligent vibe. I indulged myself for about a year.' But now, this previously naïve and self-obsessed young man had other priorities. Beverley was expecting their second child Mhairi (John had already adopted two-year-old Wesley) and the guesswork was that she would be back recording soon. In reality, Beverley was effectively finished as a recording artist and her life was soon revolving around domestic duties. She did play one successful comeback gig at London's Merlin Theatre in December 1973, backed by friends such as Linda Peters, Richard Thompson and Simon Nicol. *The Melody Maker* review talked encouragingly about her matured voice and at times brilliant guitar playing, even suggesting that Bev was 'possibly the greatest female singer in England'. There was talk of her recording an album for the DJM label in 1975, but that came to nothing. What was portrayed as a short-term retirement or domestic sabbatical for Bev turned into a near thirty-year absence from the music scene, while John's career went from strength to strength. Looking back on their albums, Bev says, in the BBC4 documentary, *Johnny Too Bad*, with more than a trace of bitterness:

> It [*Stormbringer*] was going to be my album and he was coming along for the ride . . . he wasn't content just to be a guitar player, playing with me . . . I let him take over. I did not know how to deal with it, he was quite a force to be reckoned with.

That may well be true, but any idea that John stealthily used the partnership to further his own career is a tad far-fetched. John Martyn's talents would have come to the fore with or without his wife, and many fans would argue that the two collaborative albums were in fact a diversion that actually held him back. Bassist Dave Pegg still rates the album highly, though, and adds: 'Bev was a great singer and a very lovely person but – without being detrimental to her – John was obviously the writer and musician.' Island focused all their energies on John, even footing the £25 taxi bill when John would travel from Hastings to London. Taxi driver Colin Braham, whose company usually did the run, remembers John fondly, strumming Dylanesque songs on his guitar in the back seat. 'John was always polite and well behaved when he travelled with me – though possibly a little stoned,' says the typically perceptive cabbie.

But as one musical partnership bit the dust, another much more fulfilling one was about to rise. The track 'New Day' on *Road to Ruin* was the first opportunity for John to record with Danny Thompson, the double bassist with folk supergroup The Pentangle. 'New Day' was a fairly inauspicious start to their musical union, indeed it takes a few listens to appreciate that Thompson is actually in the mix. In years to come, however, Danny would become a crucial part of the Martyn sound, the pair melding together in some dazzling live performances. Danny's mazy mastery of his stand-up bass (which he calls Victoria) became as integral a part of the early Martyn sound as the Echoplex. John came to realise that

Danny was the only musician who could easily follow his structure-free approach to live playing. The two grew together, the one learning new musical directions and feeding off the other. Chris Blackwell also saw that despite John's innate musical talent he was not a disciplined player and preferred to innovate rather than follow a set text. Blackwell helped to bring Martyn and Thompson together, realising that John needed a jazz-hardened player who would react quickly to the guitarist's inspired playing.

Danny Thompson is the son of a miner from Seaham, Northumberland, who was killed while serving as a submariner during the war. Danny moved from the family home in Devon when he was six and grew up in London. He became a professional bassist aged sixteen, playing in Soho strip clubs before graduating to Ronnie Scott's club in the early 1960s. There he played with the likes of Tubby Hayes, John McLaughlin and visiting American stars such as Art Farmer, Joe Williams and Freddy Hubbard. Danny also earned a sterling reputation with Alexis Korner's Blues Incorporated and then co-founding Pentangle, the all-star group that also featured Bert Jansch and John Renbourn. He also played numerous sessions, including, rather bizarrely, on Cliff Richard's Eurovision classic 'Congratulations!'

Martyn and Thompson went on to become the closest of companions – both musically and socially. John said he and Danny shared similar insecurities about their childhood upbringing. But if coming across Danny was a godsend there was also a slight complication. John was teaming up with a musical genius who was also a near-legendary hellraiser and boozer. Not that John needed much encouragement. Indeed, as with Hamish Imlach, John was irresistibly drawn towards the wild carouser. By the age of twenty-one, John himself was on occasion polishing off over two bottles of rum a day. As is the way with heavy drinkers, memories of when they actually met for the first time are hazy. According to John, the initial meeting place was – perhaps predictably – in a pub called The Three Horseshoes on London's Tottenham Court Road during the early days of The Pentangle. Danny has a different recollection – saying he first met John while playing with Pentangle at the Newport Folk Festival in the

USA. John and Bev were in the crowd enjoying the festival. Wherever they met, music fans should gather and consecrate the ground because when John and Danny played together it resulted in six or seven years of musical magic. It was also six or seven years of madness, punctuated by boozing of heroic proportions, fights, nudity and the occasional nailing under a carpet. Nervous hotel managers would have to get used to the pair checking in and offering a down payment of £50 to pay for 'damage to come'.

A sexual time bomb

John is a person that eats life; he is so much bigger than almost every person you will ever meet. He is not a man you can tame.

Claire Hamill

Harmony and music is more interesting to me than lyric. If I wanted to get lyrical, I would go off and read Yeats.

John Martyn

In 1971, Joe Boyd took a decision at short notice to move to Burbank, California, where he would eventually work for Warner Brothers on films such as *Jimi Hendrix: Rainbow Bridge* and Stanley Kubrick's *Clockwork Orange*. Witchseason was sold to Island Records and with it went John and Beverley Martyn. Witchseason had been paying the rent for the Martyns' London home, and when Boyd decided to leave the country, John and Beverley couldn't afford to live in the capital. Already growing sick of London, they moved to Hastings in 1971, buying a house for £7,000 with financial help from Chris Blackwell. The Martyns' new home was in the Old Town of the Sussex fishing port, standing on a steep hill just a few minutes' walk from the seashore. Before the Martyns rolled into town, the most famous resident had been Aleister Crowley, who was a regular visitor to the nearby Harpsichord House, and the notorious occultist lived in the seaside town during his dotage.

Initially, Island intended to carry through Boyd's plan for solo records for both John and Beverley, followed by a third outing for the couple together. In the event, the only one of the three projects to see the light of day was John's third solo record, *Bless the Weather*, which was released in November 1971. The slight undoubtedly hurt Beverley and – her confidence shattered – she faded into the background. The spin was that she was concentrating on domestic duties, but later it became apparent that Island weren't keen on her and were always set on John resuming a solo career. At the time, John said he was angry at what he thought was a brutal decision and there was an initial uneasy relationship with his new masters – though, to their credit, Island seldom tried to interfere or force deadlines on him. John claimed to be disgusted by the whole affair – unsure as to whether Boyd or Island Records was to blame for the abandonment of the three-record plans. He said he hoped Beverley would make another solo record, but his comment that he found it increasingly impossible to reach a musical compromise when he and Bev worked together probably said more about his true feelings about their unbalanced musical partnership. In a 2001 interview with *Mojo* magazine, Beverley gave a withering account of the whole messy episode and how it contributed to the demise of her marriage.

> Joe Boyd was pissed off because John wanted more and more control. I just got pushed further into the background. He didn't want to do gigs with me. Then I had another baby. Joe went back to the US to work on *Rainbow Bridge* and said, 'Look after Nick (Drake) for me, Bev.' So I had two babies and John and Nick! I wanted to do my own album and John said, 'They only want one of us and that's me.' He started putting me down, giving me abuse. I lost my self worth, I was just thinking: am I rubbish?

Martyn may have gained a few good write-ups but he was far from making inroads in terms of selling albums or getting airplay on Radio One, which ruled the British airwaves during the early 1970s. By his own admission, he was still a rank outsider and investing large sums of money in his work could have been throwing good money after bad. After some delay, all that was forthcoming from the initially indifferent chiefs at Island was a few thousand pounds to work on the album that became *Bless the Weather*. (Producer John Wood puts the figure at under £2,000.) The quality of the finished product actually helped to get Martyn's relationship with Island back on track and for many years he wouldn't consider recording elsewhere. The record was made in just three days, and almost two-thirds of the songs were written in the studio. Martyn gave the musicians free rein, only suggesting that Danny Thompson play bowed bass on the title track. One of the standout tracks, 'Head And Heart' was covered by America – a soft rock outfit whose popularity peaked early in the decade with the single 'Horse With No Name'. Martyn himself was a touch underwhelmed by America's interpretation of his song, saying he would have preferred a punchier Brazilian samba-style rhythm section. Gradually, other artists took to covering material from his earlier records and Martyn's publishing went into profit. When Bridget St John, an English folkie who recorded on John Peel's Dandelion label, covered 'Back To Stay' from *London Conversation*, the Island bosses started to take a bit more interest in his career. But by now he was becoming more than a little distrustful of the industry he worked in. Even though he felt quite at home on Island, he was increasingly aware that the music industry was a business first and foremost, with artistic integrity not top priority for many music executives. But in reality, Martyn was fortunate that Chris Blackwell could afford to act as his benevolent patron. Artists such as Jethro Tull and Cat Stevens had already made £2 million for Island and this money helped Blackwell hold onto less lucrative acts like John. Still, it wasn't the ideal working relationship, and Martyn confided in journalist Andy Childs of *Supersnazz* magazine that he found the industry to be ghastly and foul, and sometimes contemplated jacking it all in and farming pigs instead.

Bless the Weather marked a return to form for Martyn, with jazz affectations that would get greater rein in his next two albums. Freed from what he considered to be Joe Boyd's dictatorial approach to production, Martyn worked alongside John Wood in the control room. A creative atmosphere in the studio meant spontaneity – with some of the songs recorded on the day that they were written. The finished product was his most mature and natural record to date, brimming with hearthside homilies and delicate melodies, but with lyrics which pointed to a more sophisticated, brooding and introspective take on life. By now he was perfecting the art of simple, gentle songs of hope and regret: songs such as 'Go Easy' and 'Just Now', which were best appreciated sitting in front of a roaring fire in a smoke-filled room. But listen to the equally gentle and pastoral title track and you can hear traces of the strife to come in his domestic and professional life. When he curses the storm that takes his love away, he accurately foretells the difficulties to come. The Martyns' musical split planted seeds that would eventually lead to their marital breakdown, John having to spend increasing amounts of time on the road away from Bev to support his family. Mrs Martyn meantime stayed at home, raised the children and quietly seethed about the loss of her own promising career. As in his relationship with Linda Dunning, John was extremely possessive of Bev, while he himself was taking the traditional rock star approach to fidelity and sleeping with any good-looking female with a pulse. When he did eventually return home from his philandering and music making, John was invariably either under the influence of cocaine or trying to recover from its side-effects.

Despite the title track's deceptively clever words, overall the emphasis on *Bless the Weather* was not on creating profoundly poetic lyrics. Steve Tilston says that Martyn once told him that he 'mistrusted words'. Indeed throughout his life, John was almost always self-deprecating when discussing his lyrics. Rather than emphasise his lyrics, he preferred to play with the sounds of his voice, slurring words and sounds so the voice almost becomes as forceful as a musical instrument. Many years later, in a conversation with Levon Helm, which was printed in the *Chicago Sun-Times*, John made plain where his priorities lay: 'It's all music. Harmony and music is more interesting to me than lyric. If I wanted to get lyrical, I would go off and read Yeats.'

The ground-breaking 'Glistening Glyndebourne' polarised opinions among music critics. The journalist Nick Kent came to regard it as one of the great songs of the decade, but *Rolling Stone* considered it to be 'rambling', while *Sounds* more accurately recognised it as a masterpiece. The track showed John's increasing interest in electric music with the sustain of the Echoplex interweaving hypnotically with Danny's bass. It was written after John passed through the small country town as the local opera house was emptying out and hundreds of people in dinner jackets and evening gowns piled onto the train. The track showed that John was an artist who refused to be tied down by people's expectations of what a 'pop star' should sound like and was willing to move away from conceptions of conventional song. Instead of getting stale as most singers do by their third or fourth record, he was continuing to experiment and explore new directions. Underpinning John and Danny's free-flowing experimentation was the beautiful sparse piano of Ian Whiteman and drums from Roger Powell. Both played in a little-known group called Mighty Baby and got the Martyn gig after he had met Whiteman at a Sandy Denny session. Both Whiteman and Powell eventually moved to the States via Morocco and became Sufi Moslems. For the first time, *Melody Maker* reviewed John's work in their pop rather than folk section. The write-up was as positive as ever, listing it as one of the LPs of the month – the author advising that the record offers a pathway which is way outside common reference points.

People were beginning to take notice of Martyn by now and getting to know his philosophy on life. The track 'Head And Heart', which around that time was his signature tune, encapsulated his doped-up view on life. His aim at the time was to get a balance between head and heart, between the cerebral and the emotional. Two years later he told *NME* (21 July 1973):

I'm really hung up on heads and hearts . . . I mean, obviously they fuse together in your life, but they're two quite different things. Say you see a photograph of a Biafran child with its bones sticking through its skin – your heart is what brings the tears to your eyes and makes you want to leave everything and to go out there and feed that child. But your head says: 'Listen, man, there's millions of those and only one of you; stay here, do what you can, try and do it through the music, look after your own interests.' Initial reactions, to me, are heart reactions. I wouldn't trust head, or heart, finally though. The closest I can get is that I use my head to temper the judgements of my heart. I feel strongly that there's a great dearth of heart everywhere right now. The drug-culture has laid too heavy an emphasis on the expansion of the head. Sure, politics and practicality may prove your heart to be suspect at a given moment, but the power's still there. Like, I'm married with two kids – and, quite literally, the most important things to me are my children's smile and my woman's love. The head is totally divorced from those.

The following year, a tour with the band Bronco built on Martyn's growing reputation. The *NME* reporter who attended a gig at London's City College thought John was now one of Britain's finest innovators of contemporary folk music. In May, he was billed as one of the 'Giants of Tomorrow' at the massive Great Western Express Festival in Lincoln, along with other promising acts like Budgie, Rab Noakes and Patto. The tour with Bronco also featured the young singer-songwriter Claire Hamill, who had first met John when he played on a number of tracks on her debut album, *One House Left Standing*, recorded at Basing Street studios in the summer of 1971. The petite and attractive Hamill hailed from a small village near Middlesborough and, aged just sixteen, she had signed to Island Records. Moving to London, Claire found herself thrust into a daunting new environment, suddenly being touted as a future star and ironically supplanting Beverley Martyn as Island's favoured female solo artist. 'I had left a great big northern family and I was lonely,' she recalls. 'I used to go to Island Records every day to make the tea just because I needed people around me.' Meeting John Martyn was like coming across a kindred spirit – Claire's own father was from Glasgow and she and John were both young prodigies from broken homes. Claire's first impressions of John were of a confident young man who although 'a golden boy' in her eyes retained a refreshing degree of modesty and refused to play the star in the studio.

Speaking to me in 2007, Claire had fond memories of the tour with John and Bronco, though it's fair to say that they weren't playing at some of the most salubrious venues. In one particularly bleak Glasgow dressing room the performers had to sit on paint pots as they prepared for the show. Sleeping accommodation could be equally spartan, though Claire recalls how one kindly landlady in Stirling left out hot water bottles in the stars' beds for when they returned from the gig! As Claire and John found themselves criss-crossing Britain on the tour, her admiration for the young Scot soon grew into something more meaningful.

In those days the music business was completely chauvinistic and at the end of the tour the boys in Bronco said: 'Come on, Claire, it's time you slept with one of us.' But they never knew that John had actually pulled me on the first night of the tour! When I was first introduced to John, my manager warned me to keep away from him, but John was the type of guy you are just magnetically drawn to. Because we were both young and signed to the same label, we had shared experiences. It was all a bit new to me and I had hardly any experience of love at that stage of my life. John was wild and untamed – like a walking sexual time bomb, very sexy and a sweet tender lover as well. That was a complete juxtaposition to what he was like at times in real life, when he could be a brooding and sometimes angry and tempestuous man. Other times he was jolly, but he always had this enormous nervous energy about him which seemed to be held in just waiting to burst out. He was a huge character, being around him was always exciting, and he had this immense smouldering passion for life. He was so generous, if you sat in a bar with him the drinks were always on John and they were always triples! If he was drinking, everyone was drinking. No one could afford to keep up with John but he didn't care, he'd just spend all his money on you. As for drugs, well I had never seen such a big lump of dope in my life!

John and Claire's casual relationship lasted on and off for another few years, but Claire has no illusions that she was the only rival to Beverley for Martyn's affections.

I never had any kind of guilt about having a relationship with John because I knew that he had a girl in every town. I used to meet them; after the gig he would always introduce them to me. So I had no claim to John, it was just that when we were together we were attracted to each other and used to thoroughly enjoy ourselves. He never really talked about Beverley to me. The weird thing is I did do a gig with her about four years ago. I had never met her and I wasn't sure whether she knew about John and me. After the gig, she never said anything, but her daughter did ask if I had an affair with John and I of course said no. I had to lie, because to say yes would have opened a whole string of questions. Some people have said that she (Beverley) was going to be the female singer for Island and that I came along and stole her crown, but she was a mother with children by that point. I guess you do feel bitter about the loves you lost, especially when you are still in love with him. I am not proud of what happened, I was just so lonely and John was so sweet and protective towards me. John is a person that eats life; he is so much bigger than almost every person you will ever meet. He is not a man you can tame. I wrote a song for him called 'Speedbreaker', which has the line 'You are a man in the fullest way and no one can tie you down, you are lighter than air and faster than light and you break the speed of sound.' I was having a sexual relationship with John on a very casual basis and I didn't fall in love with him till much later. I never pursued him; I just think it was one of those things that we were incredibly attracted to each other.

We found ourselves in New York together in 1974 or 1975. I was getting a big push at the time over there and John just happened to be there and we bumped into each other. As soon as we met up, we were inseparable. He came to my radio interviews with me and we just spent all of our time in New York together. I remember him throwing a TV out of our window for a laugh when we were staying at the Chelsea Hotel! I think that around that time I fell in love with him. But I was always slightly jealous of him; he has such an enormous talent. He is a much more accomplished guitarist than I could ever dream of being. I did try to ring him when he was off around America, but in the end we just drifted apart. I had met Nick, the man who was to be the father of my kids, and the next time I met up with John I told him I was engaged to be married. That was the end of our relationship, though to be honest there had never been great commitment between us. We could never have survived together; John needs a supportive woman to help him run his life. I knew he would always have been a bigger star than I would and maybe I feared that that would have crushed my ego.

Claire Hamill had by then left Island and branched out on a long and varied career, working with Ray Davies and those gods of the twin guitar sonic assault, Wishbone Ash. The late great Eva Cassidy recorded one of Claire's best songs, 'You Take My Breath Away'. Claire still writes and performs and – like many people who have played a part in John Martyn's life – she lives in the sunny south of England. She's moved on from her days with John but speaking to her you get the feeling that their relationship remains a very sweet memory for her.

Solid Air

Musical territory that few could even comprehend existing.

Nick Kent on Solid Air

Vocally it was a step forward. I've never sung as good as on that record.

John Martyn

Whatever the merits of *Bless the Weather*, they pale in comparison to John's next album. Ask any Martyn fan which of his recordings best sums up his genius, and the answer is invariably *Solid Air*. Recorded in just seven days during the winter of 1972, the nine songs taken as a whole undeniably represent Martyn at his creative peak. A beguiling mix of homespun heartfelt romantic paeans such as 'May You Never' and dreamy, trippy hypnotic works of wonder such as the title track and 'Dreams By The Sea', *Solid Air* never fails to hit the right spot. Although subsequent albums all had individual tracks that left the listener breathless, none of them would ever come close to the consistency and class of the template for trip-hop that is *Solid Air*. The signposts had been there for all to see in the earlier records, where John had started to build on his pure folk roots and add in strands of jazz, blues and grinding, tough electric rock. All of this was topped off with John's own inimitable vocals and, on *Solid Air*, his ambition to use his voice as another instrument in the overall sound is perfectly realised. On *Solid Air* – in just under 35 minutes' work – all those elements came together perfectly to produce the unique sound of John Martyn. As the great *NME* journalist Nick Kent argued in 1980, the record 'showcased Martyn in musical territory that few could even comprehend existing'.

But the actual sound of the classic album came about literally by accident. Initially, the plan had been for John to work with some big-name musicians and produce an album in time for his first American tour. (Martyn was to open the bill for Island heavyweights Traffic and Free on a four-week tour, with the first date set for 17 January 1973.) The first sessions at Sound Techniques studio weren't really working out to Martyn's satisfaction, but then fate intervened when co-producer John Wood took a tumble negotiating the stairs leading to the studio. Wood's badly twisted ankle meant the cancellation of the recording for over a week and by then the original musicians had moved on to other projects and the recording had to move to Island's Basing Street Studio. With the record company starting to fret and John talking of doing the record in America, it was decided to call in Danny Thompson. Eventually, the reliable Dave Mattacks and Dave Pegg – both of Fairport Convention – were also drafted in as rhythm section along with saxophonist Tony Coe and the Texan, John 'Rabbit' Bundrick, who had played with Johnny Nash. Thankfully, these were talented musicians who could adapt to John's tunings and establish a rapport with Martyn that allowed many of the songs to be cut live with few overdubs.

The album came at a relatively stable time in John's life – free from the madness of city life, he seemed to be living in domestic harmony in his new home in Hastings with Beverley and their children. Speaking in 2006, Dave Mattacks recalled being impressed by John's musical abilities and his personality during the sessions.

John was very confident and his mood was positive. If there were drugs being used, I was naïve enough at the time not to notice it. It was not until a few years later that I became aware of that scene and John's predilection. I'm under the impression that – with John – the drinking and the drugs got seriously under way in the 1980s. From what I can gather, the negative aspects of excessive use of alcohol have still yet to truly dawn on John. I do, however, think he's a great writer, musician and singer. For what it's worth, I am proud to be on that record. My clearest memory of those *Solid Air* sessions is of the title track going down in Basing Street Studios with invaluable contributions from the great percussionist Tristram Fry on vibes, Danny T on upright bass and Rabbit. I recall thinking: 'This is great stuff.'

Bassist Dave Pegg agrees that – contrary to the subsequent mythologising – John had his serious head on during these sessions:

> I've never had a bad time in the studio with John. If it had been unpleasant, I would have remembered it. John wasn't doing a lot of drugs or drinking heavily. I have a reputation as being a big drinker, but we never ever got drunk with John. We might have gone down to the pub, but generally it was all heads down, serious working. The end product was a great album. I still love *Solid Air*.

Many of the songs like the warm and sensuous 'Go Down Easy' reflect Martyn's harmonious lifestyle. John's devotion and yearning for life with his family is also caught in the positively jaunty 'Over The Hill', which he recorded using a cardboard pick. Powered by Richard Thompson's effortless mandolin playing, the song was inspired by the view John saw of his home overlooking the sea as he returned from London on the early morning train to Hastings. The affectionate tribute to an unnamed friend, 'May You Never', remains Martyn's best known song – thanks largely to a cover version by Eric Clapton on the 1977 album *Slowhand*. (In 1980, Martyn conceded that Clapton's one cover had earned him more money in royalties than his own entire catalogue put together!) Depending on whom you believe, the song was written for either John's adopted son, Wesley, or for the owner of Cousins, Andy the Greek. As the journalist Rob Young pointed out, the lyrics of 'May You Never' list a catalogue of admonishments, including losing one's temper and getting hit in a barroom fight, which could have been autobiographical. John Wood has since revealed how the final version of 'May You Never' was only completed at the last minute. Martyn had been less than content with the version set to appear on the album and – at 2 a.m. on the final day before deadline – he entered the studio armed only with his acoustic guitar and effortlessly peeled off the definitive and much-loved album version in one take. Hours later, John Wood boarded the plane to New York to master the album. The record closes with 'The Easy Blues', which came about when Martyn was struggling to master one of the other songs and played the blues workout to clear his head. It was so impressive that he decided – quite rightly – to leave it on the finished product. John had been playing the song for years and Steve Tilston remembers seeing the young Scot bashing it out on a handmade John Bailey guitar, which belonged to Richard Thompson's future wife, Linda Peters, at the Volunteer Folk Club in Loughborough in 1968.

> John was brilliant that night, playing stuff like 'Seven Black Roses' and 'Jelly Roll Baker'. I remember it caused quite a stir when he told the audience that Jelly Roll is a euphemism for fucking! The barman had apoplexy, muttering something like 'I don't care who he is, if he says that again, he's out of here!' It was pretty quickly apparent that John liked to shock people.

Another mighty song, the plaintive 'I Don't Want to Know About Evil' was subsequently covered by Dr John and Beth Orton. Like many people, Orton had been won over to John's music when as a student she experimented with hashish.

In marked contrast to the cosy, delicate love songs that were becoming his trademark, *Solid Air* also features a clutch of songs which reflect the darker side of life and point to the addictions and demons that were increasingly besetting John. His growing predilection for hard drugs surfaces with references to 'users', 'sweet cocaine' and 'Mary-Jane'. (When 'Over The Hill' was released in promo-single format in 1977, the words 'sweet cocaine' were replaced with 'dry champagne'.) But as ever there's a price to pay and on 'Dreams By The Sea', with its scurrying keyboard from Bundrick, Martyn captures astutely the desolation and paranoia of drug withdrawal. Finding out what drugs were powering *Solid Air* wasn't difficult. Whereas most rock stars jealously try to keep the exact nature of their illegal habits under wraps, John Martyn was always disarmingly honest. In August 1973, he told *Sounds* that he was a believer in natural drugs, with hashish being his first prefer-ence. It helped him to see love and to 'explore himself' and find out what he 'was all about'. LSD wasn't recommended, and he denied touching downers or heroin, though even then he was developing a strong liking for cocaine. A touch optimistically, he told the interviewer that he could stop all the drugs tomorrow if he wanted to. A couple of years down the line he was snorting smack in front of the journalist David Belbin during an inter-view. Whatever the problems they caused him, John believed the drugs opened up new doors for him and helped him creatively.

Another trip to the darkside comes with the frenetic cover version of 'I'd Rather Be The Devil' – originally penned by Mississippi-born Delta blues legend Skip James. A one-time pimp and bootlegger who eventually changed his ways and studied at a Baptist seminary in Texas, James also wrote 'I'm So Glad', which was covered by Cream, although the version was denounced by James. James's beautiful voice and delicate playing on the National guitar always appealed to John. But so did James's darker side, and Martyn's take on the blues standard is suitably apocalyptic, with thundering Echoplex, bass and keyboards mixing together in a dazzling improvisation. Few performers could ever have captured the drug-fuelled paranoia of the time as potently as Martyn managed to.

Pride of place on the album goes to the sublime title track, with its dense, claustrophobic mix of concussed vocals, languid bass and haunting saxo-phone. It's the song that consistently tops polls among fans for their favourite Martyn track, but, amazingly, the words and music were done in under half an hour as John strummed his guitar in his Hampstead home. At the time, John coyly said the song was about 'a friend of mine, and it was done right with very clear motives, and I'm very pleased with it . . . It has got a very simple message, but you'll have to work that one out for yourself.' (*Zigzag*, April/May 1974) Of course, the friend was the English singer-song-writer Nick Drake, who by 1972 was well into the tragic decline that even-tually led to his death two years later. John had met Drake at a party thrown by Joe Boyd in 1969 just after the recording of *Stormbringer*. Drake moved into a suitably bleak and bohemian bedsit in Haverstock Hill, close to John's

Hampstead flat and the two became good friends (Drake was a witness at the Martyns' marriage). Nick Drake appeared on the same bill as John and Beverley on a couple of occasions, though sadly never on vinyl. John told the Dutch radio show *Moondogs* in 1983 how Joe Boyd was very jealous about keeping John and Nick from playing together. Nick would visit the Hampstead and Hastings homes for meals, card games and also to baby-sit the Martyn kids and strum guitars with John. But even John and Bev found it almost impossible to break his shell of sadness. On occasion he would stay for the weekend and then just disappear without having said hardly a word. Behaviour like this led the exasperated hosts to dub Drake 'Nick the drag'. Once, John found him silent, in a foetal crouch outside the living room. Nick's parents liked John and he visited them at their Tanworth home. In Patrick Humphries' biography, *Nick Drake*, Drake's mother, Molly, told how Martyn's presence soon had a strange effect on Nick: 'John Martyn is a tremendously vivacious, ebullient character and, at that stage, it was more than Nick could take. It was all right for one evening and the next morning he couldn't take it anymore.'

In retrospect, the two men seem unlikely companions. Over the years, John earned a reputation in some quarters for being loud and aggressive, an accusation that could never be levelled at Nick Drake. But closer inspection shows that the two men had quite similar career trajectories. Nick Drake was born in Rangoon in 1948, the same year as Iain David McGeachy. Both came from solid, respectable if not overly affluent family backgrounds, Drake's father, Rodney, having worked as an engineer in the Burmese teak industry. After the family moved back to Tanworth-in-Arden, in the heart of middle England, Nick had a happy childhood and was educated at prep school before entering the elite Marlborough College. Both he and Martyn had a supportive and musical family background. Drake and Martyn also showed promise as rugby players in their teenage years; the former was renowned as a fine wing three-quarter. He and John Martyn also shared an instinctive talent for learning to play their musical instrument of choice – both eventually maturing into supremely talented guitarists.

Nick studied English at Fitzwilliam College, but quit Cambridge twelve months before his final exams. Like John, he was drawn to the far riskier attractions of a full-time recording career in London. Drake memorably once told his mother that 'the last thing in life I want is a safety net' (*Nick Drake*, Patrick Humphries, 1998). Early in his career, Nick listened avidly to Martyn's songs, along with the music of Martyn's own heroes, Davey Graham, Bert Jansch and John Renbourn. Both young men also came under the wing of Joe Boyd, Witchseason and Chris Blackwell's Island record label. Eventually, their shared love of music and drugs brought them close together and Martyn is generally acknowledged as having got as close to Drake as anyone did during his final years. But, as the lyric for 'Solid Air' points out, even John Martyn really didn't know what was going on inside the head of his close friend. The writer David Stubbs summed up the deep emotional helplessness and despondency of the track beautifully when he wrote in *Uncut*, December 2000, that it reflected 'Drake's state of disillusion with his life, perhaps more vividly than Drake's own music did'. It's a song that perfectly details the helplessness of seeing a friend at the edge of darkness, gradually losing touch with reality.

Although a slight rivalry existed between the two guitarists, John loved Drake's shyness and his tranquil, beautiful music, which was uniquely English at a time when most contemporaries – including John – were in awe of North American groups like The Band. John also was well aware of Drake's sensitivity, how the smallest of things could upset him and throw him into depression and how Drake's nerves led to difficult live performances, which further eroded his confidence. In 1985, John told the BBC DJ Richard Skinner:

> When I first met him he was rather more urbane than he became. He was always charming, delicately witty. But he just became more and more withdrawn as time went by, in the three or four years that I knew him he became more and more withdrawn. I think he suffered from some sort of depression . . . he just slipped and slipped further away into himself and divorced himself from the mundane. It's very sad, really. And it wasn't

through lack of trying – all kinds of people tried to be friendly, and went out of their way to be nice, but I suppose he'd see through that, you see, being very bright and intelligent.

John admitted that he – like everyone who knew Drake – later felt guilt that he could have done more to help. He also thought Nick too sensitive and in need of the love and understanding of a good woman, but in the end Drake's distrust of the world set him on a course that no one could have changed.

Steve Tilston has an interesting take on the friendship between John and Nick.

When I got to know Nick briefly, and from what people like Andy Matthews said, it became apparent that John had somehow assumed some of Nick's background. When I first met John he'd refer to being at Cambridge University. I could be wrong, but somehow it didn't ring true – if pressed he'd change the subject. When I raised it with people who knew him like Hamish [Imlach] they'd roll their eyes as if it was one of John's porkies.[1] Although John was much better known, I could see that in some ways he was actually in awe of Nick. Maybe it was a residual class thing because Nick was born with a silver spoon and had a fey quasi-aristo bearing. I don't know, maybe that's too simplistic, it wouldn't feature these days, but they were different times.

Paul Wheeler remembers – as a student at Cambridge – going with Nick Drake, who was a year ahead of him at university, to visit John in Surbiton.

John had already heard something about Nick, presumably from Joe Boyd, and I recall John thinking Nick's name was 'Nick Silver' which was an amusing but also, in retrospect, rather appropriate mishearing. I think John liked to think of himself as working-class, he saw me as middle-class and Nick as upper-class.

1. During the research for this book, Martyn phoned me and admitted that he never attended Cambridge. He seemed slightly embarrassed and even relieved to have finally admitted the truth. John also used to give detailed accounts to reporters of how he attended Glasgow Art School for a few months after leaving school, but the Art School have no records of him ever being a student there!

These distinctions were not particularly true, but they were convenient. I guess my own music and personality is somewhere between John and Nick, so it was not surprising that I was a go-between. I remember John ringing me in the middle of the night when I was living at John Lennon's place, Tittenhurst Park, near Ascot [Wheeler's wife was for a while a personal assistant to the ex-Beatle]. John [Martyn] had just visited Nick and he sang me an a cappella version of 'Solid Air'. For John, there was no division between art and life.

Solid Air eventually sold over 100,000 copies, breaking even in the UK and making a few thousand dollars profit in the US, allowing John to settle his debts to Island. It remains a favourite with fans and critics alike. In appraising the record some twenty-seven years later, the critic David Stubbs compared it to Stevie Wonder's *Music of My Mind* and astutely noted their oscillation between despondency and blissfulness. In many ways, Stubbs' phrase sums up John Martyn's psychological profile, a man whose sensitivity and talent were magnified by the inevitable highs and lows of heavy drug abuse. But surprisingly, given the records' subsequent rise to iconic status, John was initially less than totally content with *Solid Air*. In July 1973, just five months after its release he met Ian MacDonald of *NME* in a Westbourne Park pub and told him:

> I'm not as pleased with it as I have been with previous ones, although vocally it was a step forward. I've never sung as good as on that record. But at the time I made it I was capable of singing even better – and playing better. It was all too rushed. The next one's going to be a lot heavier. There'll be more blowing on it from me. Previously, I've tended to let other people do most of the blowing. I mean, if you come out front when you're playing with good musicians, you're making an ego statement. My idea is that everyone, providing they're strong enough people – should impress their personality on the final sound.

He would also argue that the studio version of 'I'd Rather Be The Devil' paled in comparison to funkier live takes of the song and that *Solid Air* had only one or two really strong songs. Not for nothing has John Martyn earned a reputation as a hard man to please.

Nick

Nicky was nobody's friend really . . . He became so withdrawn that it was
very difficult to be in the room with him . . . it was a very black space that
he was in . . . we never discussed the fact that I wrote Solid Air for him.

John Martyn

I would think that it was music that drew them together and a shared sensitivity and sensibility – I think their individual talents were far more respon-
sible for their connection than a liking for hashish!

Bridget St John

The US tour supporting Traffic and Free marked Martyn's arrival on the big-
stage. Thirty-five dates in thirty-nine days meant playing to audiences way
beyond anything he had experienced in the UK. Until the trip stateside, the
largest crowd he had performed to was the ill-fated gig with Bev and a pick-
up band at The Queen Elizabeth Hall. British concerts invariably meant
playing at venues like the North London Polytechnic, where addled heads
would sit cross-legged on the hard floors, slyly toking on illicit drugs and
supping flat, warm beer. At one show in Bolton – which he described as the
worst he had ever played – he felt like smashing his guitar and attacking
somebody because of the audience indifference. (The bad memory stuck
with John, and on an *Old Grey Whistle Test* appearance several years later he
bad-mouthed the folk of the Lancashire town in an amusing – if slightly
unsettling – rap between songs.) But mostly British audiences were now
getting the message and an appearance at the Reading Festival in August, on
a bill topped by Genesis, was one of the best sets of the day, according to
NME. Armed with his electric guitar, John confused the audience somewhat

by talking in a strong Cockney accent between songs. After only a few months playing with Danny, John's voice had morphed into Cockney. But the same paper – reviewing an Edinburgh concert – correctly pondered that his approach to music would never allow him to make it big.

John was realistic enough to know that his music would never get widespread acclaim.

> There are some people who are never going to understand what I'm on about . . . I don't envisage myself having mass appeal. There was a time when some people around here thought I was going to be another Cat Stevens . . . I soon stamped that one on the head! You have to be yourself in your songs, and money doesn't come into it. I'm just not a pop musician, never going to be one, and that's that. I'm trying to make converts, but so many of the routes in for them are blocked off. There comes a point when you must live all the things you talk, otherwise you don't sleep easy. In fact, you're just not a happy man, and I'm really interested in being a happy man more than anything else. For me, the way I've gone, it seems inevitable that a large part of my life has got to be devoted to music, and I'm trying to involve myself less in the paper chase . . . I'm existing somewhere between the music art and the music industry. (*Supersnazz*, October 1973)

On the American tour, the smallest show was for 6,000 people and the largest drew a crowd of 24,000. Still relatively young and inexperienced, the challenge of facing such large crowds armed only with a guitar and some boyish exuberance could have killed his career stone dead. But American audiences seemed more aware of what he was trying to achieve and loved the shows. The Stateside crowds gave him incredible feedback – applauding after key instrumental solos where some British crowds would tend to just sit and show what Martyn felt was a lack of true understanding of his purpose. In America, he felt he was accepted more readily, even though his sets were relatively short – thirty minutes – and electric. It was felt his acoustic sound would have been lost in such vast venues. Todd Tolces attended one of the two sell-out shows at San Francisco Winterland and told *Melody Maker* readers how John went down surprisingly well in front of a crowd notorious for giving short shrift to solo artists. By now, Martyn was such an accomplished performer that he often played whole songs with his eyes shut to help 'get into the feel'. Dabbling with cocaine throughout the tour, Martyn later confessed that the jaunt had brought moments of real elation alongside acute depression. Physically, too, he was left drained by the constant gigging and infections picked up along the way. In a Boston bar, John risked a slightly more serious condition when a man brandishing a .38 gun shot at him. John had been drinking, dressed in a white suit with a red carnation, with a lady friend in the bar – which had predominantly black clientele – when he did something to annoy the man.[1] Monk Moncure met up with his old friend during the US tour and was shocked to find how much he had changed since their first meeting in Woodstock.

> John called me when they were in New York City and I met him in his hotel room and he looked like a different man. He was drinking and Island Records would not give him a dime. I got the feeling that he was being kept on a leash. They would not give him a dollar to spend. I got the impression that he was now chasing after women that he shouldn't have been chasing after. He was someone who needed to be looked after.

After the tour was complete, John took an eight-day break in Britain and then returned to America for a set of club dates to help build on the encouraging sales of *Solid Air*. Then, during the first three weeks of February 1974, he had the thankless task of supporting progressive rock's hottest act, Yes, in vast outdoor concerts to crowds of up to 50,000. John failed to bond with the headline act and he told Rob Fitzpatrick of *The Word* magazine that the tour was a nightmare

---

1. Later in his career, a man armed with a light-gauge shotgun would shoot at John in an argument over a woman. On another occasion, in Chicago, a man aimed a shotgun at John's head. John also claimed that one of his wives once took a shot at him, thankfully missing him completely. Verifying the accuracy of all these claims is of course impossible but one friend of John's scoffed at Martyn's 'self-mythologising', saying 'ask him to show you his bullet wounds!' On the other hand maybe the gunshots just all missed their intended target!

I *hated* that band. They were snotty, horrible people who thought they were intellectuals. I quite liked the drummer, Alan someone or other (White) but the guitar player (Steve Howe) I never could stand at any price. They came from Scarborough or something (actually, London) and played Beach Boys covers – then they got into this 'the frogs in the forest are flying away' shit and it was just horrible. And they didn't give a *fuck* about me; they didn't listen or care about what I was doing.

After these shows, John had the unsettling experience of entertaining a handful of fans in small clubs on days off from the Yes tour. The quest to break America would later see John support acts as disparate as Lou Reed, Dave Mason, Jackson Browne and Linda Ronstadt.

If Island Records were expecting the follow-up to *Solid Air* to exploit John's more commercial side with a collection of tracks like 'May You Never', they were in for a surprise. Released in October 1973, on the back of a nineteen-date tour of the UK with Danny Thompson, *Inside Out* was like a two-finger salute against the industry he was increasingly coming to distrust. Also in his sights when he recorded the album were the folk establishment who, he said, played jigs by rote and thought Nina Simone too rhythmic. He called it his one and only concept album – a pure celebration of the powers of love. Reflecting his infatuation with Pharaoh Sanders, John wanted to experiment with tones and notes and he went ahead and did it, even if he was later to admit that it could have been done with more technical ability. This was an uncompromising set of songs and the sleeve artwork – with a storm raging inside the silhouette of John's head – spoke volumes. The album title alluded to John's belief that the music was his inside feelings coming roaring out into the open. Even gentle, lilting numbers like the ultra-laid back opener, 'Fine Lines' and 'Ways To Cry', are rendered completely uncommercial by John's strange vocals, which are often indecipherable. At the time, he thought it was his best record to date. When I met him in November 2004, he still believed it was his strongest album, the one where all his influences came together best, adding that back then he 'didn't want to be stuck into being straight'.

Like its own successor, *Sunday's Child*, *Inside Out* emerged out of a background of a seemingly contented domestic life but this time the recording sessions were legendary for their length – often lasting days on end – and their intensity. John produced the record himself, and wanted things done simply and directly, with little in the way of cutting or editing. The writer Jerry Gilbert recalled arriving at the end of one such session at Island's number two studios with the sun rising over the Westway and various session musicians looking the worse for wear. Martyn was demanding more playbacks of certain tracks while management tried to vacate the premises for the next band to record. Gilbert said Martyn still hadn't got any sleep when he met him twenty-seven hours later. Bassist Dave Pegg witnessed the aftermath of an even longer session: 'I saw Danny Thompson at Island studios one afternoon and he said he had been downstairs doing a session with John for the past 57 hours! He looked fine, but I think he was quite glad to get out!'

The tour of America with Traffic had forged bonds with that band and three of their players – Stevie Winwood, Remi Kabaka (aka Rebop) and Chris Wood appeared on *Inside Out*. As a result, the album – especially on the track 'Look In' – was his funkiest to date, full of rhythmic delights. On occasion it's also dominated by stunning free-form jazz improvisation. The eight minutes twenty-one seconds of 'Outside In' was his most ambitious work yet, and soon became the fulcrum of his live shows. Originally called 'Inside Of Him' or 'A Man Walks Inside', it explodes into life with John and Danny's swirling instrumental currents and then segues into some sublime interplay between Chris Wood's mellifluous sax and Remi's thunderous drums. This is intense, raw music drawing comparison with other innovators like Tim Buckley and one of Martyn's heroes, John Coltrane. Coltrane was certainly an influence, but John preferred to cite the immaculate chords of McCoy Tyner as his real hero around that time. He also likened the unsettling screaming on parts of his new record to Pharoah Sanders' screaming horn playing – a cathartic release of bottled-up anger. John had first heard Sanders' album *Karma* in 1972 and was wowed by the combined intensity and gentleness of his playing. Although in thrall to these jazz legends like Sanders and Miles Davis, John resolutely refused to be part of the UK jazz scene. He despised the cliques, petty jealousies and backbiting of the jazz crowd just as much as he hated the folk scene. At times, like on the track 'Make No Mistake', the intensity is unsettling, with Martyn bellowing out the simple message 'It's love!' over and over again. On 'Ain't No Saint' he sounds like a drunk railing against the world, shouting 'Just get it together'. He himself knew that this was the antithesis of commercial pop and predictably it was music that many listeners found too complicated and too inaccessible. If the inclusion of a traditional Celtic instrumental lament, where a fuzz box and phaser on the guitar ape the sound of the bagpipes, doesn't quite work (how was John to know it would sound like the dreaded 'Mull Of Kintyre'?) then it's no great problem.

Reviewing the record in *NME*, Ian MacDonald concluded it was the result of six years' striving towards reaching an optimum means of personal expression. 'Like all really good things *Inside Out* is new – which means it needs some hard work to sort out. On the other hand, like all new things, it means a vitamin shot in the jugular for the culture that kicked it off. The scene being infinitely healthier for the presence of blasts of solid air like John Martyn.' The perceptive MacDonald noted the paradox that in realising his long-promised potential he had produced an uncommercial work forcefully out of key with these times. Jerry Gilbert for *Sounds* thought the album was eminently serene and 'glistens with the glory of love'. *Melody Maker* gave the disc an unreserved recommendation and argued that John was now a jazz singer. The record won Martyn a Golden Disc award from Montreux and on 5 July 1974, he played most of *Inside Out* at the London Rock Proms in Olympia – a three-day festival which also featured Captain Beefheart and Fairport Convention. Despite woeful acoustics, which sent the music roaming all around west London, *NME* thought John's set consolidated his reputation as one of 'the most innovative performers in modern music'. Beverley joined him and Danny onstage for the final encore in front of an appreciative audience of just 500 fans in a building with a 10,000 capacity.

John himself found the intensity of the recording process for *Inside Out* exhausting and vowed to relax more and get rid of some bad habits. As the writer James McNair has pointed out, the album was fuelled by a cocaine blizzard, and certainly around this period rumours were rife that hard drugs were coming to dominate John's life. The writer Nick Kent tells a story of a Martyn gig when the singer's mood darkened visibly on stage after being handed a note saying that the night's expected drug supply had fallen through (*NME*, 29 November 1980). The dark moods became more frequent as he watched the inexorable decline of his friend Nick Drake. Near the end, it was painful for John just to be in Drake's company and to witness his mental distress. Drake continued to visit the Martyns but to no avail. As Beverley recalled, one visit ended on a peculiar note that adds to the Drake enigma.

> Nick would come and stay sometimes and we'd write together, but there was nobody there for us after Joe [Boyd] left. One night Nick and John went out, I don't know where, and when they came back Nick said to me: 'Can't you see what he's like? I'll take you away.' I just thought this is too weird, I'm going to bed. And in the morning, Nick left. I had a bad feeling. When we got the phone call I just went to pieces. I took it very badly and got very ill. (*Mojo*, May 2001)

Nick Drake died of an overdose of the anti-depressant Tryptizol on 25 November 1974. He was just twenty-six years of age. He died despite the efforts of psychiatrists and of friends such as John and Chris Blackwell, who talked together often about how they could help Nick. Danny Thompson, who had played on some of Drake's greatest recordings told *Q* magazine in September 1989: 'I tried everything with Nick: I was horrible to him, I was nice to him, I was patronising to him, anything to try and get something out of him.' It is often said that Nick and John were like brothers – often arguing, but bonded by a love of music and each other. But to say that John was Drake's only true friend is probably inaccurate and also underestimates the difficulty that even John had in breaking the protective shell that Drake had built around him. John told me:

> Nicky was nobody's friend really. He was a very solitary figure. He didn't set out to be solitary but he just ended up that way. I didn't like to see him

suffer, but he was a classic example of a manic-depressive, there was nothing could be done for him really. To be honest, we never discussed the fact that I wrote 'Solid Air' for him. We used to play songs to each other; we both still had a lot of youthful enthusiasm back then. He became so withdrawn that it was very difficult to be in the room with him. It was a terrible quandary and you would really feel for him – it was a very black space that he was in. He didn't like being there at all, but he never asked for help, because he was too strong for that. He found it really difficult to communicate. He would turn up at your door anytime of day or night with nowhere to go, usually in the fucking pouring rain! When he played live it was just soul destroying to watch him. It was like watching a man being stripped naked.

The story of Nick Drake's gradual decline from happy teenager to the almost catatonic adult who – it's assumed – ended his own life has been already told by Patrick Humphries in his eminently readable biography. Drake only ever recorded three albums, which sold barely 20,000 copies in total, in his lifetime, but the timeless beauty of those records and the nature of his death at such an early age have made sure that the cult of Nick Drake lives on. He's the quintessential lost soul of British rock music in the 1970s, with only perhaps Paul Kossoff – another good friend of Martyn's – coming close to Nick when it comes to tragic endings to careers laced with brilliance.

Martyn's closeness to Drake and his inability to stop his downward spiral remained a sensitive topic until John's death. John always felt that the excessive publicity given to Nick's death bordered on the macabre and bad taste, so he spoke sparingly about his old friend. If he did, he invariably ended up slating the way Drake's career and death had become almost mythical. He disliked the way 'parasites' in the music business took advantage of such an innocent. He objected to the way precious memories of Nick just became anecdotes to be bandied about. He also hated the way that Drake had been virtually ignored during his lifetime but now 'pseudo-intellectual ponces' were championing his work. John's view was that if those people had paid attention to his work during Drake's lifetime he might not have died. By ignoring him, they had effectively helped to kill him. An exasperated Martyn once even talked about faking his own death to see how the industry vultures would then move in.

Martyn had never been so exposed and so close to someone with such ingrained psychological problems. In a rare mention of Nick, he told how a few months before his death Nick had given a clue to his despair when he revealed how angry he was by his lack of commercial success.

> He did say that to me once and that came as a great surprise! Because he never appeared ambitious, never ever, you know? You would not think that ambition was in him. But he once, about four or five months before he died, in fact told me. I said: 'What's the matter, old boy?' And he actually said he was disgusted that he had not been more successful. Which surprised me because I had not seen hitherto any hint of ambition in the man. It was very, very peculiar. ('*Moondogs*', Dutch FM Radio, April 1983)

Bridget St John had observed Nick and John's friendship since the Cousins days and offers interesting insights into what brought the two men together.

> I would imagine that it was music that drew them together and a shared sensitivity and sensibility – I think their individual talents were far more responsible for their connection than a liking for hashish! Either of them could probably have found that anywhere else quite easily, but I think that in those musical days it felt very good to connect with kindred spirits, and while I think Nick and John were very different personalities I do think they shared a lot in common musically. I visited John soon after Nick died. John was living in Hastings at the time, and my memory is that he was very sad and troubled by Nick's death and, at the time that I saw him, John did not know really what had happened. It's very hard when you are so young to lose a good friend who is also so young and with whom you also share a connection through music.

Sitting in a smoke-filled bedroom of Glasgow's Radisson Hotel in the summer of 2006, John told me how he received the news of Nick Drake's death and of his unusual reaction.

I was lying in my bed in Hastings and the phone went, I think it was Paul Wheeler who gave us the news. I laughed! For which my wife never forgave me. I don't think I've ever cried for Nicky. It seemed so obvious at the time that it would come. It was inevitable. He was surrounded by a loving family, they adored him. He was just too distant. You know when candyfloss is very, very finely spun and it hits cold air? It turns very brittle, but it looks kind of soft at the same time. Nick was like that – a very brittle character.

At which point John's voice tailed away.

Koss

Those dates with John Martyn reminded me of a few things I'd forgotten – the power of an audience. There's no better high than that.

Paul Kossoff

Paul and John are both very sensitive characters, John may not always appear that way but he is a very sensitive soul. Those types of guys tend to be the casualties in our business unfortunately.

John Glover

Following the tragic death of Nick Drake, Martyn threw himself back into the never-ending loop of tours and albums. His fifth solo album, *Sunday's Child*, was a rush recording over six days at Island Studios during August 1974, with Martyn under pressure from Island bosses who were eager to release it almost immediately. Martyn worked round the clock to meet their demands (one energy-sapping session lasted for fifty-eight hours) and the album was completed just the day before he was due to go on holiday. Then, much to his anger, Island decided to delay the release. Martyn was not a happy man, telling reporters – without a trace of irony – that the delays 'really got up my nose!'

When it eventually saw the light of day on 24 January 1975, eighteen months after *Inside Out*, *Sunday's Child* earned lots of critical acclaim. Much less intense than its predecessor, *Sunday's Child* was, according to John, his cooling-out album. It's a richly rhythmic record, with great variety of songs and sterling playing from the likes of John Bundrick on piano and tabla player Keth Sashe. Neil Spencer of *NME* called *Sunday's Child* a very important and undeniably masterful work from one of the true heavyweights of the singer-songwriter scene. Spencer felt John's confident approach compared favourably to both Dylan and Lennon and argued that it was about time his talents got the credit and prestige they deserved (*NME*, 8 February 1975). The ever-critical Martyn later argued that the record was nothing devastating, though even he admitted that it had some strong songs. Many of them are ultra-mellow celebrations of domestic life and the joys of being a dad. He and Bev were now well settled in their south coast home with their two children (their third child, Spenser, was born in May 1975). The album cover has a charming photo of John, cradling his daughter Mhairi, whom he nicknamed his 'Little Miss Wisp'. Beverley sings backup vocal on 'My Baby Girl', which was written about Mhairi. Those devotions to family life may have been too saccharine for some, but listen to the lyrics of the opener, 'One Day Without You' and they suggest that John's love for his wife was now almost bordering on obsession, wanting to keep the object of his affections to himself. The conclusion that 'every bird that sings is born to fly' perhaps presaged the difficulties lying ahead in his marriage.

Having already shown his mastery of folk, jazz and the blues, Martyn now decided to show his prowess at playing scuzzy rock music on the twelve-bar boogie, 'Clutches', and on 'Root Love'. Geoff Barton of *Sounds* made the improbable comparison between the latter song and the Glitter Band's guitar sound! Barton thought that John's songs 'have seldom before had the same consistent excellence' (*Sounds*, 1 February 1975). Far removed from that grungy sound was John's magical take on two age-old traditional tunes. The inclusion of the Scottish favourite 'Marie's Wedding' surprised many but it was one of the songs the McGeachy family used to sing together around the piano in their Glasgow home. There's also an affectionate nod towards the English folk tradition with the best track on the album, the immaculate 'Spencer The Rover'. The tale of the weary traveller returned to the warmth of his family obviously appealed to John, who was forever touring the country to earn a crust – a manic lifestyle which was accentuating his alcoholism and drug dependency. John had fallen in love with the song after hearing Robin Dransfield play it at the Glasgow Folk Centre in the mid-1960s. Robin told the *Big Muff* website how the 'manic, enthusiastic, bubbly-haired' Scot had pleaded with him to teach him the song. This he did on the stairs of the club and later at fellow folkie Alex Campbell's home. *Sunday's Child* also contains a cover of the Porter Waggoner hit 'Satisfied Mind' and closes with the excellent 'Call Me Crazy' with its hypnotic Echoplex climax, which bears more than a passing resemblance to 'Small Hours' from the *One World* album.

To promote the new record, Island announced a 22-date tour of the UK during January and February. John had now graduated from the club scene and fifteen of the gigs were at universities with the tour climaxing with two sell-out shows at London's Victoria Palace. It was to be the first of three UK tours in 1975, with European shows – including the Montreux Jazz Festival – to add to the exhausting mix. The Montreux gig led to a legendary all-night booze binge with Irish guitarist Rory Gallagher and The Chieftains. But John thought that charging £12 a ticket was a rip-off and thought the whole festival was just a moneymaking concern and not the cultural feast he had hoped for. Audience reaction in Europe was generally favourable and John invariably got good crowds in France and Belgium. Germany was more problematic and audiences expecting singalongs to 'The Wild Rover' sometimes left in their droves. Things weren't helped by Martyn singing 'Let the storm troopers chase every Kraut from the place' during 'Singing In The Rain'!

Danny Thompson and the improvisational jazz drummer John Stevens of the Spontaneous Music Ensemble provided able backup for John on the first UK tour. Danny had played with Stevens in a number of jazz sessions and initially recommended the drummer to John. Martyn admired and learnt a great deal from the exuberant Stevens, rating him as the best drummer on the British scene. At some of the shows the trio was joined on stage by the troubled guitar genius Paul Kossoff, who was attempting a comeback after a long spell away from performing. Born in London in 1950, Paul Francis Kossoff had exhibited a natural musical talent from an early age. When just eight years old, he was given a plastic Tommy Steele guitar and instruction book, and within a few years he was studying classical guitar. But whatever his talents, Paul had other, darker interests.

His father, the renowned actor and biblical broadcaster David Kossoff, commented in *Heavy Load: Free* by David Clayton and Todd K Smith: 'He [Paul] was attracted all his life by dangerous pursuits, by larger than life characters and by the wicked rather than the good.' Paul was expelled from his London school after experimenting with Purple Heart pep pills and had a drug problem even when playing with an early group, Black Cat Bones. Despite subsequently earning adulation playing lead with Free, Paul's problems continued. Distraught at the death of his hero, Jimi Hendrix, and exhausted by endless touring, Paul became a depressed, insecure figure, increasingly paranoid and ever trying to escape his problems through illegal means. Just like Nick Drake, Paul Kossoff was a troubled genius and almost inevitably he too came into Martyn's inner circle.

Free were also on the Island label, and Martyn was a long-time admirer of the quartet's powerful take on electric blues and supported them on several tours, including one in Scandinavia. Indeed, Free were the first rock band to really impress Martyn – who thought no other white rock 'n' roll group could play the blues with such power. During a 1972 gig at the Sundown in London, John had played a spirited version of the classic Free song, 'Little Bit Of Love'. In an interview with Brendan Quayle he confided:

> They were amazing – I was really moved, genuinely moved, no one else had such an effect. It was insane, they were so young, absolutely no one has ever come close to that kind of music. It was a cross between musical integrity and genuine soul. (CD liner notes, *London Conversation*)

He also liked the band members as people, admiring their humility and the way they kept in touch with real life rather than playing the superstar game. Kossoff had played back-up guitar on the 1971 session for the single version of 'May You Never'. At the time, Chris Blackwell fancied that a reworked version of the song might become a hit and Kossoff, Rabbit, Simon Kirke and Tetsu worked on the drug-fuelled session which Martyn subsequently disowned, but which was released nonetheless at great expense and only sold a handful of copies. The two guitarists got on well that night, drawn together by a similar taste in drugs and jamming together on a late-night session on a song – 'Time Away' – which eventually ended up on Kossoff's *Back Street Crawler* album. (An eighteen-minute version of the track called 'Time Spent/Time Away' appears on Free's box set, *Songs of Yesterday*.) Playing with Kossoff was a release for John who always fancied himself as a bit of a frustrated rock 'n' roller.

When Free first split up in 1971 Kossoff was asked what he intended to do. He gave the disturbing, though prophetic answer: 'Probably a lot of drugs.' Many around him thought he had a death wish, not eating properly and taking up to twenty-two tablets of the hypnotic sedative Mandrax a day, which led to seizures, memory loss and slurred speech. By the time he came to play on the tour with John, Kossoff was dabbling with heroin. Like Nick Drake, Kossoff was in a fragile state of mind, made ten times worse by a crippling drug addiction. His manager at the time was John Glover who had worked for Island Records between 1964 and 1974, arranging tours for Island artists, before branching out on his own. (Glover also managed Martyn and Beverley for three years during the mid-1970s.) Glover wanted to build up Kossoff's confidence, raise his profile and get him back playing live again, but if he and Martyn had any hopes of saving another friend in need, they were to end up sorely disappointed again. John Glover recalls:

When I was with Island, Free was my baby. I managed them in the 1970s and Paul Kossoff was always good mates with John. They were attracted to each other through their love of playing – they were both great guitar players, though at the time John was more into acoustic playing and he didn't really get into the electric till later. When Free broke up the first time and Kossoff got really out of it, he was living just around the corner from Island Records and John used to pop in and see him. They both worked together in Basing Street Studios on stuff like the *Back Street Crawler* album.

Around 1974, Paul went through a very bad stage and I rang John and told him I was trying to get Paul to do something, but that he wasn't confident enough to go on stage himself. John obviously knew that Paul was in a bad state and he said he would love it if he came on stage with him. John and Paul absolutely loved playing with each other. Paul was desperate to get back on stage and John gave him that opportunity. John was very fond of Paul and around that time John wanted to experiment more with his guitar playing, he wanted to stretch himself more.

To ease the pressure on Kossoff, he was not named on the bill and the idea was for him to join the other musicians on stage for an elongated encore. At venues like London Victoria Palace and Bristol University Blues and Folk Club, Kossoff ambled on stage to deafening applause for the final couple of songs – the blues 'So Much In Love With You' and 'Clutches'. Exchanging fluent guitar licks with Martyn and vigorously contorting his face as the guitar sound got shriller, Kossoff invariably stole the show, even though the drugs sometimes adversely affected his playing. His family attended the London gig, with his father later sending Paul a telegram saying how glad they were to see him performing live again. John had a different memory and said Kossoff senior actually mistook Paul for his elder brother, calling him Simon by mistake and so knocking Paul's fragile confidence still further. John Martyn held controversial views on Kossoff senior, believing that he treated his son badly and calling him an unpleasant martinet. Although the appearances were limited to a couple of numbers, the mere fact that he wanted to play live was encouraging to all those who were so worried about Kossoff's health. They hoped that it would mark a rebirth in his career. A picture in the Teasers section of *NME* of 15 March 1975, showed Paul on stage with John at the London show. The paper called it the 'nice event of the month' and hailed the public reappearance of Kossoff, looking healthy 'after months of bad problems, including drug busts'. Certainly Kossoff seemed reinvigorated by the shows, saying they reminded him of how much he missed live work. In a reverse-charge call to Steve Clarke of *NME* he explained: 'Those dates with John Martyn reminded me of a few things I'd forgotten – the power of an audience. There's no better high than that.' Sadly, the words weren't a sign of a sea change in Kossoff's outlook on life.

John Glover says keeping an eye on Kossoff was never straightforward:

When they played together during that tour it was just fabulous – some of the best playing I had seen from Paul. But unfortunately during that tour,

Paul did on several occasions get totally out of it. I don't think he was using heroin at that time, I think it was pills like Mandrax. The great thing about dear old Koss was that he could talk anybody into doing anything for him. After the Leeds show he went into the local hospital, Jimmy's, in the middle of the night and just convinced them to give him a prescription for Valium for a nervous condition and then just took the whole lot. We lost him once at Watford Gap service station. Paul just dropped a whole lot of pills, wandered off from the car and just disappeared – we got him back the following day from a police station.

The unlikely support act for this tour was one of Martyn's contemporaries from the Cousins days, Wizz Jones. Croydon-born Jones had earned his spurs busking in Europe with an unknown young singer called Rod Stewart, and subsequently Wizz became one of the finest guitarists on the scene and an early influence on Eric Clapton. Although Jones graduated from the heady 1950s and 1960s Soho scene, he was never really into drink or drugs in a big way. Jones had first seen John Martyn play a floor spot at a club called The Dungeon near Tower Bridge back in the mid-1960s.

I was incredibly impressed by him because he was so young and such a good performer – a good singer and a clever guitar player. Then I got to see him more often when he started playing at Cousins, when he was the first guy to muck around with the Echoplex. That was a really exciting thing to see. It was a very, very creative period for him. At that time Beverley had been singing with a band called The Levee Breakers. One night at Cousins she told me she had met this young guy who was a really good guitar player and I remember telling her I knew him and that he would be a lot better when he stops talking so much and calms down a bit! At that stage of his career he was speaking all the time on stage – like verbal diarrhoea.

As you can imagine there were a lot of fireworks on that tour with John and Paul Kossoff! By that time John Martyn was getting quite infamous for being a heavy sort of bloke. We met somewhere in Soho before the first gig and John said: 'I've got a bone to pick with you—my old lady says you think I need to stop talking so much!' I thought: Here we go; the tour hasn't even started yet! I ended up doing a short set before they came on, but most of the audience would either be in the bar or impatient for John, so it was not a particularly successful tour for me. There was one night after a show, John and I went to a party together and he was really up for it, dancing and bopping with everyone the minute he walked in. I really admired him for that, because I was much more introverted.

In fact, I was a lot older than him and I think he kind of looked up to me, so we never actually came to blows, but I did get to see the rock 'n' roll lifestyle that he was living at that time. I remember thinking: 'I cannot handle all this', so generally I would use my own transport to head home after a gig and then just meet up with them at the next town on the tour. I remember after one gig in Bristol, I left them all at the hotel and started driving back and I stopped at a service station and there was Paul Kossoff wandering around in a completely terrible state – utterly out of it. That tour was a cut above what I usually did, which was folk clubs. It was quite exciting for me – like a novelty. John was a fantastic player. On that tour he had quadraphonic sound alongside the Echoplex – those sounds whistling around the hall were just absolute dynamite. For me that was a real peak in his career. After that I lost touch with him, he was going further and further into that electric sound.

Martyn recalled how Paul's addiction affected the tour.

We took him out and had to shake him down every couple of days, and half the gigs he made and half the gigs he didn't. When he didn't make them it was because he was out of the game. What really pissed me off was that with good medical attention he really could have been all right. There is no question of that in my mind. He could go down to a hospital at six o'clock in the morning and hustle pills out of anybody, and he used to do that all the fucking time. He was determined to get hold of the shit. I used to stay up until about seven in the morning just talking to him and eventually I'd crash out because I'd be knackered. I'd wake up about half past nine and there'd be no Koss . . . and you'd know that the next time you saw him five hours later, he'd be loaded. I used to lock him in rooms, seriously, and physically me and Danny would turn him upside down and empty his pockets out! We used to have terrible fights. He'd bite your ankles and fucking attack you and kick yer nuts in. He was a terrible man when he was like that. I really liked him, but what can you do with someone like that? A very difficult character to deal with. And very, very sweet – very pleasant, very witty and very bright. But a highly volatile character. And very, very shy . . . and it seemed so sad. (*Heavy Load: Free*, David Clayton & Todd K Smith)

The journalist Allan Jones recalls finding John prior to the Leeds University show slumped in a tiny dressing room, which resembled an off-licence storeroom, looking like he'd been drinking since the dawn of time. Jones ended up being threatened by an equally inebriated Danny before witnessing Martyn and Kossoff fighting like madmen after the latter had cracked a bottle over John's head. The article ends with John kicking Kossoff as he lay prostrate on the ground (*Uncut*, July 2004). All in all, it wasn't exactly the summer of love.

After the tour, Kossoff moved for a while down to Hastings to live with John and Beverley. Martyn told the Free biographer David Clayton:

He was trying to keep dry; he was doing a fairly good job. He was just drinking a bit. I wasn't allowing him out and we didn't allow him access to any shit at all, except drink. So he'd have two or three brandies in the afternoon and he'd be alright until the evening, then he'd go out and drink till he got to the point where he could sleep because he found it difficult to sleep without the drugs.

John Glover, who these days manages slightly more sedate acts such as Go West, Tony Hadley and ABC, recalls:

John and Bev were nice people; they invited him down to Hastings to try and rehabilitate him to life. Paul and John are both very sensitive characters. John may not always appear that way, but he is a very sensitive soul. Those types of guys tend to be the casualties in our business unfortunately. It's a tragedy of the music business that you have people like them who are absolutely fabulous talents but in other ways are a bit of a wreck. They push the self-destruct button all the time.

Despite John and Beverley's best efforts, Kossoff's health deteriorated and a demoralised Martyn soon lost another friend. Paul died on board a flight from Los Angeles to New York on 19 March 1976. He was only twenty-five.

Ironically, an autopsy showed that at the time of death he had no drugs in his system – the cause of death was cerebral and pulmonary edema. John Glover was on that flight and, thirty years on, he has these thoughts on the Martyn/Kossoff relationship.

> John did his very best to help get Paul through it all, which was really nice of him. On tour, John himself was good as gold. He got drunk occasionally, but then John is a full-on boy. John is as mad as a hatter, but he is incredibly talented and I'm a sucker for talented people. There would be the odd night when he was just too gone to perform, but most nights you saw John play he was just magical. He has a temper on him, but sometimes you have to put up with a little bit of madness just to get the genius. I regret Kossoff died and I tried everything I could to stop him dying. He was a nightmare for me in many ways, but I wouldn't have missed a minute of it. John can be a bad tempered old drunk but he is a fantastic talent. He was very fond of Paul and his death did affect John a lot.

John had begged Paul's record label not to send him out on tour with his band, Back Street Crawler, who he thought were a bad heavy metal outfit. In October 1994, John told *Mojo* magazine:

> I mean, look, when Paul Kossoff went out on the road that last time, I begged his management: I said, 'Please, don't send him out on the road, you're gonna kill him.' Gosh, he was a good player. Lovely man, sweetheart, far too good for the likes of me. Delightful little fella. But, God, he was fucked up.

The lengthy and ultimately futile attempt to divert Drake and Kossoff from the road to ruin hint at a compassionate side of Martyn's character which was seldom seen by the general public. Asked about the caring side of his nature which manifested itself in the way he tried to help Nick and Paul, John replied:

> If you don't care for people you are a lesser person, if you don't do the right thing in those circumstances you are lacking in fibre and aren't a part of

decent society. It is cool to be cool, people have been cool to me and I possibly didn't deserve it.

Interestingly, tapes do exist of some of the fabled live shows with Paul playing guitar, though John was never keen on them seeing the light of day. He later commented that the juxtaposition of upright bass and heavy electric guitar didn't work for him. A song written by Martyn about Paul, 'Dead On Arrival', was eventually released on the *Live at Nottingham* CD in 2005. The lyric – 'there's nobody else in the world but yourself to blame' said it all.

Danny

We were just kindred spirits, that doesn't mean bad, good or anything else; it just means he had all that energy that I had. I've been with other people who just couldn't keep up with that energy and just flaked.

Danny Thompson

They were an unbelievably aggressive musical pairing, who made sublime music – full of madness, mayhem and unpredictability. But, man, I wouldn't have been anywhere near them.

Ralph McTell on John Martyn and Danny Thompson

By 1975, Martyn had been in the music business for almost seven years and was undeniably a critic's favourite. The endless touring circuit also meant he now had a loyal following – in July 1975, readers of the influential *Zigzag* magazine voted him Britain's Eleventh Best guitarist ahead of the likes of Rory Gallagher, Jeff Beck and the Rolling Stones' Mick Taylor in a poll topped by Eric Clapton. His growing reputation also led to a prestige appearance on 16 March alongside the likes of Kevin Coyne, Procul Harum and Frankie Miller at the closing-down party for London's ill-fated Rainbow Theatre. (An album of the final gig, *Over the Rainbow*, appeared later that summer.) But John's record sales were still no more than respectable, failing to make any impression on the charts. By now he was starting to feel a dual disenchantment both with life in the UK and with the music industry in general. Recording and touring for three years had meant that he was away from his wife and kids for long spells – he didn't intend to make the same mistake with his new son. He and

Bev were considering selling their Hastings home, which was 'too near civilisation' and also lacked a garden for their children to play in. With the exception of Danny Thompson, Martyn was still unhappy with the standard of musicians on offer in the UK and at times he talked about moving back permanently to Woodstock. A move Stateside would make more sense economically – allowing him to meet the increasing demands of US audiences for him to tour there. There was talk of recording an album at Electric Ladyland studio in New York with Herb Lovell, who had worked on the *Stormbringer* album, and also plans for John to produce and play on a proposed new disc by Beverley. On other occasions, he talked of taking time off in Morocco and the prospect of a move to the healthier, sunnier climes of Jamaica was also mentioned as an alternative to the grind of life in Britain. On one occasion, he mentioned the prospect of becoming a social worker, which would certainly have been something to behold.

When a twenty-date tour of Britain was announced for September it came with a caveat; the tour, which would open with a major show at London's Theatre Royal, Drury Lane, on 21 September would be John's last for the foreseeable future. A planned year's sabbatical was in the offing, with John intending to travel, spend more time with his family and write fresh material. Disillusionment with the music business was also obvious in his decision to release a new album, *Live at Leeds*, on a mail-order basis. Available in a signed limited edition of just 10,000 copies from 12 September, the record would come in a plain white sleeve which parodied The Who's album of the same name, with the title in black on an otherwise plain cover, and would cost £2.50 plus post and packaging. Fans were advised to write to John with payment to his home at 10 Coburg Place, The Old Town, Hastings, in Sussex, and many even called at the house and bought it over the doorstep. Island – who for some mysterious reason weren't keen on a live album release at that time – issued a press release saying the arrangement would be a one-off and would have no bearing on John's long-term contract with them. Indeed, Island still 'owned' John and the album still had Island Records stamped on it. Without their permission it couldn't have been released and John was aware that no other company would have allowed him to carry out the project. But without the label's backing, the Martyns were left to deal with the marketing, production and design of the LP. In a move that mirrored Led Zeppelin's occasional preference for back-to-basics album covers, Martyn initially demanded that the *Live at Leeds* cover and centre label should be bereft of information. It was a sign of his disquiet over losing control over the design of some of his earlier record sleeves. Island refused to accept that demand, but they gave the go-ahead for the limited release and promised not to re-release it again for ten years. (It has since re-emerged many times, most notably in 1987 and on CD for the first time in 1992. A deluxe version in 2002 stretched to four sides of vinyl.)

In the end, the album's release was plagued with problems – none of which was caused by Martyn. EMI were in charge of pressing the record and ended up delivering poor-quality (jumping) master cuts seven weeks behind schedule. The release date came and went, and the letters requesting the album started piling up. When the albums eventually arrived from EMI, John was away on tour and Beverley was left with the unenviable task of sending out records to customers already angry about the seven-week delay. The task of personally signing all 10,000 copies also proved problematic and exhausting! But overall the experiment reinforced the bond between John and his fans. They invariably wrote supportive letters with their orders, some even advising him to use the money to buy a round of drinks for Danny Thompson if no albums were left! Others were even more bizarre. As John explained to *NME* of 29 November 1975, one fan wrote:

> Since I left the institution your albums have been most comfortable in times of loneliness and despair . . . I have a twenty-six-inch photograph of you on my lavatory door which I occasionally keep in my wallet along with a photograph of Jean Paul Sartre playing lacrosse in the nude. Occasionally I compare the two, and when I do I laugh like a dragon!

Naturally the album became a real collectors' item – legend has it that even John didn't have a copy of the original himself.

The recording of the Leeds University gig of Thursday, 13 February 1975, showcased John and Danny playing drunk, at full throttle and at the peak of their powers – one track, 'Inside Out' clocked in at just over eighteen minutes. Danny told me how prior to the gig he had been drinking pints of crème de menthe and whisky.

> The dressing room was awash with the stuff. When I heard that the concert had been recorded, I thought 'Blimey!' And yet when I heard it I thought it was one of the best live recordings I ever did. John Stevens fitted in admirably. If we had used a rock drummer he would have been completely baffled by our improvisation. John Stevens wasn't at all fazed, he lived on it.

Danny believes that the beauty of his music with John Martyn lay in its spontaneity.

> We never practised before a tour and, although we would talk about other music that we liked, we never discussed or dissected our own music. We would never finish a gig and say: 'Oh that bit you played there etc . . .' Our music just sort of grew and no two nights were ever the same – that was the beauty of it, it was spontaneous, contemporary improvised music. Like most people who are great, John is his own man; he's an innovator and has his own way of playing. I call him 'Wild Finger'; he has this very strange technique where his hand just glides about all over the fingerboard, seemingly without purpose. Then you hear what he is playing and it becomes this beautiful thing.

Interviewed before John's death, Ralph McTell remembered being blown away by the pair's music, but also being amazed by their wild lifestyle. McTell believes that the latter was rooted in insecurities.

> I was watching an old film of John recently and even then he sounded brash, but when I hear it now he sounds like a man not terribly sure of himself. He doesn't know if he's Scots or whether he's Cockney. He became Danny Thompson for a while. Danny is a right Cockney geezer and a tremendous

musician. They formed a wonderful musical partnership but John slowly metamorphosed into more of a Danny than Danny was! In the end he paid the price for it – Danny's still got two legs! They were an unbelievably aggressive musical pairing, who made sublime music – full of madness, mayhem and unpredictability. I don't know of any of the wild men of rock 'n' roll who could compare to them and the things they got up to. But, man, I wouldn't have been anywhere near them. Sometimes I get a bit mumsy when I think of them – I cannot believe how they survived such drunken and drug-fuelled strength of feeling. At one point they had John Stevens and Paul Kossoff in the band – four madmen! I think the roadie dumped them all once because he couldn't stand it any longer!

I found some of John's behaviour like the overt joint-smoking on stage not cool. And overt bravado and deep aggression do not impress me. I remember seeing John play once and after a couple of numbers, someone in the crowd shouted out: 'For Christ's sake, relax, John!' And he replied: 'It's not my fucking job to relax!' Sometimes people are in awe of such dark passion – like he's telling you 'this isn't a game up here, I'm playing from my soul, and this music is coming from a very dark well'. Some nights he was absolutely stunning and some nights he wasn't. Some nights he was right in the groove, others he was on another planet. That band was one of the most exciting I've ever heard. You never knew if they were going to get through it all or if John was just going to lose it. There's a very anarchic side to his music that is very hard to contain and orchestrate. John's strength for me is in his playing – the open tuning – 'Oh, I don't know what note this is but it seems to fit with that note' and working it all into some stunning piece of music.

Steve Tilston was one of many people who commented to me how Danny's influence on John was more than just musical.

In 1972 I remember seeing John at a BBC studio where we were both recording sessions for John Peel. I hadn't seen him for a while and in the meantime John had metamorphosed into a real Cockney Sparrow, even his body language had changed, flicking his shoulders back like a real East End geezer – struttin' abaht like a sparra on a shit 'eap, and doing all the rhyming slang. He'd become an exaggerated version of Danny Thompson. It was very funny though. He saw these people and became greatly attracted to them, then started to take on their persona – almost like a benign incubus or something. One time we stopped with Hamish Imlach up in Motherwell, and we went for a lunchtime drink in the local pub and John was doing the full-on Cockney thing, and then he would go up to the bar and order drinks in a broad Glasgow accent. He was totally oblivious to the fact that there were several very hard, broken-nosed locals in the bar, their faces like thunder because they thought he was taking the piss. There was never a dull moment in the man's company, a genuine larger than life character.

Wizz Jones was another who witnessed the musical partnership up close.

John and Danny were absolutely amazing together, it was a perfect partnership. The two of them together were just absolute dynamite. I think Danny was almost like a father figure to him, very much a role model for him. Although John was from Glasgow, he developed a Cockney accent like Danny. He was almost trying to out-Danny Danny. They were an inspiration to me, and I wrote a song, 'Poacher's Moon', about them a few years later. The song came about when Danny told me how he and John had this really emotional sometimes violent relationship. Once, on tour with John up in the Highlands of Scotland they ended up fighting when they were down to their underpants and up to their waists in freezing water fishing in the middle of the night!

Prior to Martyn's death, Danny Thompson told me how the fact that he was ten years older than John contributed a great deal to their relationship.

That's why he talks like me and does all my mannerisms. People ask who's the real Cockney out of the two of us and I say 'Well, I'm from London and he's from Glasgow – work it out for yourself.' He's not naïve and he's not stupid, but if he goes to the West Indies he comes back talking like dat [adopts Caribbean twang]. I was on a plane once to Scotland with him and when we took off from Heathrow he was talking like a Cockney and by the time we touched down he was speaking in broad Scots! Who is this bloke?

They call him an enigma, but I think that is just a polite way of saying that he is a complete loon! Of course I was a bit of a lad in those days. We were just kindred spirits, that doesn't mean bad, good or anything else, it just means he had all that energy that I had. I've been with other people who just couldn't keep up with that energy and just flaked. It's not a question of stimulants or booze; it's just that naturally he is that type of person.

Martyn and Thompson's concerts and their hell-raising lifestyle during the 1970s have since taken on an almost mythological status. Both men had sizeable alcohol habits and each constantly encouraged the other on to even greater carousing. John's old friend from Shawlands Academy, Davie MacFarlane, once met Martyn and Thompson at the MacDonald Hotel in Glasgow and was amazed at the pair's drinking capacity. Strung-out on post-gig adrenalin, they were downing treble vodkas and orange one after another with John making regular trips to his bedroom for a line of something to add to the mix. Davie told me with a nice touch of understatement: 'That was the first time I thought his drinking was getting out of hand, at times like that you just could not keep up or compete with his drinking. But then again away from the stage Iain was an entirely different person.'

Danny's days in the folk supergroup Pentangle had set a precedent for fine music topped off with plenty of madness and boozing. With the aid of the hotel night porter, Danny and the band would clean out the wine cellar of just about every place they stayed in on tour. His time with John was equally alcoholic and invariably led to shenanigans. John recalled one episode:

We used to drink a great deal together. I got really drunk one night and woke up and he had nailed me under the carpet. I couldn't move my hands or feet. I was very dry and had a hangover and I said [raspy-voiced] 'Danny, please . . . get me, get me a drink.' So he stepped over my helpless body, went to the phone and in a very loud voice said: 'Can I have a glass of orange juice for one, please? Breakfast for one, please.' I was screaming blue murder by this time. I was furious! He met the guy in the hall, so the guy couldn't get into the room and see what was happening. He sat in front of me and downed the orange juice and had the breakfast. The following evening I got my revenge. I got him really drunk while I remained sober. I watered down my drinks. He was so drunk, he just got to bed. I put his watch up five hours. He'd only been asleep about fifteen minutes. I shook him viciously and I said [in a rushed voice] – 'Danny, Danny, come on, come on, we gotta go, oh fuck man, the gig, we're gonna miss the gig, come on man, we gotta get a flight, come on man, come on, come on, we gotta go!' He just went 'Blaaahhh' . . . I said, 'I'll see you in the lobby.' I went down to the front desk and got myself another room and locked myself in there. I snuck downstairs and there he was, wandering around aimlessly, with his big double bass and half of his shirt hanging out. It was about two in the morning, you see. He was under the impression it was half past seven. It was wonderful! Things like that went on all the time. We had sort of a running battle. (*Dirty Linen*, October/November 1992)

A typical Martyn/Thompson show would start with 'May You Never' and proceed at great pace fuelled by endless bottles of beer and other relaxing agents – invariably the latter being provided by members of the audience. Not surprisingly, things sometimes got a little bit abstract. Rod McShane of *NME* reviewed a concert by the pair at Croydon in the summer of 1975 and estimated that a third of the ninety minutes spent on stage was taken up by conversations between the musicians and banter with the audience. Yet no one felt short-changed and McShane thought it was one of the most completely satisfying concerts he had ever attended. The exchanges between John and Danny were often more than a touch on the blue/obscene side and more than one commentator thought the swearing and belching rested uneasily beside the emotional gentle music they could produce together.

Danny has fond memories of a bizarre encounter with some nuns in Hastings.

We were drunk as usual on the stone jetty in Hastings, which slopes into the sea. It was a very hot, sunny day and we were just walking, enjoying a couple of bottles of Mateus Rosé. He put the bottles onto the end of a nylon fishing line and lowered them into the sea. And just before they reached the bottom they went plop and dropped off the nylon wire. So he says: 'I'm going in, are you with me?' So we both stripped off completely naked and dived off into the sea, to the absolute horror of all the fishermen that were there. After swimming about, I tried to climb up this sloping wall which was covered in barnacles and ended up getting completely cut to pieces. So I swam to the beach and started walking back along the jetty to get my clothes. So John then tries to throw a mate of his into the sea, and this bloke is frantically trying to stop getting thrown into the sea and the bloke breaks his finger. The bone was sticking out of his skin. So we flagged down this car and asked them to take him to hospital, and the car was full of nuns and there we were both standing there with nothing on!

Both John and Danny were naturally funny characters even without the addition of generous amounts of booze and in John's case, dope (Danny never partook, preferring alcohol). Martyn was an incurable giggler and a more than passable impersonator – veering into wild versions of the Glasgow hard men he came across in his youth. Danny played the part of straight man. The duo once entertained an audience of 700 fans in Bolton by playing naked. They had a bet that the other wouldn't have the nerve to take off an item of clothing after every song. In the end, the double bass and acoustic guitar provided much needed protection for the audience – though the view from the back of the stage took some beating. John once got three encores for a show in Spain despite falling off the stage due to drink. At another gig, he vomited into a bucket during a guitar solo! A typical exchange came when the pair played Edinburgh's Empire Theatre in 1973. At one point, John came to the edge of the stage to get a light for his joint from a member of the audience and bumped into a wire crash barrier. He turned, bemused, to his bassist and asked what the wall was for. 'It's to protect the audience,' replied Danny, opening another bottle.

That throwaway line had a trace of truth to it. By the mid-1970s, John was getting the reputation for being an unpredictable and occasionally heavy individual. A photo shoot for the *Live at Leeds* album showed how he was changing. The record's working title was *Ringside Seat* and to promote it John and Danny did a boxing photo shoot at Thomas à Becket gym in London's Old Kent Road. For some reason, John started to try and throw real punches. The playful sparring quickly turned serious and Danny eventually had to show how he had once been regimental boxing champ during his National Service days.

On tour, John got a reputation for not paying bills or menacingly asking for cash owed to them – behaviour more akin to a small-time gangster. Dave Pegg recalls how the money upfront demand backfired on John when he played at the Lisdoonvarna Festival during the late 1970s. Pegg was also on the bill, playing with Richard and Linda Thompson, and he found himself in the hotel room next to John and his then current lady.

We all went off to the gig, but the sun had gone down and the weather turned really cold. John was in the bar backstage with just a shirt and jeans on for many hours before he went on to perform. His minder came in to warn him that it was really cold on stage, but John had left his coat in the hotel. There was an Irish guy sitting next to him at the bar that was a big fan of John's and he offered John the loan of his jacket. He kept saying it would be an honour for him if John would wear his jacket on stage. John wore it on stage, but at the end of the night he got paid in cash and put the money in the pocket of this jacket. He went back into the bar and eventually gave this jacket back to the punter – with the cash still in the pocket! The punter decided then that he wasn't that big a John Martyn fan after all and he promptly disappeared. Back in the hotel, when John realised, he had a complete fit about it – there was an awful lot of noise, expletives flying left, right and centre. To make matters worse he had to fly out to another concert the next day, but the local airport was fogbound and he ended up missing the next gig! He was not a happy budgie.

At one Glasgow concert, Danny took offence when a particularly persistent heckler kept upsetting the flow of musical improvisation, calling the two bearded men 'teddy bears'. The double bassist lay down his instrument, clambered up into the balcony and forcibly ejected the troublemaker before returning to the stage and continuing the show. As Danny explained to Q magazine in September 1989: 'If he was in my house and we were having a party, I'd chuck him out, so he had to go. I've never been afraid to offend people when necessary.' Another Glasgow gig, at the QM Union in May 1976 ended with John leaping into the crowd to join in a Wild West-style brawl. John had made the mistake of praising Glasgow Celtic – not a wise decision when the hall was filled with Rangers fans celebrating their team's 3–1 win over Hearts in the Scottish Cup Final that day! Mick Doonan of support act Hedgehog Pie remembers that a couple of hecklers were getting out of order and spoiling the enjoyment of the show for the large audience. Halfway through a song, Martyn stopped playing and pointed at the hecklers and invited them outside. 'Two of the hecklers followed him out and a couple of minutes later John came back into the building with a smile on his face, having obviously given the hecklers something to think about. He walked back onto the stage to a roar of approval from the crowd and picked up the song where he had left off!'

Martyn wasn't always victorious though. He and Danny came to blows in a Hull hotel once, leaving John with two black eyes and a bandaged thumb. When Danny introduced John on stage as 'Old black eyes is back', the audience dissolved in mirth, with – to his eternal credit – no one laughing louder than Martyn himself. But beyond the looning about, there was a subtle, close friendship and dependency between the two men. John may have joked that they kept each other insane, but he would also be the first to admit that around that time he couldn't perform without Danny's reassuring presence in the background. For his part, Danny thought their relationship was perfect, unique and spontaneous – a blessing from heaven. To this day, he still holds John in the highest esteem, though he always fretted about his old friend's drinking. 'He used to phone me up in the middle of the night telling me he loved me, so I used to say to him "Well if you love me, do me a favour, and *please* stop drinking.'" Back in the 1970s, the wild lifestyle eventually took its toll on Danny. He lost his way and had to break up the partnership. The drinking stopped being fun for him and became like a job – needing half a bottle of vodka in the morning before he could face the world. He gave up the booze for good in 1978 and eventually converted to Islam in 1990. That he and John survived the mad dog days, when many others who partied far less died, is something of a miracle. Danny said goodbye to the wild days, quoting the old Bedouin saying 'We pitch our tents far apart, so that our hearts remain close.'

Glasgow drinker

. . . if I drink I'm sometimes very aggtessive.

John Martyn

When anyone tried to compliment him on his talents, he would belittle his music with frustrated self-contempt.

Nick Kent

By the end of 1975, it's safe to say that the early cosy idealism of John's career had been replaced by a deep disenchantment with the industry he worked in. At times he talked about jacking it all in and claimed that there were so many rotten aspects of the business that he was in danger of losing his voice speaking out in protest. He was sick of the session musicians who would only talk about money, of the agents who were no better than leeches and the managers who boasted about ripping clients off. People were lying to him about contracts, and agencies were allegedly hanging on to money that was rightly his. From now on, he would demand cash or a cheque in his name on the night of the concert. But with a young family to feed, John couldn't afford to turn down work. He was faced by the conundrum that doing the thing he loved so much was actually doing him great harm. Even Beverley, despite all her grievances against her ex-husband, admits that he worked bloody hard to provide for her and their children. When, in late 1975, an interviewer with *Liquorice* magazine told John he had done sixty dates in the UK alone that year, his response was blunt and telling.

> Is it that many? No wonder I'm fuckin' tired . . . it's boring me to death . . .
> It's lovely when you're on the stage, right, really good when you have a play,
> but all the driving about the fuckin' motorway and going to poxy hotels . . .

John loved performing so much that the idea of giving up live dates for good was out of the question: he would go mad with boredom. In any case, he needed the money. Although good sales of *Live at Leeds* had helped things financially, he had just over £7,500 in savings to show for the years of touring and recording. It was, by his own admission, the unhappiest time of his life so far. To use the Scottish vernacular, he was 'scunnered with life'.

The endless touring was also putting a stress on his marriage. John told reporters that he still loved Bev more than anything in the world and would die for her tomorrow if necessary. He no doubt did, but in reality he was still playing the field once the opportunity arose. Many years later he looked back with regret at his infidelity on the road, where every young girl he met seemed to want to bed him, and his wife back home was conveniently forgotten. He ruminated on the temptations of life on the road.

> You're 4,000 miles away from home and what are you going to do? . . . I was
> a nice laddie . . . but easily led. Actually it was a pure joy . . . At twenty years
> old, young girls are saying 'Come to bed with me,' and you tend to forget
> your wife for that extra half hour. The infidelity I regret. But that's the only
> thing. It's just a lie – everybody regrets lies. (*iCast* website, May 2000)

As his mood darkened, John was increasingly trying to alleviate the pain through booze and drugs. When it came to alcohol, John confounded racial stereotypes about the Scots: he was never a big lover of whisky and preferred white spirits like vodka and Martini. Then there would be times when he would take a liking to Brandy Alexander or Mount Gay Rum and drink that for days on end. As for drugs, well smoking hash was a constant throughout his life. But back in the mid-1970s he was also using just about anything else he could get his hands on. Cocaine and heroin were the drugs of choice: in one interview, he talked of using eight grammes a week of both drugs, though he did rather optimistically say that he could stop at any time. (*Liquorice*, January/February 1976). He told the Nottingham University journalist Dave Belbin how he was now refraining from taking cocaine before a show.

> Occasionally, if I'm very unhappy, I'll take some horse (heroin). But equally occasionally, if you were to offer me some (coke) after the gig tonight, if I was on top of the world and I wasn't drunk, I'd probably say 'Yes', because I enjoy it; I actually do enjoy getting high. I don't count this as a drug [referring to the joint in his hand]; I don't think it's more dangerous as a drug than alcohol. Also, if I have this, I don't smoke nearly as many cigarettes, and I'm a better person. I'm more peaceful; if I drink I'm sometimes very aggressive.

In truth, Martyn's drunken rages and his insistence that Beverley concentrate on her domestic chores rather than attempt a musical comeback were increasingly causing problems in the marriage. One former babysitter from this era told me how she had to field calls from America where John would rage about his wife not being at home looking after the kids.

> John didn't like her going out when he was not around and I remember him quizzing me about who she was with. He did like her to stay at home with the kids, but she would be out playing gigs at the Six Bells pub in Chiddingly. In a way, John came across as a typical male chauvinist and a bit of a bully towards her.

The drug scene was also to affect his domestic arrangements. Around this time, the heroin scene in Hastings was getting just a bit too close for comfort and this was one of the reasons for John moving his young family thirty miles inland – to Heathfield in East Sussex. Unfortunately, it was a case of frying pan to fire. The new home on the small town's Tilsmore Road was named Kenyata and had once been a smart country house. But in the mid-1970s it had a reputation as a drug den and was well known as a place for scoring. It would later be the scene of a major drug bust (not involving the Martyns) and was eventually pulled down to make way for a new housing scheme. At the time, John settled well into Heathfield and when he was not touring he became a well known regular at the local pub, The Star.

Increasing levels of paranoia were the inevitable consequence of the drink and drug abuse. When in sober mode, John was invariably amusing and spiritually alive, but when inebriated he could turn loud, obnoxious and difficult, or sullen and depressed. Friends described him as a stereotypical Glaswegian drinker, whose mood could change suddenly and violently. With his nerves shredded by abuse, simple things like ordering a pint in his local pub were becoming a challenge for John. He talked openly about the need to get help from a neurologist and confided that he feared being ordered to give up everything. He sounded like a man increasingly isolated – only Danny, Beverley and a couple of other friends were considered close relationships. In November 1975, an emotionally drained and disillusioned Martyn announced that he was to take a one-year break from touring in the UK. Physically, the years of touring and drink/drug abuse had left him ill; mentally, the deaths of Drake and Kossoff left him sure that he would be the next casualty unless he put the brakes on.

Sensing that John was in a fragile state, Chris Blackwell invited him, Beverley and their kids to stay in Jamaica – though John had to pay his own way, using up much of his savings in the process. The four-month trip saw John chill out at Blackwell's home in Kingston, which looked onto a scenic mountain range. John had never been to the Caribbean before and the whole trip was a bit of a culture shock for him. He enjoyed the experience, even though the ongoing political strife on the island allied to the threat of muggings and the undercurrent of racial tensions meant he often stayed put in the home. From his base he could hear the sounds of pigs being slaughtered, and he grew to hate the way the whites still lorded over the blacks when it came to money and influence.

After a while he got bored and started doing session work. He played lead guitar with Burning Spear on the album, *Man in the Hills*, which was produced by Jack Ruby, and also worked with Lee 'Scratch' Perry and Max Romeo. Blackwell made the introductions and Martyn immediately took to the talents of the locals, thinking they were intuitively hipper than western musicians. Playing with the local musicians helped reinvigorate John. He especially enjoyed working with the eccentric Jamaican genius Perry – admiring his creativity and ability to coax the best out of musicians, while being undeniably 'round the fuckin' bend'. The pair shared an interest in repeat-echo and John soon introduced Perry to the joys of Echoplex. Martyn claimed to have been one of the few people to understand Perry's bizarre behaviour, though even John must have wondered as to why Perry filled bathtubs with dead fish and seashells and cuddled trees! On another occasion he found Perry taped to a tree yelling 'Tree, I love ya man!' These rum and reefer-filled sessions were great fun and were meant to help keep John in cash, though payment sometimes came in the form of coffee liqueurs, hookers, blue movies and counterfeit US currency. When Perry later visited the Martyns' home in England he cooked up a red snapper curry with goat peppers which were so potent that John nearly ended up in hospital. Years later, visitors to John's Scottish home would see a photo of Perry proudly on display by the fireplace. Perry met John again when they were both in London during 1977. Perry's thoughts on the art of sex as told to guests at Chris Blackwell's were the inspiration for one of Martyn's best-loved songs, 'Big Muff', which John and Lee co-wrote sitting at the breakfast table and which was named after a fuzz-box they used at the time. Contrary to scurrilous rumours, the track is not a tribute to Beverley. The Caribbean trip also inspired Martyn to record another slice of prime reggae – the self-mythologising 'Johnny Too Bad' – a track originally recorded by The Slickers which featured in the classic movie *The Harder They Come*.

Although 1976 was to be a fallow year in his career, John never stuck to his promise to take a whole year's sabbatical and during the long hot summer he appeared at a few prestige events. On Sunday, 4 July, he topped the bill at the Open Air Theatre in the heart of London's Regent's Park. Without his favourite sidekick, Danny Thompson, John took to the stage in the steep-tiered venue on a stiflingly hot summer's evening to the roars of a capacity crowd. Rod McShane of *NME* thought the lyrical imagery in standards such as 'Bless the Weather', 'Spencer The Rover' and 'Over The Hill' gained an added strength floating on the balmy evening breeze. As a steady stream of fans handed him beers, smokes and even guitar strings, John kept them entertained with amusing long raps between songs, taking requests, giving light-hearted abuse to his roadie or anyone who had the nerve to leave the audience early. The hot summer night was the perfect setting for John's sultry music and his final number 'I'd Rather Be The Devil' was, in his own words, 'hot and nasty'. The audience demanded two encores, but due to Greater London Council Sunday night curfew rules they only got one – 'Singing In The Rain'.

Later that month, he played another mesmerising show at the July Wakes – a three-day folk festival at Chornock Richard in Lancashire. Chosen to close the entire event, John played for over an hour on Sunday evening – this time with Danny backing him. Hugh Fielder of *Sounds* described Martyn as the avant-garde of the folk genre and was greatly impressed by the volume and dynamics of the star's electric box of tricks to conjure up an orchestral sound from a single amplified acoustic guitar. The highlights were 'Bless The Weather', 'May You Never' and 'Inside Out'. On 29 October 1976, he played a solo gig in Nottingham as a benefit for *Liquorice* magazine. By now his concerts rarely featured songs from any of the first four albums.

In early 1977, Island released the compilation, *So Far So Good*, which marked the end of John's first decade as a professional musician and took in tracks from his eight album career with the label, including a live take on 'I'd Rather Be The Devil'. John had little say in the track listing, but the album eventually went gold. According to Nick Kent, the award did nothing to cure John's worrying levels of disillusionment.

He kept attempting to smash the framed artefact in a fit of disgust partly at the music business and partly at himself. When anyone tried to compliment him on his talents, he would belittle his music with frustrated self-contempt.

Iain with his mum and step-dad, mid-1950s (*John Martyn*)

Infant Iain, c.1949 (*John Martyn*)

Young Iain on houseboat, c.1951 (*John Martyn*)

Iain on Triumph motorcycle, c.1957 (*John Martyn*)

Iain and Linda (age 16), September weekend, Millport (*Linda Dunning*)

Left. Iain and Linda (age 18) in a pub, Charing Cross, Glasgow (*Linda Dunning*)

Below. Iain and Linda meet for the first time in 37 years. Taken backstage at the ABC Glasgow, April 2006 (*Linda Dunning*)

John and Beverley Martyn, c.1970 (*Redferns Music Picture Library*)

John Martyn at home with Mhairi in Hastings, 8 August 1974
(*Brian Cooke / Redferns*)

Nick Drake, Hampstead 1972 (*Redferns Music Picture Library*)

Paul Kossoff, New York 1975 (*Redferns Music Picture Library*)

Posing for the *Inside Out* album sleeve in July 1973 (*Brian Cooke / Redferns*)

Arrsan Ahmun, John Martyn, Alan Thomson and Spencer Cozens, July 2004
(*Spencer Cozens*)

Julianne 'Daisy' Flowers, John Martyn's long-term partner during the 1990s
(*John Neil Munro*)

A modelling agency shot of Annie Furlong taken by Tony Higgins, a Dublin photographer (*Michael Furlong*)

The final shot of Annie in Kenya before she died in 1996 (*Michael Furlong*)

Annie and John Martyn at their wedding in Edinburgh in 1983 (*Michael Furlong*)

John Giblin, Spencer Cozens and John Martyn in Inistioge bar
(*Spencer Cozens 2007*)

John and Gizmo the dog, November 2003 (*Spencer Cozens 2007*)

John Martyn, Blackheath, 3 December 1994
(*David Sinclair, www.jazzphotographs.com*)

John Martyn, May 2005 (*Spencer Cozens 2007*)

John February 2005 (*Spencer Cozens 2007*)

John and Teresa (*John Martyn*)

John Martyn, Henley-on-Thames, June 1998. He was being photographed for US magazine *Magnet* and sang throughout the whole shoot (*Pete Millson, www.petemillson.com*)

Only *Inside Out* was left unscathed by all this self-directed bile. (*NME*, 29 November 1980)

To coincide with the compilation, John's first UK tour in over a year kicked off in Canterbury, on 11 February, with a major gig at London's New Victoria theatre nine days later. This time out he went solo, as Danny had other commitments. In any case, John was increasingly happy playing more electric guitar. Vivien Goldman of *Sounds* caught one of the gigs at Belfast University and found a performer still living on the edge and suffering for his art. John was sick from food poisoning and nerves before going on stage. The skin on his fingers was cracking and bleeding and he had to use an anaesthetic by his side to treat the fingers after every song – by the end of the show his guitar was spattered with blood. His dislike of the industry was still evident as he rubbished contemporaries like Jansch and McTell and other unnamed 'sycophantic musicians'. Singles were dismissed as 'cheap, disposable, nasty and tasteless'. And once again he complained about being skint. John was by now one of the old guard under attack from the new wave of British bands, and he generally had little time for the movement. He admired the energy of The Sex Pistols and went to a handful of New Wave concerts, but overall he felt it was just fashion. He was angered by the fact that many of the new musicians had been hawking their wares about for years in old bands. On one occasion – outside a posh hotel in London where John went to play poker – he locked horns with the Pistols' bassist Sid Vicious.

> He kept having a pop at me and the woman I was with, calling me a washed-up middle-aged pop star. He was just so rude and ridiculous – a really dreadful person. I told him to stop, but he wouldn't, so we went outside and I beat him up a bit. The ironic thing was that John Lydon used to come to my gigs and cheer me on.

1–0 to the Old Wave.

By now, John's drinking bouts were beginning to cause real problems for those around him. On a trip to Australia in August 1977, he was meant to share the bill with Bert Jansch – another guitarist whose reputation for musical brilliance was also being drawn down by alcoholism. Both men were managed by Bruce May, who later recalled in the book *Dazzling Stranger* how Martyn and Jansch got into a fight on the plane to Perth. Bert's muddled reasoning was that he had to hit John first because he knew that John was going to do the same to him before the end of the tour. The efforts of the tour manager to calm matters by buying a bottle of Scotch just made things worse. For some unknown reason, John had placed a life-jacket in his hand luggage and when the tour manager carried the bag off the plane for the sozzled star he ended up being arrested and thrown in prison. Jansch and Martyn weren't much smarter – John had a burst lip and Bert's finger was dislocated as a result of the drunken star wars. Bert had to sit out the rest of the tour, but made a bizarre appearance on stage at the Sydney Opera House, sweeping the stage with a broom while John played on unaware. According to Bruce May, he was lucky to get both men home in one piece. Perhaps the friction between them was partly because Bert had once dated Beverley Kutner in the days before she married John. Bruce May's brother, Ralph McTell, remembers:

A large amount of vodka was drunk on the plane, a fight broke out and John twisted Bert's arm up so he couldn't play for three weeks. The roadie was later arrested for trying to steal a life-raft, and John ended up having to do the shows in Australia on his own, while Bert seethed and tried to disrupt things in the background.

During the Australian tour, one attempt at humour went down like a lead balloon when John told a radio DJ that Beverley had been killed in a car crash the week before. The radio station imposed a blanket ban on John Martyn records. At a concert in Canberra, John did his bit for Anglo–Australian relations by telling the audience they were backward and racist. All in all, it wasn't the happiest of tours.

One World

I think when he and Beverley split up his life started to really fall apart. He once said to me that he had never written a good song since Beverley left him.

Phill Brown

I've had moments when I have looked in his eyes and been really scared just being in his company. Everyone will tell you that if they are honest.

Dave Pegg

Despite his increasingly chaotic lifestyle, John still managed to conjure up another sublime album. *One World* was recorded during July and August 1977 at Chris Blackwell's Woolwich Green Farm in Theale, near Glastonbury, Somerset. Island's mobile recording unit was set up in a courtyard one hundred yards away from the main house, with John and recording engineer Phill Brown living in a converted stable block nearby. Blackwell produced the sessions and, on his suggestion, microphones were set near to the water that surrounded the home to pick up the sounds of waves lapping and of the resident geese. Martyn would later pay tribute to Blackwell's refined production. Besides being his boss and close friend, John thought Chris had a better judgement and objectivity than he did when it came to deciding which songs were strongest. Among the usual suspects providing musical backing to John were Danny, Steve Winwood, John Stevens, Kesh Sathie and Dave Pegg.

Phill Brown had been house engineer at Island's Basing Street Studios during the label's seminal years of 1970–76 and in an interview for the first edition of this book remembered meeting Martyn back in 1971 and being very impressed by the young Scot.

> You look at him now and in a sense it is sad to see what has happened to him because back then he was a charming guy and he looked great. He was with Beverley and it was all very positive. Over the years he slowly built up a reputation for being quick-tempered and easily riled, but I kind of got on with him at that time. He was a bit of a drinker, but he was very together and very cool back then.

Brown reflected on how Chris Blackwell played an integral part in the making of the *One World* album.

> Blackwell was a great positive guy by John's side. I didn't see them as really good mates; it was a bit more like the relationship between benevolent patron and talented artist. Blackwell really believed in John and he got involved in *One World* because he wanted to help him and to move things on. It was Blackwell's idea to get everyone out to Woolwich Green Farm. It had been a derelict house when he bought it in the 1960s and did it up. Apart from the entrance driveway, this old gravel pit filled with water surrounded the house. It was pretty isolated; there were no other houses around. If you stood outside in the middle of the night you could hear the Paddington to the West Country trains in the distance, and maybe see the odd light in the distance, but you certainly wouldn't have any disturbance from neighbours. I was out there previously doing overdubs on a Robert Palmer album, and Chris subsequently had the idea of getting the mobile out there to do an album with John.
>
> The recording was done pretty quickly – I think we were just out there for three weeks. On a typical day we would get up about eleven in the morning and have some breakfast. Blackwell would be seeing to business in his house and betting on horses, and then he would stroll over about two in the afternoon and we would get started. Sometimes we would work through till four or five in the morning. 'Small Hours' was recorded at four o'clock in the morning. The train you hear in the distance is the first mail train out of Paddington! The idea of pumping it out through the PA system and miking it up across the water – all

that is a very important part of the guitar sound in *One World* and on 'Small Hours' you can hear that it really was recorded outdoors.

When they weren't working, the musicians whiled away their time sailing a rubber dinghy on the lake or lazing in the sun. This idyllic set-up produced some wonderful languid music but a steady supply of opium also helped to set the mood and curb some of Martyn's excesses. Phill Brown recalls that during the sessions, John was together and focused on the job in hand. Occasionally, though, his darker side would become apparent.

> John has always been the same; he's very up and down. You could meet him one night and he'd be the best thing you've ever seen, he could change your life. But the next night he might be so drunk that he couldn't really speak to you. The recording process was a bit like that ⸗ but we had this opium and we all kind of floated on that. Most of the time he was very up, concentrating on the songs, and there was a good vibe – John is a very funny guy when he is in a good mood.
>
> But I remember one day Chris and I were talking in the mobile about how we could get the best out of John and he was standing outside and overheard us. When I came out of the mobile he was very angry with me for talking about him behind his back – but all we were doing was discussing, as any producer and engineer might, how to get the best out of this guy. I managed to talk my way out of it, but over the years John has had a tendency to be quite violent. You have this guy whose music and his attitude to life through his lyrics are so beautiful who then almost turns into the very opposite of what he is writing about. Back then, everyone was prepared to put up with it – over the last ten years I get the impression fewer and fewer people are. It's a different era now and you cannot really get away with that type of behaviour any more.

The end product of all their labours was one of John's best-loved and more commercial albums. John enjoyed working on the record and a number of its songs were mainstays of his stage shows for the rest of his career. His admission that he seldom listened to it after its release meant little, as John tended to do this with all his records. As ever, it was an album of great variety. 'Smiling Stranger' and 'Dealer' shone more light on John's ever-present drug habit, with their exploration of the love/hate relationship between pusher and user – 'the spit and polish on a fat man's shoe!' But in complete contrast the album contains some of Martyn's most commercial work to date in songs such as 'Couldn't Love You More', 'Certain Surprise' and 'Dancing', which has a touch of Dire Straits at their most innovative. The bossa nova feel to 'Certain Surprise' – with a show-stealing cameo from Rico on trombone – probably harks back to the days with session men Ed Carter and Mike Kowalski, who had turned John on to Latin music.

As in many of his songs, 'Certain Surprise' finds John in confessional mode, telling us with commendable understatement that silence has never been his thing: 'I love to shout and sing about my love.' On 'Dancing', the lyrics are a plea – presumably to Beverley – asking that she understand how a music man must live the wild life. Dave Pegg has fond memories of the *One World* sessions, though that particular track did cause problems.

I remember having a very difficult time with it, because I'm a kind of spontaneous player and the first thing that comes into my head is usually all I can play. I love the bass line on 'Dancing', in fact I have the single on my jukebox at home, and it's one of the tracks I am most proud of. I loved the tune straight away and I came up with the bass line that was eventually used, but John initially didn't like it and was asking me to play something different. And I said no, because to be honest that is the way I hear it. I think John wanted me and Dave Mattacks to be black really! I think he booked the wrong people, because you cannot get two whiter people than DM and me! I remember John saying play anything but the sequence C, A minor, F and G, and I said: 'Listen, I'm from Birmingham!' Anyway, John grew to like the bass line.

The outstanding title track has Martyn teasing out the socialist lyric over a delicate, beautiful instrumentation. It was a rare example of John's lyrics branching out from the painfully personal to reflecting his anger at the injustices he saw in the world. John, who described himself as a lifelong socialist, albeit a smoked-salmon one – he would dedicate a later song, 'Mad Dog Days', to Margaret Thatcher – told the writer Dave Belbin:

> You either believe in it or you don't – regardless of political boundaries it is one world whether you like it or not; just because people look different on the other side of the world doesn't mean to say that they are different. Because they eat different things, smell different, doesn't mean to say they are different at all, they're just the same as thee 'n' me.' (*Gongster*, 24 January 1978)

Martyn also had a refreshingly liberal view on race relations. Danny Thompson tells the story of how John once head butted two burly white diners at an Indian restaurant in Birmingham who had been racially abusing one of the waiters. John did so despite the fact that there were twelve men at the other table! When interviewed for this book, John selected the title track as the song he was most proud of writing – the best example of what he would like to be musically. As he often did, John made sure the final track on the album also left an indelible impression. 'Small Hours' was a spell-binding display of Echoplex at its best, with some local geese providing backing quacking. It was to be the last vinyl outing for the Echoplex – and what a way to sign it into oblivion. As Ralph McTell has commented, if that song does not move you then there really is something wrong with you. *One World*, with a lovely cover designed by Tony Wright, deservedly reached the UK charts, albeit a modest number 54. For once, the hard-to-please Martyn voiced contentment with the finished product – the opium had worked its spell and he remembered: 'You can really tell we were somewhere else when we made that record. I was really pleased with it.'

Phill Brown later became a close friend of Martyn, living just two villages away from the singer's new Heathfield home. Prior to Martyn's death, Phill reflected on how John's domestic difficulties eventually caught up with him and contributed to his later problems.

> When I knew Beverley she was really just a mother, living at home and looking after three kids and dealing with John's life as good wives do. But I

think when he and Beverley split up his life started to really fall apart. He once said to me that he had never written a good song since Beverley left him. That may be a bit extreme, but his best writing was definitely from the time when he was with her. His voice is still great, but he has lost a bit of the old spark. I really love the guy, I think he is an amazing wasted talent, he should be huge. I guess when he finally dies he will have wonderful obituaries. *One World* is one of the best albums I worked on. I love the songs and the lyrics and I love the whole vibe of the album. It has really stood the test of time. When you look back on him when he was young, it is kind of sad to see the way he has ended up. If he is bitter about the business, I'm not surprised; anyone who stays in the business for any length of time will feel that way. I think he felt manipulated at times and pushed into situations he did not want to be in – but he might have brought it upon himself to a certain degree.

When he wasn't on the road, John would chill out in local pubs around the Heathfield area such as The Six Bells and The Kicking Donkey. Invariably he was driven to those inns by Simon Climie, a local teenager fresh out of school who was also a promising guitarist. Simon, who went on to earn chart success during the 1980s as one half of Climie Fisher, hit it off with Martyn and was in awe of his talent.

John wasn't driving at the time, so I became his chauffeur for about six months and we would also have jamming sessions back at his house. Without meaning to be, he became my mentor. I couldn't help but admire the guy: he had this amazing purity and brilliance to his writing, singing and playing. The band I was in at the time played a lot of local pubs and occasionally Bev would do a song or two with her Guild guitar and John would come on and play on his Martin. To us they were like the royal family, they were both so spectacular artistically. When John and Bev were entertaining they were a lot of fun.

Simon himself went on to have massive success both as a producer and songwriter for major artists such as Aretha Franklin and Eric Clapton, but he still rates John incredibly highly as a person and a musician.

John is a big personality; I think he is one of the kindest, most big-hearted people I've ever met. He's the sort of person you would want as a friend and not an enemy. I've had some great hit records with my own stuff, but I've never seen myself as a poetic person up on the same level as John. He is one of the true geniuses that I have met in the music industry.

An American tour in the spring of 1978 saw Martyn share the bill with Eric Clapton, playing solo to crowds of over 20,000. Both he and Eric were drinking to excess for most of the five-week tour, often drunk on stage, where armed security with guard dogs kept them from the audience. It wasn't a wholly enjoyable experience, with Clapton's fans less than receptive to John's music. He was stuck alone on stage in cavernous half-empty halls while fans milled about finding their seats and eating popcorn. The only saving grace was that the humiliation only lasted half an hour and he was well paid for it. He later said that only one in five of the gigs were enjoyable; the rest were more likely to induce suicidal feelings. He told the journalist Rob O'Dempsey: 'It was definitely Christians to the lions; my seed fell on stony ground!' (*Musin' Music* magazine, 12 November 1984). Clapton paid him extra if he got off stage on time – which left more opportunity for John to get to know the local groupies while Slowhand did his stuff on stage. Eric also showed his appreciation of John's talents by gifting him a Musicman amplifier. Another gig on John's US jaunt saw him supporting Foghat at the Kansas City Cow House. The concert descended into *Spinal Tap*-type farce when he had to make a quick exit as the venue caught fire. It was one of John's worst nights on stage. The friendship between John and Clapton endured, and the two stars joined Hamish Imlach on stage once in 1979 in the rather unusual setting of Dorking Folk Club. Their rendition of the old Blind Gary Davis number 'Cocaine' and Hamish's signature tune, 'Cod Liver Oil And The Orange Juice' went down well, even though the audience seemed blissfully unaware they were being entertained by inebriated rock royalty!

*

By the end of the 1970s, John and Beverley's decade-long relationship was in terminal decline. By his own admission he felt trapped and, as a result, the devil within him emerged. On one occasion, Beverley threatened to leave him unless he underwent therapy. John met the wife of Scots therapist RD Laing, who promptly told him there was nothing wrong with him. After his wife started divorce proceedings and took custody of their three children, John told *NME*'s Nick Kent how the marriage finally ended.

> She cited her reason for wanting a divorce 'officially' in terms of me being 'grossly negligent towards my family owing to a desire to constantly further my career' . . . Just one morning it exploded. It was like 'the egg's too hard-boiled'. Slap, I'm staring at all these divorce papers. I mean, it had been going on for a while but . . . the end was just boom! That was that. (*NME*, 29 November 1980)

He was now getting a reputation around the music scene as an angry and difficult character. Steve Tilston, who hadn't seen much of John since the Cousins days, suddenly got an up-close insight into how his old friend was changing.

> In 1979 I did a fifty-date tour opening for him. I would do a forty-five-minute set before he came on. He was still very friendly and we got on well, but he had become pretty famous by then and there was a marked change in his personality. He was drinking a lot more and a lot of white powder found its way up his nostrils. On stage, he was great, but his personality would change easily. The way he would treat people – like the soundmen who were working for him – I found it a bit hard to take. He treated these people almost like he was a baron and they were his retainers. Then he would go on stage and sing about one world and love. It made me cringe a bit.
>
> I don't suppose he and Beverley were getting on that well. I remember him ringing her constantly from his hotel room in Aberdeen. One of the last times I saw him he organised a meeting at the Half Moon pub in Putney with Beverley and me and my first wife. He thought Bev would get on with her as she was Jewish too. He looked to me like a man vainly trying to hold something together, but not making a very convincing attempt at it. I was aware of it, because I was trying to do a very similar kind of thing in my

marriage. After that tour, I didn't see him again. I didn't like what he had become; I just thought I didn't want to be around this person any more. He'd become famous, but he'd lost a lot on the way. He would talk about violence a lot. He was mixing with a rough crowd on tour. His driver, he would refer to him as 'his assassin'. This guy was a real East-End thief, a whippet-like man. In actual fact, he and I got on like a house on fire. At a gig in Southampton, John and this fellow had a set-to and the little bloke was yelling 'You drive me fucking crazy, I can't take it any more.' He pulled a knife on John who was dancing around trying to make light of this, kicking out at the blade in a balletic kind of way because it was obvious he wouldn't use the knife. That was the last we saw of the guy. He just left the tour and John got another nefarious character to take over. The new guy had court cases pending to do with importing illegal immigrants across the Channel. John was always drawn to this kind of bloke; I must admit they had a certain nefarious attraction.

Dave Pegg concurs that around this time John was almost like a Jekyll and Hyde character.

John has obviously done a lot of work under various influences, which is part of his art. I've had moments when I have looked in his eyes and been really scared just being in his company. Everyone will tell you that if they are honest. You don't like to see people that are really nice acting in that kind of way, when he is a different person from the one he was the day before. I felt kind of threatened in the way that he was talking to other people and to me. But to be honest, people tell me that I have done that to them. When I had bad drink experiences I hear stories about myself and I cannot believe them. But I've never actually seen John be violent to anyone.

When he played at our (Fairport Convention) Cropredy festival some years ago, we saw the Jekyll and Hyde side of his character again. He did the festival with Danny, but he had a dreadful problem in that he had brought the wrong guitar with him. He spent the whole of the gig shouting at people because the guitar sounded so bad. It was like a cheap Stratocaster copy and the battery had gone in it and it really wasn't our fault. It was his own fault or his roadie's fault. It just got worse and worse, and I think Danny just walked off at one point. It all really didn't do much for John's reputation. However, we all still love him – he is a fantastic writer and a great musician. I wish him well.

In a later interview with Rob Young, Martyn owned up to having an obstreperous side to his nature.

I think you have to fight with people all the time . . . For a while I had the reputation of a real bad boy; this man was going to punch you out, shoot you or fuck you. I deliberately cultivated it, because it kept people away from me. I want people away from me, basically.' (*Wire*, June 1998)

In the case of his marriage, he was to have the opposite problem. Tired of all John's excesses, Beverley had taken out a restraining order to keep him away from their old home. The whole debacle eventually contributed to her having a nervous breakdown. In the immediate aftermath of the break-up, John embarked on an alcoholic bender of mammoth proportions. But through all the pain and madness emerged his last truly great album – *Grace and Danger*.

Grace and Danger

I would do it differently now but back then I was too busy being sad. It's all about Beverley.

John Martyn on Grace and Danger

To me, it was an album that summed up where John was in his life at that time, it certainly came from his heart, that's for sure.

Martin Levan

John once said that every record he had ever made – good, bad or just plain indifferent – is totally autobiographical. If you want to get a grasp of the state of mind of this self-confessed emotional fool at any given time, a trawl through the lyric sheet invariably gives the best indicator. *Grace and Danger*, released in 1980, was the prime example of how he preferred making records to keeping a diary. Written as his marriage finally imploded in a spectacular way, it's an achingly emotional account of the last rites of his years with Beverley. When it comes to documenting the demise of a once strong love affair, perhaps only Dylan's *Blood on the Tracks* comes close to the bare-boned confessional intensity of *Grace and Danger*. But it's a mark of John's talent that not only could he write such an emotional record but also that he should make such harrowing subject matter sound so magical and beguiling. Out of all the pain came his most commercial record to date. For John, writing about the break-up was cathartic and almost like a form of very public confession. But it couldn't have been easy for him to tell the world how he had to beg before the object of his devotion before she would even say his name. The intensity of this set of songs meant that *Grace and Danger* very nearly never saw the light of day. Island's chief, Chris Blackwell initially delayed the release for up to a year. His reasoning was that the lyrical content was just too honest – he found it upsetting and depressing. Blackwell loved the music, though, and still carries a copy of the CD with him wherever he travels.

The fact that he put his helplessness and despair on display to the general public showed that Martyn was at heart a very brave individual. The album could have ended up as an acute embarrassment; instead it's now generally regarded as one of his finest works. Twenty-five years later, John himself was still aware of how strong a record it is, citing it and *Inside Out* as his personal favourites, although he told me: 'I would do it differently now, but back then I was too busy being sad. It's all about Beverley.' When I asked about his views on her, he replied:

> If you speak to her you'll have to expect a whole dose of vitriol. She's a dear old lady now; she'll say I was a terrible handful. Lovely girl, bless her – she didn't deserve me. I came from the bottom of the pack. She's too sensitive for her own good. We weren't getting enough money. I was only getting £100 a night. Once you pay expenses off that and you're left with £30 and we had a house the size of your manager's ambition! But it was good fun though.

Others wouldn't use the word fun to describe the end of the Martyns' marriage. In a BBC documentary, John asserts that Bev was too gentle a person for him. When I put this to one friend of the couple, the reply was coruscating.

> John is a fucking liar. He's a very, very clever man but he invents things. I think he has had serious problem with his women, to do with all kinds of hang-ups that he has from childhood. Beverley is not someone I would describe as gentle, she was cynical, she was tough, and she was quite analytical. She is certainly a very strong girl and not soft and gentle. She was an attractive prize. They had children together and no one stayed with him as long as she did. They had a very intense and fiery relationship – some of the things that went on were horrible. On occasion, the kids would have to hide outside under the hedges in the fields by their home. It was fucking rough

out there, terrible things went on. It was testament to Beverley that they were together for as long as they were.

In the same BBC documentary, Bev gave a withering put-down on John's behaviour near the end, saying that he was no longer a 'nice little boy'. By now his alcohol and cocaine predilections had become addictions and the resulting violent mood swings were helping to shred his marriage.

Bridget St John had known John and Bev since the Hampstead days when she occasionally babysat young Wesley. Bridget, who now lives in America, recalls how she saw at first hand some of the pressures that were tearing the couple apart.

> I think in the beginning they had a good thing going – but I think once more children were born and Beverley was necessarily a mum first for a while and a musician second, that took a toll on their relationship on all levels. I think things got very difficult and the last time I visited them as a couple in Heathfield shortly before I came to the US it was clear things were rocky. I think it was hard for both of them – they both loved music, but they had children to raise and a living to make, and the demands and conflict of doing both destroyed what they originally had.

By 1978, John was separated from his wife and was living a peripatetic existence, though his 'crash pads' would not have been familiar to the average homeless person. At times he stayed at Chris Blackwell's Basing Street house, which had a bath the size of a small swimming pool, and at other times he crashed at the home of his friend Phil Collins. Collins' own three-year marriage to his childhood sweetheart, Andrea (both had been students at the Barbara Speake Stage School together), was under irretrievable strain as the workaholic drummer emerged from the shadows into an international star. Aside from a fledgling solo career, Phil was still the drummer with Genesis and also their new lead singer following the departure of Peter Gabriel. As if that wasn't enough, he had his own band, Brand X, and countless sessions and tours to keep him busy. While on one tour, Andrea became close to a local decorator, which didn't exactly ease tensions in the home they shared with children Joely and Simon. The common marital problem cemented a friendship between John and Phil, two musicians who admired each other as people and players and also shared an infatuation with the music of Weather Report. The Collins house – Old Croft in the village of Shalford near Dorking – was eventually dubbed 'Heartbreak Hotel' by the two musicians. John was drinking too much of just about whatever booze was on offer. This time the bender lasted for all of seven months – though his inability to come to terms with the break-up with Bev fuelled his alcoholism for years to come. According to John, that period was intensely difficult for both men – with much weeping and regrets to go with the alcohol. Both emotionally traumatised, they took turns to make long phone calls to their respective partners in vain attempts to save the relationships. When they were both suitably miserable and desperate they decided to put it all down on vinyl. Collins had long thought John was a unique performer and admired his ability to create a powerful sound from simple three-chord songs. Initially he was just a fan turning up at concerts, but then he became more actively involved. John, for his part, was in awe of Phil's musical abilities and staunchly defended him when critics took a swipe at his post-Genesis career. Ray Coleman's biography of Collins reveals that it was Martyn who introduced Phil to Eric Clapton in 1978. Clapton, in the throes of alcoholism himself and downing a bottle of brandy a day, had apparently never heard of Collins, despite him having been a member of the phenomenally successful Genesis for years.

Collins' close involvement with the *Grace and Danger* record has seen him often mistakenly credited with producing the album. In fact, the producer was Martin Levan, who would later gain a sterling reputation doing musical theatre sound design for many of Andrew Lloyd Webber's shows. More recently, he opened a recording studio near the Brecon Beacons in Wales and started the Red Kite record label. Levan recalls:

My manager at the time was Bruce May, who was also John Martyn's manager, and he got me involved in *Grace and Danger*. I first met John towards the end of the 1970s and we did the recording over about a week at Dick James Music studios in Holborn, London, which, unfortunately, is no longer there. There was John, Phil Collins, Tommy Eyre and John Giblin and myself – that was it, just a small group of us, and we were all there pretty much all of the time. Part of the reason it is a great album is that all the people who worked on it were tremendously sensitive to John's mindset and his music.

The time spent recording was fine, really good fun, I had a ball actually. The only disappointment was one day near the end when Eric Clapton came down to work with us. That day there were some pretty heavy egos flying around. We didn't really get anything out of it. It was a real shame. I did try to edit some of it, but it was basically just a day spent jamming. Sometimes you can get bits from a jam session, but on that occasion – to be honest – it just wasn't there. Where are the tapes now? Island would have owned them and what's happened to them, I just don't know.

John was great to work with all through the recording process, he was together and focused. I had heard lots of stories about him, but we got on fine and I had no problems with him. I never knew John or Beverley before this, so I was a total outsider when it came to their private life. I think John was staying at Phil's place for a while and they worked on some of the demos there. If my memory serves me correctly, Phil had split up with his wife around that time, so maybe John and Phil's friendship grew partly due to them sharing a similar situation and comforting each other in that regard. They were both going through similar emotional rollercoaster's at the time. Phil was an absolute sweetheart in the studio. He was delightful to work with and when necessary he came forward with ideas, but otherwise John would run it all. John was the dominant force in the studio, but a lot of that was due to Phil's professionalism – he's a patient man in the studio and knew it wasn't his album, it was John's.

In the studio, everyone got on really well and there were no real problems. John wasn't drinking too heavily to my knowledge. I'm a pretty patient person in the studio anyway and I really believed that the artist has to be allowed or helped to get their art out. It's his art, not mine. I am there to facilitate that process. You need lots and lots of patience with these guys, although there are always some moments when you do have to be quite firm. John liked to be very free in the studio, he didn't like to lock too many things down. He would do some of his vocals without having even written them down. He would have sketches or ideas and may have a few lines written out, but there were certainly some tracks on that album where the vocals were not written down word for word. He had a special talent for improvising his vocals. Of course John ran the session, but Tommy Eyre and John Giblin were both given plenty of freedom to introduce ideas. The budget allowed us plenty of time to work through the numbers in the studio. I had worked with John Giblin a couple of times before, principally with a superb guitarist called Gary Boyle. But if I remember rightly, in this instance, it was John who had suggested we use John Giblin, which was fantastic.

Very soon after we finished the album, I heard that Chris Blackwell didn't want it released. Bruce May had met Chris, who told him he thought it was just too sad. It didn't seem that way to me, but perhaps it was for people who knew the family and what was going on with Beverley. It was pretty deflating for me because I thought it was a lovely album. There was a time between completion and the eventual release where I had convinced myself that it might never see the light of day. Bruce May also felt it might never be released. In those days I was pretty busy jumping from one project to another and I just tried to put *Grace and Danger* to the back of my mind. It was great news when it was eventually released and it was the right decision – it would have been a tragedy for it not to see the light of day.

To me, it was an album that summed up where John was in his life at that time; it certainly came from his heart, that's for sure. And my position was to help make the best version of that as I could. I mixed it on my own at Morgan Studios. It was the first album I had done with John and whilst he was still building his own confidence in me he came in the first day of mixing and stayed for a few hours. Then he said he would leave me to it and that was it. For me it all came together during the mixing process where I began to realise that it was a very special album. I never worked with him again, obviously his association with Phil continued and they made the next album together. At the time John's head was really into the idea of working with Phil, they hung out together and in a sense it seemed natural that they would work together again.

Though he and John never worked together again, Levan's own contribution to such a classic album should not be overlooked. Ralph McTell believes:

Martin Levan worked unbelievably hard on that album. The way he put things together must mystify John, because the next album John did – which was with Phil Collins – didn't have anywhere near the magic of *Grace and Danger*. Martin Levan is one of the great unacknowledged producers, one of the kindest, most patient guys you could meet, and he needed to be when he was working with John.

Those who were there say the sessions went smoothly, although on one occasion work at Morgan Studios was cancelled when Martyn's coke supply went missing. All the furniture in the studio was shifted to try and find the little bag, but half an hour later it still hadn't been found and that was that – the end of the day's work.

Grace and Danger was John's most polished work to date and there was little in the way of the experimental edge that had characterised parts of his mid-1970s records. Even the guitar gets rolled into the lush ultra-smooth jazz sound, with John Giblin's dreamy bass a standout. Musically, on tracks like 'Looking On', the album can be seen as the summation of Martyn's love of Weather Report's richly textured, gentle sound. Indeed, back in the mid-1970s, he told *Supersnazz* magazine that Weather Report were the best band in the world, but predicted accurately that it would take five or six years for him to achieve his goal of playing like them. John had been an admirer of the band's keyboard wizard, Joe Zawinul, ever since his time playing with Cannonball Adderley. Lyrically, *Grace and Danger* is a near-to-the-knuckle account of John alone, still unable to come to terms with the loss of his love and still – especially on the almost maudlin 'Baby Please Come Home' – hoping for reconciliation. At times, as on the title track, you can almost taste the bitterness in John's voice. He always believed that he wrote his best work when he was most screwed-up, and this album is the proof. The only really upbeat song is his cover of The Slickers' 'Johnny Too Bad', a riff-laden, self-mythologising slice of reggae with additional lyrics by John, which was released three times as a single. Martyn first heard the song on a Jamaican jukebox. Beverley, ironically, contributed lyrics to the track 'Our Love'.

The gorgeous opening track, 'Some People Are Crazy', had lyrics based on the fact that the name John Martyn triggers wildly contrasting emotions from people. When I told him that some former colleagues reacted with a mixture of terror and hatred when I approached them for an interview, John smiled sweetly and said:

That's wonderful! Some people are crazy about me; some people just cannot stand my face! A lot of people just do not like me. See, I always tell people if I don't like them and they are not used to that. You are supposed to love everybody – but in all honesty, I don't suffer fools gladly. I do not like any form of dishonesty. I have told lies all my life to avoid confrontations and nastiness, but nothing that would harm anybody. I think I am just a touch too outspoken and I'm rather proud of it, to be honest. These people, their 'Get Well Soon' cards just get lost in the post. If they were my real friends, I would still be hanging with them and sending them Christmas cards and I don't. They were a transient part of my life. There's always a reason for me discarding them.

Listening to him, you got the impression that John was a guy who revelled in his own notoriety. In a way, he would prefer to trigger a negative reaction than no reaction at all.

By the completion of the recording, John was in a dreadful emotional state and barely in control of his own actions. By his own admission he freaked when the release was delayed, pleading with Island to put it on sale, saying it was what he was all about – 'direct communication of emotion'. Released in October 1980, the new album won immediate praise from critics – even *NME* found it hard to pick faults with it. Martyn was one of the few survivors from the 1960s and 1970s who could still earn the respect of Britain's leading music weekly, which back then was much more interested in punk and ska bands. The paper's Angus MacKinnon loved the jazz tinges of the record comparing bassist John Giblin – formerly of Brand X – to Weather Report's Jaco Pastorious and also likening ex-Sensational Alex Harvey Band keyboard player Tommy Eyre's style to that of Herbie Hancock. He also saw similarities between John's clipped guitar work and the groundbreaking 1950s piano playing of Thelonious Monk. Both players loved to leave spaces in the music 'to work around and off a theme, rather than over it'. What both men leave out is almost as crucial as what they left in, argued MacKinnon. He ended his review by writing:

> It's always been tempting to use the consistency and quiet, careful innovations of Martyn's work as a stick with which to thrash at the monstrous dumbness of so much contemporary rock 'n' pop. To do so is to render Martyn a disservice. *Grace and Danger* is perfectly capable of recommending itself on its own considerable merits. It's also the best album I've heard all year. (*NME*, 25 October 1980)

The album – like its predecessor, *One World* – reached number 54 in the UK charts. Phil Collins of course didn't do too badly out of his spell in the marriage doldrums – his 'divorce album', *Face Value*, went on to sell over ten million copies and made him an international superstar. Whether it's a better record than John's is debatable. One can only wonder how John felt to see his own record stall in the lower reaches of the charts while Collins' effort was embraced by the general public in a huge way.

In 1979, John had moved to Scotland to help care for his father, who had suffered a stroke and who was also drinking heavily. As the only son, John felt it imperative that he answer the call. John settled in Moscow, a tiny village seventeen miles south-west of Glasgow of just a dozen homes, seventy inhabitants, and with no pub or shops. His father's illness coincided with the break-up of Martyn's marriage and both factors expedited a move away from his home in Heathfield, Sussex. Beverley remained in that house and got custody of the three kids, but by then John had tired of living in England, telling *NME*'s Nick Kent that his wife had learnt to live with 'middle-class ponces'. Changed days indeed from the early years of domestic bliss in Sussex, which inspired classics such as 'Over The Hill'. John said he was now happier to live with the honest, hard-nosed Scots. At least in Glasgow when they ripped you off, they do it 'neat, sweet and petite' (*NME*, 29 November 1980). Never a great lover of city life, he found that the forced move north had unexpectedly reinvigorated his love for the peacefulness and the culture of his native land.

In November 1980, *NME* sent its star writer, Nick Kent, to Glasgow to track down Martyn. Kent and Martyn met up in a suitably shabby city centre pub where the exotically dressed and dreadfully pale Kent stood out like a festering thumb amid the 'slug-bound' old soldiers propping up the bar. Both singer and scribe were soon 'heading steadily out of the realms of dreary sobriety'. Martyn, who was labouring under the additional strain of Valium after a visit to the dentist, soon passed out. Then a friend who was sitting in on the interview, proceeded to vomit copiously. As Kent memorably noted: 'It's 6.30 in the evening – werewolf hour has officially begun.' But Kent did manage to later glean from Martyn that setting his emotional heartache to vinyl had been a cathartic experience. Having worked his way through the 'rampant confusion, heartache, lovesickness, caution and remorse', John had finally reconciled matters, realising that even when love went badly wrong, love was and always will be worth it. Now he said that, aside from his kids mistaking him for the new man in Beverley's life, the heartache and resentment had passed and things were fine. 'That hurts, but otherwise it's old history.' The title of Nick Kent's eventual article – 'John Martyn: The Exorcism' – was well chosen.

*

Despite being approached on a couple of occasions, Beverley could not be persuaded to contribute to this book (The Martyn children also proved elusive). According to her website, Beverley is working on her own autobiography which should make for fascinating reading and shed much more light on a marriage that started so happily but which ended like an overture for World War Three. Until her book sees the light of day, it's also worth checking Lee Barry's book *Grace and Danger* for Mrs Martyn's take on the marriage's demise. But be warned it's not an account that shows John up in a very favourable light – he comes across as a violent, schizoid bully.

Almost famous

I wasn't married . . . I thought let's go for it, let's make some money, and let's make a band.

John Martyn

If John had been really together as a person he could have been as successful as people like Sting, Jimmy Page or David Gilmour. He was a true original . . . a charming fuck-up.

Sandy Roberton

By the early 1980s, John was starting to adopt a fresh approach to live performance and to the music industry in general. For the only time in his career, the perennial maverick seemed set on stardom. His musical partner for the previous seven years Danny Thompson was no longer part of the equation having given up alcohol and the wild days in 1978. Their final date together saw Danny arrive on stage worse for wear after drinking all day with Billy Connolly and cause a rumpus, smashing an instrument while falling about during one of John's quieter numbers. Relations between the pair cooled and they didn't play together for years afterwards, with telephone calls going unanswered. John himself had tired of playing acoustic guitar alone night after night on stage, and from 1980 onwards he would invariably play with a full band behind him. At a showcase concert at London's Apollo Victoria Theatre in November, John's band included Phil Collins, Max Middleton and twenty-year-old bassist Alan Thomson (who had played previously with John's cousin in the Glasgow-based Arthur Trout Band). Like his new boss, Alan was a big Weather Report fan. Drummer Jeff Allen, who had played with East of Eden and also on sessions for Bonnie Tyler, Barbara Dickson and BA Robertson, was also now playing live with Martyn.

The idea of John abandoning the old acoustic set was anathema for many fans and indeed John himself had never been wholly convinced by the idea of playing with a band. The disastrous gig alongside Bev and a pick-up band at the Queen Elizabeth Hall in the early 1970s certainly discouraged him. Indeed, he called it the most humiliating night of his career. For a long while during the 1970s, Martyn thought that excessive electrification and volume negated the rhythm and melody of his music. (Those fans that believe his early songs sounded better played acoustic in intimate clubs, still wish that John had stuck to that maxim.) A promotional tour for Island with the band Bronco introduced him to the realities of travelling around the country with a band for the first time and he concluded that the emotional and internal stresses of a group just weren't for him. But by 1975, John was toying with the notion of playing with a small electric band, although he only envisaged playing in local venues around his then hometown of Hastings. By then the prospect of alleviating boredom by playing lead or even rhythm guitar in a 'dirty rock 'n' roll band' was beginning to appeal. In November 1977, he played a one-off gig at London's Rainbow Theatre with Stevie Winwood, drummer Pierre Moerelen and bassist Mike Howlett, the rhythm section of European prog rockers Gong. Despite only having two rehearsals, John enjoyed the experience, even though the lack of practice led to mixed reviews.

By 1980 his conversion was complete and he was soon enthusing about the exchange of ideas and good company that a permanent band brought. From now on, fans at concerts would have to get used to John playing louder and faster on his Gibson SG, his Fender Stratocaster, or his 1954 Les Paul Gold Top with 'less of the ponderous rhythms'. (John had two Gold Tops – gifts from Joe Walsh and Paul Kossoff.) On occasion he toyed with the idea of going back to solo performing, but he found the experience less enjoyable. By and large, going to see John Martyn from now on would mean seeing him perform with a band. John's electric playing had lots of undertones and overtones; he wanted to create a 'confusing' – as opposed to clean – sound. His comment to me that he did 'not like clean chords' is another example of him deliberately avoiding conforming or commercialism. Danny Thompson eventually came to realise that the move towards a band was inevitable.

> When he decided he wanted to go in the direction of a band, it wasn't that I was getting the sack or moving on. It was just that you have to find the energy to do something else. Whenever something becomes like a recipe and a bit safe, it is then time to move on. It wasn't something we sat down and discussed – it just happened.

John loved the power and precision of an electric guitar – others weren't so convinced. Though not on a par with Dylan going electric, the reaction to Martyn hooking up with a band was not wholly positive. At some gigs in Canada, he got yells of abuse when he started playing electric during shows. The star got letters objecting to the new sound and throughout his career many a die-hard Martyn fan still hankered after a return to the days of acoustic guitars, Echoplex and Danny T. Another cause for disquiet among fans around 1980 was the sight of John onstage in a suit and tie! The days of cheesecloth shirts and faded denim were consigned to history and despite the howls of protest from female fans, John, at his most curmudgeonly, refused to ditch the new look. Another change came when, from the early 1980s onward, John's guitar sound seemed to become downplayed and his records became awash with – admittedly fine – keyboards and saxophone sounds. In 1994, he explained his theory on guitar playing to the journalist Paul Tingen.

> I write songs and I play them and that's it. I'm not into this whole guitar hero thing and don't want people to see me like that. My approach to playing the electric guitar is based on the way I play the acoustic – I hardly ever use a pick, even though I know how to use it. I don't play like Van Halen or people like that. I don't have the chops for it anyway, but I've got the brain, I know about harmony, and jazz players like what I do, which is great. But

it's not necessary to be the fastest man in the world. You can say as much with a few notes as with a whole stream. (*Guitar*, 7 August 1994)

Instrumental in all those changes was John's new manager, Sandy Roberton, who had made his name in the music business running the pre-eminent blues label Chess Records and their publishing companies during the 1960s, before co-founding Blue Horizon Records. The new label's first signing was Peter Green's Fleetwood Mac and it went on to become a hugely influential presence on the UK blues scene. After leaving Blue Horizon, Roberton moved onto producing artists such as the singer-songwriter Ian Matthews, who covered a couple of John Martyn's songs, including 'Man In The Station' on his *Stealin' Home* album. Around the time that Chris Blackwell was stalling on releasing *Grace and Danger*, Martyn approached Roberton with an offer.

> John just turned up at my house one day and said that it was obvious I was a fan of his work and asked if I would be interested in managing him. That knock on my front door changed the next few years drastically! I listened to *Grace and Danger* and just thought it was a gem of a record – with an amazing mood. John poured his heart out on that album and the musicians involved created the perfect backdrop.

Martyn parted company with Bruce May and thus Roberton began radically reshaping Martyn's career. He helped to secure the long-overdue release of *Grace and Danger* and was instrumental in recruiting Allen, Middleton (the former Jeff Beck Band keyboard player and session man with BBA and Kate Bush) and Thomson to be John's new band. Roberton also got John an agent and arranged TV appearances for the star, including an improbable guest spot on the BBC show *Pop Quiz*, which was hosted by DJ Mike Read. (John's appearances on the show from autumn 1984 have recently been posted on YouTube.) Although Roberton worked with John for a couple of years, it was a difficult relationship. Roberton told me how he was introduced to what he calls 'John land'.

At the time he was living in Scotland with a musician's sister and they had a child together. I remember he picked me up once at Edinburgh Airport and he drove to Oddbins where he stocked up on his favourite Mount Gay rum. Afterwards he cooked me the hottest curry I had ever eaten and then proceeded to finish off all the rum.

After a spell of aimless post-Beverley depression and excessive boozing, things were beginning to look more positive for Martyn. Besides being a success with the critics, *Grace and Danger* had also sold respectably. Along with Jeff Allen, Alan Thomson, ex-Level 42 and session man Danny Cummings (who had been introduced to John by Tommy Eyre and Max Middleton), the touring was also going well, with showcase gigs in Britain after his first concerts in America and Canada for four years. In June 1981, work was underway on the follow-up album with Phil Collins – one of the biggest names in the business at that time – taking care of production. But because Collins also drummed on the record, Sandy Roberton had to do a sizeable share of the production chores. The new album would be John's first away from the Island label. Sandy Roberton had reviewed John's Island contracts and decided to 'get him out of a deal which was not very good for him'. With the aid of Roberton and Phil Collins, John had signed a long-term worldwide deal with WEA International. In America, the next two Martyn albums would be released through WEA on the Genesis label, Duke. Aside from insisting that Collins do the production on the upcoming album, WEA made few demands on their new charge. His fourteen years at Island came to a less than amicable end when they and Martyn failed to reach agreement on how much he should be paid for the next album. John felt the manner of the offer – which he considered to be paltry – was insulting. He recalls that the message was delivered by an Island minion in an impersonal phone call and led to an exasperated Martyn slamming the phone down. An added complication was that he and Island no longer saw eye to eye on his career development – with the record company wanting John to concentrate on the jazz niche which he had built or return to a solo career. They were also unwilling to finance a full-scale band to back John permanently. John saw it differently. He was bored with playing solo and was keen to expand his career in different directions with a band.

John was no fan of the jazz revival of the early 1980s, pouring scorn on the zoot suit and porkpie hat-wearing West End trendies at the forefront of the movement. But Martyn had an enduring respect for the real thing. Seeing Miles Davis play in a club in Harlem, where John was one of the few white faces, was one of the highlights of his life. John also shared the bill with another of his big heroes, Charlie Mingus, at the Bijou Café in Philadelphia. The predominantly black audience was less than attentive to what the Scot was playing.

> Charlie had just had a stroke, but he and his band were diamond people. It was at the height of black power and I was very paranoid. He befriended me because I was the only white boy in the place and I was very young and I was getting a really rough fuckin' time, and he stood up for me. I just kept getting blanked. It was like playing to cardboard and I just lost the rag and smashed the guitar against the wall. He just said to me: 'Look at me, I've been playin' fifty years and I'm still wallpaper, who the fuck do you think you is?'

In a later interview with Rob Young, John talked of his disillusionment with the jazz scene in general, finding it even more cliquish and competitive than the folk scene. Finding out that his hero, John Coltrane, was as fallible as everyone else, 'pissing up and down the bars and beating their missuses up', didn't help matters, although it's a description that could have fitted John Martyn at times equally well.

> I've never been interested in tricky and difficult time changes, because nine times out of ten, they're merely an excuse for the musician to show off. It's a bit precious and nineteenth-century Vienna. There are guys like Oscar Peterson, for example, who are absolute genii, but I couldn't eat a whole one. Same with Django Reinhardt and Stephane Grappelli: beautiful, but I couldn't eat a whole one. It's hard enough to eat a packet of myself for two hours every night. (*Wire*, June 1998)

John felt the move to Warner Brothers would allow him to reshape his life, later recalling: 'I wasn't married . . . I thought let's go for it, let's make some money, and let's make a band.' Aged thirty-three, John Martyn was facing new challenges and opportunities, but one old problem refused to go away. In October 1981, during a four-month world tour – he told *NME* that the divorce from Beverley meant he was no longer independent financially. He had to earn £280 a week just to meet the terms of the financial settlement. An exasperated Martyn told the paper:

> I have four children in wedlock, all of whom I maintain. But, in fact, the children have little to do with this settlement: it's all for Beverley, whom I still like. I don't see why it should have to be so acrimonious. I didn't even want the fuckin' divorce in the first place: unreasonable behaviour on my part, apparently. Basically, what is being said is that not only have I got to support my former wife, but they're also going to cut off my fucking nuts!

He also explained how money was now needed to pay his three permanent musicians, and their back-up helpers. Selling more records was now a necessity. 'When I was solo I earned a great deal of money. I had no overheads, and I was selling out large gigs. But now it's not just for the sake of my own ego that I need to sell more records than I do!'

Any bitterness he felt towards his ex sat uneasily with his continuing infatuation with females in general.

> Actually, I've fallen in love three times in my life, and to those women I'm utterly faithful . . . I love women, I must confess. They are my weakness . . . But then I'm a romantic . . . The problem is they're so beautiful, aren't they? They've caused all the problems in my life. Every single problem can be put down to women. Dreadful things. It makes me sound like a misogynist. Actually, I've never caught the clap in my life . . . So far I've got away without having to pay to learn. Women are beautiful. Children even more so: that's the hang-up with me. I'd love to have loads more. I'd like to surround myself with children – they genuinely are such an inspiration.

The release of *Glorious Fool* on 18 September 1981 marked a real change in the perception of John's work amongst some critics. True, most writers were as supportive as ever: *Melody Maker* and *Record Mirror* thought it was one of the albums of the year, and a genuinely passionate work. *Music Week* called it a superb distillation of John's talents and *Time Out* reckoned it was his best-ever work. Even *The Times* and *The Guardian* liked it – the latter making the perennial prediction that it would mark an end to his cult status. Indeed, the record was a commercial success – reaching number 25 during a seven-week stay in the UK charts. But *NME*, the paper that really mattered back in 1981, gave *Glorious Fool* a ferocious kicking. The fact that the reviewer Graham Lock was a fan of John's early work and also admired *Grace and Danger* and the move towards a band format, made the review even more telling. Lock dismissed the album as a rabid mediocrity, bereft of the inventive guitar of old and full of 'arty synth noises that rumble and whine to no good purpose'. The songs were dismissed as either pretty fripperies or melodramatic bluster. But for Lock, the saddest aspect of the work was that most of the songs were 'simply second-rate', lacking the originality and passion of old. He concluded by proclaiming that the drive and depth of our man's best work had been replaced by ordinary upmarket competence and asked: 'Whatever happened to the glory of love?'

Twenty-five years on, it's generally agreed that Lock got it just about right. On *Glorious Fool* the super-smooth production and the, at times, intrusive playing nullifies much of John's talents. Some tracks are instantly forgettable and others just repetitive or over-reliant on synthesisers over guitars. Martyn and Phil Collins cemented their friendship in the studio, with John later praising Collins for his musical sensitivity and feeling guilt that he couldn't match his prodigious work ethic. But the 1980s Genesis feel to the project just didn't sit well with Martyn's songs.

Still, you cannot deny the strengths of numbers such as 'Hold On My Heart', the anti-war 'Don't You Go' and the reworking of *One World*'s 'Couldn't Love You More', featuring Eric Clapton. It's also unfair to overlook the sheer effervescent energy of songs like 'Perfect Hustler'. The title track of *Glorious Fool* was dedicated to Ronald Reagan, the bumbling incumbent in the White House at the time the record was made at London's Townhouse.

For the first time, John's alcoholism was starting to have a detrimental effect on the recording process. He had taken up residency in rooms on the first floor above the studio during the recording, occasionally appearing in the early hours as the other musicians – Phil Collins, Alan Thomson, Max Middleton and Danny Cummings – were completing work on the backing tracks. Decked out in his dressing gown, the inebriated Martyn would insist that then was the ideal time for him to add the vocal track. One song on the new album – 'Amsterdam' – was written in November 1980, after John had got word that a close friend had hanged himself there over an unrequited affair with a local high-class hooker. John had advised the friend not to go to Amsterdam and the song is Martyn at his angriest – grunting and roaring over the loss of another friend, spitting out the vocal in front of a taut, funk backing and wild guitar breaks. The tragedy hit Martyn hard. As the lyric says, if he knew his friend had been drowning he would have thrown him a line. He told *NME* that if he could have had a brother he would have chosen the unnamed man. The reporter, Nick Kent, thought John was a 'quietly tormented soul'.

Sandy Roberton recalls:

> *Glorious Fool* wasn't that successful, but we kept on touring in the UK, Europe and Canada. To save money, I tour-managed and even mixed the up-front sound some nights. John's intake of alcohol, cocaine and heroin was legendary at that time and I had to try and keep him on the rails so he could travel and perform. Warner Brothers asked for another album, but there was limited budget and, frankly, at that stage I doubt whether there was anyone on the planet that could have handled John in the studio, so he asked me to produce the next album.

1982's *Well Kept Secret* was an even bigger success than its predecessor – eventually reaching number 20 in the British charts. Produced by Sandy Roberton, and featuring stellar musicians such as Pete Wingfield, Jim Prime and Lee Kosmin alongside guests, including jazz great Ronnie Scott, who played tenor sax on 'Never Let Me Go', it's generally considered to be one of John's weakest efforts, even though it did stay in the UK charts for seven weeks. When the album saw the light of day on 27 August 1982, it found an unlikely admirer in *NME*'s Danny Baker. Better known as a soul aficionado, Baker was in fact a long-standing admirer of Martyn's work. In fact, he once wrote that either *Solid Air* or *Inside Out* would be one of the three records he would want to save if his then home in Rotherhithe was to burn down. (For the record, his other saves would have been *I Am* by Earth Wind and Fire along with Todd Rundgren's *A Wizard, A True Star*.) While admitting that Martyn was now coasting and much more predictable, he still thought the new album was a classy effort, full of warm and intelligent songs. He picked 'Could've Been Me' and 'Hung Up' as the outstanding tracks. But Baker undoubtedly spoke for many when he pined for the magical sound of Danny Thompson's stand-up bass of old (*NME*, 4 September 1982). Perhaps the best appraisal of *Well Kept Secret* came from John himself, who admitted to being so sozzled that he barely remembered anything about the recording.

A compilation album, *The Electric John Martyn* – with American mixes of some tracks – also sold respectably well. But it was becoming clear that WEA's attempts to tame the perennial rebel were causing friction. In particular, Martyn was less than impressed with doing the promotional circuit in America – sometimes doing four interviews and a couple of visits to local radio stations each day. He despised the whole experience, saying it was like being nailed to the floor. (Remember, this was a guy who was once nailed to the floor inside a carpet while drunk!) 'Nothing used to infuriate me more than playing a mediocre gig and finding the record company backstage going "Fantastic!" and wanting to shake my hand.' John's dislike and distrust of the music business was by now ingrained and it's a feeling that he held till the bitter end. He told me:

The music industry is not pretty, there's a lot of hypocrites and strangeness. There's a great quote from Hunter S Thompson, which I used to have on the back of my business cards, that goes: 'The music business is a cruel and shallow money trench, a long plastic hallway where thieves and pimps run free, and good men die like dogs. There's also a negative side!' For me, that just about sums up the music business.

Martyn was on more familiar ground back in the UK, and plans were revealed for a massive tour there for the autumn of 1982, covering more than thirty venues. But his wild lifestyle almost put the tour in jeopardy. In June, he was hospitalised after trying to jump a fence, which collapsed beneath him, impaling him. John had wanted to take a naked swim near his home but ended up breaking several ribs, one of which pierced a lung. En route to the hospital, he stopped off at a local pub and got so drunk that the hospital staff refused to treat him till he had sobered up. The ensuing delay meant that Phil Collins was unable to fit producing *Well Kept Secret* into his schedule. Some gigs in the USA during July were also abandoned. Although the British dates went ahead, it was to be the first of various mishaps to dog the star. The 1982 tour also saw ex-Stone the Crows founder member Ronnie Leahy play keyboards with the band. The Manchester cult band Durutti Column supported him on the English dates, while north of the border, a new group, Danceclass, did the warm-up honours.

To tie in with the tour, John's first-ever songbook, *Open Window*, was published, featuring the words and music of thirteen of his best-known songs. The final date of the tour at London's Hammersmith Odeon – where Phil Collins appeared for the show's finale – got a critical mauling from *NME*'s Richard Cook, a longtime fan left disillusioned by the new polished, predictable sound. John's backing musicians – Jeff Allen, Danny Cummings, and keyboards player Jim Prime – came in for particularly vicious, if undeniably eloquent, criticism.

In this dislikeable group, with its flat-handed drummer, superfluous percussionist and preposterously insensitive keyboardist, Martyn simply plugs in his heavy metal guitar. It's tiresome, it's lazy, and it's wasteful. Even his vocals, which once ticked the tenuous line between the leery and the remorseful, fall from a fugitive murmur into an incessant growl. Although it's a cheap catch-all criticism, this 'not as good as he used to be' tack, the complete dispersal of Martyn makes him someone I do not even recognise any more.

Only bassist Alan Thomson escaped the vitriol. Cook thought that *Sunday's Child* was now just tame and tired.

Sandy Roberton's time with John didn't last much longer. He's refreshingly honest about *Well Kept Secret*.

> It's a good album and I'm sure it was John's biggest selling album, but it's certainly not his best, it has nowhere near the character, style or feeling of his classic albums. I made that album with John being AWOL most of the time. Phil Thornalley and I performed miracles getting that album made. John was a mess and hardly turned up at all, but luckily Jeff Allen and Alan Thomson were team players and we all just got it made. We delivered the album and we got a massive tour organised and toured the album. Around this time, John moved back to Scotland – he had been encamped at the Chelsea Arts Club and was basically homeless.

On the US leg of the tour the tensions between Roberton and Martyn came to a head in a vicious fist fight. Sandy recalls:

> We had a massive fight one morning because he just would not get out of bed to drive to Chicago. He broke my ribs and I gave him the biggest shiner you've ever seen. The band and I left him at the motel and drove to Chicago, but to his credit he got to Chicago and played the show with one eye shut. After the tour we came back to the UK, but by this time I had had enough of dealing with John's constant money problems and his drug and alcohol intake.

While John traveled to Nassau to lick his wounds, Roberton quit and eventually moved to America, where he now runs World's End, the largest management company for record producers in the USA. Looking back on his time with John in 2007, he still had affection for his old sparring partner.

> Even after all this time, I still think John is one of the all-time best. The four albums he made after his records with Beverley are among my all-time

favourite albums. But I see what he looks like now and what his music sounds like now, and all I want to remember is seeing John play with Danny Thompson and making some of the coolest music you'll ever hear. If John had been really together as a person he could have been as successful as people like Sting, Jimmy Page or David Gilmour. He was a true original, but his private life took over his professional life. He was a charming fuck-up. But one thing you can say for certain is that he was never boring! He has certainly lived life more than most.

Bringing it all back home

I am more comfortable now than I have been for a while. But I mean, I would not say that I'd remain that way. It's always a bit dangerous if you are too comfortable, I think.

John Martyn

John himself is a stunning musician, we could spend a whole day trying to do one electric guitar solo, but then at the end of the day he would pick up his acoustic and do the best finger-picking you will ever hear.

Brian Young

Undeterred by the criticism of his new style, Martyn launched into another bout of touring. He left the UK on 19 January 1983, for a set of gigs in Australia, followed by a prestige slot at the Sweeteaters Festival in New Zealand alongside Talking Heads and UB40 on 29 January. Back home, he soon headed off for a six-week European jaunt in mid-March, followed by a string of dates in the UK in April and May and then on to North America. By now, he was playing regularly with two fellow Scots, drummer Jeff Allen and fretless bass expert Alan Thomson, whose melodic touch was much admired by John. (Alan had switched from lead guitar to bass after joining Martyn.) By now, Martyn's shows were lasting well over two hours and sometimes included a solo set by John. The US tour was an uncomfortable one – though the gigs were invariably wonderful, the band sometimes had to travel up to 800 miles between shows and often were exhausted by the time they took to the stage. John blamed his management for the fiasco. He eventually broke free from them, accusing them of sharp practice and being parasites. In response, they issued an injunction, making it impossible for John to play and the whole affair had to be settled in the courts. John said they weren't so much managers as asset-strippers. 'The thing was just to work you into the ground and get as much money out of you as possible.'

November 1983 saw the release of a live album, *Philentropy*, taken mainly from recordings at the Oxford and Brighton Dome shows in autumn 1982, along with some from a London show from spring 1983. John can be heard singing parts of Coltrane's 'A Love Supreme' on one track. It was released on his own independent label, Body Swerve, which seemed appropriate as, without the promotional backing of a major label, it failed to register with many fans. Indeed for many long-term fans, Martyn's output during the whole of the 1980s pales in comparison to the great works of the previous decade. He seemed to disappear from the music scene for long periods (either on never-ending world tours or because of his alcoholic inertia) and when he did return his music seemed jaded and increasingly irrelevant. *Philentropy* was an attempt to recoup some of the costs of running a five-piece band – one sell-out concert at the Hammersmith Odeon actually ended up with John losing £60. The financial pressures also resulted in an occasional return to solo sets – including one at the Glastonbury Festival of 1984.

In 1983, John married for the second time, to Annie Furlong, the manager of an Irish recording studio, and the couple settled in Scotland although their marriage received a lot less attention than John's time with Beverley. Partly that's due to the fact that the couple were together during a fallow period of John's career. They met in Dublin in 1981 and married at an Edinburgh registry office two years later, with a reception at the George Hotel to follow. They lived together in Roberton until the end of the decade – years that saw John's most uneven and poorly received albums. His ongoing alcoholism and distaste for the music industry led him to go off the radar for long spells and so the outside interest in his domestic life waned. But the lack of attention on his second marriage was also due to Martyn's reluctance to talk in detail about his life with Annie. When I asked him about her he would only offer the following:

She was vivacious, coquettish and permanently drunk. We were told to both stop drinking and we did for five to six weeks. She was lovely but wild. She was delightful company but very difficult to deal with. I don't think anyone truly understood her. She was a troubled soul, but quite lovely.

Trying to ascertain exactly what went on behind the closed doors is difficult, especially now that both individuals are dead. Undoubtedly there were happy times: Martyn dedicated his 1986 album *Piece by Piece* to her and some of those who visited the Roberton home recall John and Annie as a seemingly contented couple and good hosts. John's quote to me also hints at the genuine affection he had at one time for his wife. But it also glosses over the fact that this was another of his relationships which was plagued by what are diplomatically called 'domestic' disputes. One visitor to the Roberton home arrived for a weekend stay to find an ambulance and a police car outside the house with Annie sitting in the former and John in the back of the cop car. Annie's brother Michael recalls one particularly violent episode when he had to pull his bruised sister away from Martyn's hotel room after a wedding.

Friends recall Annie as a slim, beautiful girl with long, thick wavy brown hair, fine bone structure and appealing green eyes. When I asked people to describe her to me, the words most regularly used were kind, intelligent, thoughtful and refined. She hailed from County Wexford but moved to Dublin where she worked in a library before becoming front-of-house manager at Windmill Lane recording studio, which is presumably where she met Martyn. Through her work, Annie had a rich and varied social life with many friends. She met John when he was in the midst of his post-Beverley frenzy – an alcoholic, a ferocious coke addict and serial womaniser. If Annie didn't know what he was like when she met him, she soon found out. John's old school friend Davie MacFarlane told me: 'I remember around that time John punctured his lung and ended up in hospital. A woman called Gillian turned up one day on his ward to visit him, asking to see him and saying she was his fiancée. The nurse had to tell her that there was another woman in the ward already and she was also claiming to be his fiancée! This was Annie Furlong.'

When she married John, Annie was a vibrant, happy individual and it should be stressed that she did not have a drink problem back then. Eight years living with John changed all that. Michael Furlong contrasts the intelligent, spirited and beautiful 27-year-old who left Ireland to live in Roberton with the woman who returned to Dublin eight years later. 'By then she was a broken and anxious woman, the emotional and physical abuse she took from Martyn along with their hard drinking had taken its toll.' It would seem that John's second marriage at times brought out the same worst excesses in his character as those on display during his time with Beverley and also – later on – with Daisy Flowers. He comes across as a bullying chauvinist who wanted to confine his woman at home. Annie's younger cousin, Mary Furlong told me:

> John told Annie that getting married again would make him feel more secure. His start in life had made him a very troubled and insecure man. I thought he was intelligent, very talented and also a great cook, but I did not like him because he was a controlling bully. He isolated Annie, making sure that it was difficult for her friends and family to see her or stay in touch with her. She was a strong character but he was stronger and in the end she could not win and so she became more and more like him. In the end she herself drank too much and became as dramatic as him. John Martyn would always encourage her to drink more and then would rubbish her for drinking in front of others. When she left him she went without any of her possessions just to get away from him. That must have done even more damage to her confidence. It took guts to move away but she must have known that things were not going to improve with John; in fact they were probably going to get worse. She just took the moment and left him.

Annie returned to Dublin and tried to get her old lifestyle back but the damage was done and she never really recovered from her time with John. She did marry again and settled in Kenya with her new husband

Brian Macoun. But she continued to be plagued by the alcoholism that had set in during her marriage to John. For some reason, John persisted in telling people that Annie died in a car crash . . . in fact she died from cerebral malaria in 1996 and is buried in Kenya. It was a sad end to an episode in John's life story that does not show him in the best light. Of course there are two sides to every story and John's version of events died with him. Others who would not be quoted directly told me a different version of events, arguing that Annie, once she started drinking heavily, was a real handful and put John through a lot.

More generally the whole question of the violence that seemed to mar some of John's relationships is a difficult one for a fan to come to terms with. Finding out that your idol has feet of clay is not pleasant. But it would be wrong to ignore the weight of evidence given by his three long-term partners. It's also telling that when the first edition of this book came out and detailed some of these accusations, John made no attempt to deny them. He also, to the best of my knowledge, took no action when even stronger allegations were made by Beverley Martyn.

From all the available evidence it's hard not to agree with Annie's brother Michael's verdict: 'Talent should rarely be used as an absolution for the ignorant and cruel treatment of others. Perhaps we should all aim to be less starry-eyed about celebrity and instead place greater value on "simple" qualities like kindness and respect towards our fellow human beings.'

*

In 1984, Martyn's collaboration with Robert Palmer, *Sapphire*, was released on a new-look Island label. The label gave their prodigal son a big push, sending him to Compass Point Studios in Nassau to make the record. John had just come out of his court case with his former management team, and Chris Blackwell arranged for the trip to Nassau. Soon after arriving though, John fell out with the original choice for producer, sacking him in an argument over lyrics and so leaving the entire project in doubt. The production team were arguing and not taking responsibility. By all accounts, too much rum was being taken and the atmosphere among those present was caustic. Robert Palmer was called in and effectively saved the album, which was finally recorded between February and May 1984. To save time, Linn Drums were used for the first time on a Martyn album. For some hardcore heads, using such modern technology was anathema, but John said that not to move on and explore new types of music would have been even worse. Whoever was right, it was a sign of the times that the LP credited four people on Linn Drums and five keyboard players. John liked Robert Palmer's fearless approach to experimenting while recording. But despite Palmer's sterling efforts, John recalls the album as being long and difficult to make, and once his part was done he shot back to Scotland to get over the ordeal.

Brian Young, of Ca Va Studios in the West End of Glasgow, played a major part in the salvage job on the album.

> *Sapphire* was the first of John's studio albums we were involved with; he brought that over after doing it in Compass Point in Nassau. I think there was a lot of pressure on him over there and it was too easy for him to sort of chill out and not do too much work. Chris Blackwell told him to go wherever he felt comfortable. He had already done work here, so he brought all the tapes here and we overdubbed and overdubbed and mixed, and that was it. When we were in the studio, we didn't hang about; we were a vehicle for him.

Young and Martyn went back a long way to gigs in student unions during the early 1970s. Back then, Young was a member of a progressive rock band, Northwind, who briefly flirted with fame and made many appearances on the same bill as John and Danny. Those were heady days for all concerned and Brian has recollections of absolutely stunning live performances from the duo, though, predictably, exact memories are a bit foggy. When Northwind failed to capitalise on live dates in Germany and an album for EMI (recorded at Sound Techniques in London, where John did much of his best work) the band imploded. Instead, Brian Young turned to production, starting up Ca Va from his basement before eventually settling at the Bentinck Street site where almost all of Scotland's top acts have recorded. Ca

Va did some mixing and dubs on the *Philentropy* album, but Sapphire marked the start of a long relationship between the studio and Martyn.

In 2005, Brian Young told me:

> Working with him here at Ca Va, he was fine. I think he was with Annie Furlong at the time and everything was tickety-boo with them together. They were great company and I have some lovely videos of them walking together around here on lovely sunny days. They were living in Roberton at the time, although during recording they often stayed at the Lorne Hotel – they were famous there for getting in late and getting up late! John's favourite pub was a wee working man's bar near the Lorne. When John came in here to work, he was here for months. He doesn't suffer fools gladly but he can kind of tolerate them. We might have brought in session musicians and if it didn't work out with them John would just walk out. John himself is a stunning musician. We could spend a whole day trying to do one electric guitar solo, but then at the end of the day he would pick up his acoustic and do the best finger-picking you will ever hear. He was just always looking for melodies and themes in his head.

Brian reveals that John's approach to recording had changed from the old days:

> Because we had the technology, we could spend a lot of time on recording. John was always progressive, always expanding. He would start with an idea and then it was dubbed and dubbed and dubbed again. He would put a guide vocal down and virtually when you think you have completed the track, John would add to the track or maybe scrap all the previous ones and write a whole new song around the new track. That was great in most instances when he did that. It would be a shame about the old song that was scrapped, but maybe it would come back in another form. But he was allowed the studio time to be like that – he was almost writing in the studio.

Many critics thought the end result bland. But through the wash of synthesisers and synthetic drums, John's supreme song-writing craft shines through. He described 'The Fisherman's Dream' as his first hymn. That track was to have featured ten women from a Scottish choir, but that plan didn't work out and they eventually ended up on another song, 'Climb The Walls'. John told *Musin' Music* magazine: 'All these wonderful ladies with an average age of about fifty, all called Maisie and Meg and stuff, with blue rinses . . . they were wonderful . . . puffs of talcum powder everywhere.' The Judy Garland track, 'Over The Rainbow', emerged late one night during recording and was included for 'pure devilment'. John always liked the original, especially the veiled references to drugs, with characters sleeping in a field of poppies to wake covered in snow. The album subsequently peaked at number 57 in the UK charts.

1986's *Piece by Piece*, a collaboration with Edinburgh-born keyboard player Foster Paterson, reached the giddy heights of number 28 in the UK. To augment the duo, old favourites Alan Thomson on fretless bass and percussionist Danny Cummings sat in on some tracks, as did the saxophonist Colin Tully. They had all been on Martyn's UK tour earlier that year. Martin Stephenson and the Daintees played as special guests on the UK tour. Even at the age of thirty-seven, John was as addicted to touring as ever. The alternative of staying at home was considered far too dull. By now, John had found that touring with musicians over a long period was the only way to learn from them. His bond with his fans was as strong as ever – battle-hardened veterans of the Cousins era were now bringing their kids to see John play. Paterson wrote the music for the title track, which was loosely based on the story of a miner who was taken back to the surface after a pit tragedy 'piece by piece'. John considered the original lyric inappropriate and the duo wrote fresh words for the song. The album was released at a positive time in John's life and he spoke enthusiastically about its melodies and musicianship, even going as far as calling it his best record to date. He was happy to be back with Island records and seemingly content with Annie. The songs were unashamedly sophisticated – sounding not unlike artists such as Sade and China Crisis (both of whom were admirers of John's work). John himself disliked the description 'smooth', but was quite happy to hear it described as mature, slick,

FM-friendly soft rock, reasoning that he was hardly likely to sound like U2 at his age.

John likened the track 'Lonely Love' to some of the youthful flippant songs on *The Tumbler* album. He had wanted to write a commercial pop song, which the likes of Aretha Franklin could easily cover. He said the track 'Serendipity' was a hymn to good luck for professional gamblers. 'Angeline' was released as the first commercially available CD single along with a few of John's greatest songs and a cover of Dylan's 'Tight Connection To My Heart' which John recorded in one enjoyable morning studio session. The album closes with the intriguing 'John Wayne', with perhaps John's most vengeful ever lyrics – aimed at his former manager, Sandy Roberton. While he was penning them, Martyn realised how indignant he was and decided that he was sounding like John Wayne – whom he considered to be a 'self-righteous twit' – in the film *True Grit*. The addition of Wayne to the lyric added a bit of humour to things and turned the song into a diatribe against the all-American Wayne/Reagan dream. But the words remained chilling and threatening. They must have made his former manager shake in his cowboy boots. John sang the lyrics in one take while considerably drunk.

Overall, John seemed optimistic about the future. Besides the tour with his band, 1986 also saw him play live with his old sparring partner, Danny Thompson. John was ever hopeful that his music would eventually reach a much wider audience and earn him lots of money, but if it didn't – well, it wasn't really that important. He seemed keen to spread his wings – eager to rise to the challenge of writing hit singles and making conceptual videos for the MTV generation. He also wanted to play a bigger part in Island's management of his work – during his first spell at the label he was an infrequent visitor to their HQ. Now he was more interested in how the business worked. There was talk of an album with Ry Cooder and Jim Keltner and another with the jazz bass player Charlie Hayden. He was also enthusiastic about having been commissioned by Blackie Publishing to do three of the twelve songs for a children's cassette and book. In a promotional interview with Trevor Dann for the new album, he hinted, however, that his newfound contentment might not last: 'I am more comfortable now than I have been for a while. But I mean, I would not say that I'd remain that way. It's always a bit dangerous if you are too comfortable, I think.'

Those words turned out to be somewhat prophetic. The final few years of the 1980s were fairly unproductive ones for John Martyn. Fans had to wait more than four years for another studio album – the only commercial release during that period being the 1987 *Foundations*, a live record of the Town and Country Club gig the previous year. Mark Cooper in *Q* magazine thought the record found John coasting into MOR territory with keyboards and saxophone filling in the spaces which had previously leant his music its haunting quality. September and October of 1987 also saw John undertake a UK tour marking the twentieth anniversary of his first shows. On 4 July he had also jammed with Eric Clapton and Ringo Starr at the twenty-fifth birthday bash for Island Records at Pinewood Studios. Though his career was deep in the doldrums, the presence of such greats in what was effectively John's backing band showed that he was still well-respected. But although there were some concert appearances in the following two years, live activity over this period paled in comparison to his usual prodigious work standards. The spell out of the limelight was by his own admission one of chronic alcoholism – at times he was polishing off more than two bottles of rum a day. By now, there was no need for mythologising about his alcohol intake – the addiction had taken over. He was also still in thrall to cocaine in a big way and getting involved in far too many bar-room brawls for his own – and everyone else's – good. There were also ongoing problems with his record company.

In 1988, Island finally severed links with him, after rejecting the tapes that would eventually became the 1990 release, *The Apprentice*. The rejection angered Martyn, who believed in the product's worth and was not used to having his songs binned. He even re-recorded the record at his own expense in Glasgow. Andy Sheppard's improvised sax featured on four tracks. Sheppard was recruited at short notice, as he happened to be playing with a Dutch jazz band in Glasgow at the time. But it was all to no avail.

Clive Banks, who was in charge of the label while Chris Blackwell was away, wasn't too keen on the material. Banks declined to be interviewed for this book, as did Island's long-term PR chief, Rob Partridge. E-mails to Chris Blackwell went unanswered, though it's said that the Island founder still has a strong affection for his old prodigy. But overall it would seem that the bad memories of John outweigh the good ones, and few who worked with him on the management side back in the 1970s and 1980s remember him fondly. John's 1988 solo tour and the concerts with Foster Paterson the following year went ahead without major label backing. He and Annie were by now settled in Roberton, near Biggar, Lanarkshire, with Punch, their Staffordshire bull terrier, in a spacious cottage complete with a recording studio. The tiny village has a population of just sixty and few amenities. It was remote, but if John had his way he would have lived even further away from the city and the hassles of the music industry. The rejection by Island left him at his lowest ebb and his drinking eventually led to an ultimatum from doctors to either sober up or die.

When he eventually emerged into the public view, John looked remarkably well considering the amount of abuse he had given his body over the years. He had put on a healthy amount of weight and the angelic look had long since gone, but when he met up with a reporter from *Q* magazine he was drinking orange juice and boasting of a healthy lifestyle, swimming forty lengths of his local pool to stay fit. He talked frankly about his drink problem, how waking up with a hangover and needing three large drams to face the day had become untenable. He explained to the magazine in May 1990 that 'alcoholic' is the last word you use about yourself when you finally realise that you have a problem.

As soon as you finally admit to yourself that you are dependent and that's what's holding you together, then you can either do something about it or carry on and die. Most of the time with Danny, it was a prerequisite for going on stage that you had to be loaded. The justification that we used to use was that it would open your mind and then you'd play better. With hindsight, I'd probably say we were getting out of it to have fun and perhaps to hide our insecurities. I don't believe in acting like that any more. But I do believe that without having belted various mind-expanders and uppers and downers, I wouldn't have come up with the same stuff.

He also told *Guitarist* magazine:

It's all very easy to fall into, and the trouble really starts when you're playing all the time. You end up doing it night after night and eventually your body starts to scream for it. That's really the point at which you should stop, but you feel so bad that you just have to go for your first drink, and that's you off again. It's a very dangerous vicious circle.

He proudly stated that the wild days were now a thing of the past. But the fact that his interviews were often held in licensed premises told its own story. Like many alcoholics, John thought he could resist the temptation on offer. Inevitably he could not and was soon back on the booze. In the meantime to help keep things straight, John had enlisted a trio of young musicians – Spencer Cozens (keyboards), Miles Bould (percussion) and Dave Lewis (sax). Bould was heavily influenced by jazz; in fact he had been given a set of congas as a three-year-old child by Dizzy Gillespie, who was a friend of his father. All three recruits were more into the music than partying and their playing brought a jazzier feel to live shows, allowing John to experiment more with his singing and guitar playing. Adding a family slant to things was his sixteen-year-old son, Spenser, who was sound manager on the 1991 UK tour and also occasionally played with his father on stage.

Aged forty-two and a veteran of twenty-one albums, John's newfound optimism and contentment partly came from living in tranquil, rural isolation, where he could indulge in his love of fishing, gardening and cooking. But the old beatnik fascination with the open road, the desire to play music and tour was stronger than ever. Enforced breaks from the circuit were bad for John – he ended up vegetating in front of the TV or doing other 'wrong things'. He loved singing and was working on improving his vocal delivery

– with less slurring, and clearer vocals. By his own admission, his singing had become too wimpy and now he wanted to sound louder and deeper. It was a welcome admission, as on much of his 1980s work John's vocals had taken on a lachrymose, unsettling quality, which negated the natural power of his voice. His vocals were no longer integrated into the overall sound like another instrument. Instead, they put many listeners off and made listening to John Martyn a difficult chore.

His love of black music had been apparent from early on in his career when he cited Tamla stars and Stevie Wonder in particular as inspirations. By 1990, rap singers, and the soul stars, Jonathan Butler, Bobby Brown and Alexander O'Neal, were high on his playlist. John also felt pride in the Scottish music scene, having a particular affection for The Blue Nile. He was known in the village for walking around whistling and humming. As one young child commented, he was 'that man who's always singing'. He later told a reporter that everyone in Roberton took turns to be the village idiot – his turn came when he wore an oversize hip hop jacket. The devotion to performing was also still as strong as ever. John said he still loved the idea of the wandering singer – 'the man with his guitar, against the world'. He told John Perry that 'out of ten gigs, two must be diamonds, really sparkle, three should be really good, three OK for the crowd, but you know there were holes, and two can be thrown out for the dogs.' (*International Musician and Recording World*, March 1989) But the joy of what he called emotional communication with his audience remained – he loved to see the way his music moved people and brought back good memories from their past.

Highs and lows

He was sporting a great big black eye . . . He was in Hastings for a month, very, very drunk for most of the time. He just seemed to have one set of clothes.

Susanne Mead recalling Martyn's visit to Hastings, summer 1991

John is a full-on guy, a wild man. He's always been larger than life. One of the first gigs I was with him I saw him drink a bottle of Bacardi in one gulp.

Andy Sheppard

The new sense of optimism came through on *The Apprentice*, which was recorded at Ca Va Studios and eventually released on the Permanent label. Angered by Island's rejection of the original album, Martyn had – at great personal expense – completed it on his own. Brian Young remembers how the split with Island occurred:

The idea was that his manager would look after his management and we would record the album – which took a couple of months – and then go out and try and tout it to other record companies. We got really good feedback, people were raving about it, but at the end of the day his manager decided to put the album out on his own label, which was Permanent. Maybe there was something about John's character at the time that precluded a major deal, though he was very sociable and could get on with gigs no problem at all. Kenny Macdonald, his personal roadie, was looking after him well. But these were really excellent days, great days. John was probably at the point in his career where he needed to move somewhere else apart from Island. He was doing great writing with Fos Paterson and Island was definitely going in a different direction. He had had a great personal relationship with Chris Blackwell, though; he could pick up the phone and speak to him at any time.

In the end, John's self-belief in the strength of the material was justified and the album sold over 35,000 copies. Living in Scotland seemed to have reawakened John's socialist roots, and there was definitely a move away from purely autobiographical writing towards more socially aware songs and the need to highlight injustices. The title track was based on the anger he felt after meeting a Carlisle man who was dying from cancer after years of working at the Sellafield nuclear plant. The apprentice was a fan of John's work and, after signing some albums, Martyn shared a drink with the man who told him how he was terminally ill. Seven months later John received word that the apprentice had died and he started work on the song. 'Patterns In The Rain', with its impressive string arrangements, was co-written by Foster Paterson. 'Look At The Girl' was written for his nineteen-year-old daughter Mhairi, who of course had been the inspiration for 'My Baby Girl' all those years ago. The song 'Send Me One Line' was penned for the film *84 Charing Cross Road*, but did not make it into the movie's final cut because John forgot about it and missed the deadline. *Q* magazine thought *The Apprentice* was the work of a master of his craft who had at last integrated his solo talents into a band format, hailing it as his best record since the halcyon days of *Grace and Danger*.

Eleven consecutive sell-out shows at London's Shaw Theatre in early spring – with Danny Thompson, the Irish singer Mary Coughlan and Dave Gilmour of Pink Floyd as guests – were followed by a thirty-date tour of the UK in May and June. Gilmour and Martyn had been friends and admirers of each other's work for years and the Floyd had watched many a Martyn show – John in turn had all the band's records. The guitarist featured on the video that resulted from the Shaw Theatre shows, adding tasteful guitar to 'John Wayne', 'Look At The Girl' and 'One World'. The video captures the build-up from John's solo acoustic openers, 'Easy Blues' and 'May You Never', through to the gradual addition of band members. Reviewing the video, *Q* magazine's Monty Smith took objection to John's loud blouse, his Acker Bilk beard and clunky shades, but thought the band en masse sounded like an entire orchestra playing with exhilarating force and enormous confidence. Smith was particularly taken with the songs from the new album – 'Deny This Love', 'The River' and 'The Apprentice' – which he compared to Springsteen's narrative, blue-collar songs. John also played at the Big Day festival in front of a 2,000-strong crowd at Custom House Quay on 3 June, part of the 1990 Glasgow Year of Culture celebrations. Sheena Easton and Wet Wet Wet topped the bill.

But as ever with John, those highs were soon followed by predictable lows. Just a few months after the sell-out shows with Dave Gilmour, John was back on the booze with a vengeance. In the summer of 1991, Martyn found himself back in Hastings, eventually staying there with friends for more than a month at various homes. His main hang-out though was the Lord Nelson pub, just a few minutes' walk from the Coburg Place home which he had first moved to twenty years previously. In fact, John had played in the pub with Beverley in the early 1970s to appreciative audiences. The pub is a regular haunt of the local fishing community and in 1991 they welcomed John back and looked after him well during his stay. Though the sabbatical in Hastings was one long alcoholic bender, John did find time to show his generous side by playing a local fundraising gig.

Susanne Mead, who ran the pub, remembers him turning up one day in June:

He had just played at the Heineken music festival in Brighton and had made his way here to hibernate for a while. He was sporting a great big black eye, which I think he got after the Brighton concert, and he spent his time here moving from place to place. He kept getting phone calls from Scotland telling him to come home, but he was in Hastings for a month, very, very drunk for most of the time. He just seemed to have one set of clothes. My abiding memory of him was finding him sitting cross-legged in front of our fridge devouring lobster after lobster. He called the pub his headquarters and he knew all the fishermen who drank there, and they gave him a place to stay in their homes. It was like time had stood still and he was back with his friends and they just welcomed him back into their circle like an old friend. In the pub he would drink Bacardi and Cokes by the pint.

Around that time we had started a pub football team called the Nelson Tigers and he agreed to do this concert on the beach to raise money for the team, which was very nice of him. It was a fantastic afternoon. We only advertised it on the Thursday, but it was quite amazing how word got out and on the Sunday people came from two hundred miles away to see him play. The concert started at closing time in the afternoon and went on till 8 p.m. John really gave all he had and we raised about £500 to help pay for strips and insurance for the team. We always have a carnival here in August with a rock concert on the beach and he promised to do it in 1994, but he never turned up. But the following year he showed up and did the concert – so he did keep his promise to us.

With the help of friends, John got back on the wagon and headed back to Scotland. The arrangement with Permanent continued with the release of *Cooltide* in November 1991. John felt at ease with the small label – there was less pressure on him from bosses and more time to spend with Annie in Scotland. His work was still a critics' choice. The magazine *International Musician* in 1991 called him a touchstone of excellence and argued that 'were he black and American, John Martyn would be a legend as great as Herbie Hancock, Smokey Robinson and Tom Waits rolled into one'. John was by now at ease with the ever-present cult status and glad that the pressure to reach a bigger audience was long gone. His own faithful following would always be there and John was also still touring incessantly – although now he had to rest up in bed for days on end at the end of a tour.

The *Cooltide* album marked the end of John's long association with Foster Paterson, who had tired of life on the road and opted instead for spending more time with his family. In his place as John's musical permanent partner of choice came another keyboard player, the classical and jazz-trained Spencer Cozens. The twenty-eight-year-old had studied at Berkeley and Goldsmith music colleges and was recommended by bassist Alan Thomson – the two having played together with Julia Fordham (as had another Martyn man, drummer Miles Bould). Cozens replaced Paterson on some gigs in Britain and Germany and then accepted the invitation to work on *Cooltide*. Spencer and John holed up in the latter's barn in Scotland for a few weeks working on demos with guitar, keyboard and an

R8 drum machine. The jamming session resulted in a clutch of songs – 'Cooltide', 'Jack The Lad' and 'Father Time' – which all ended up on the album. Spencer, who had been a fan of John's music since the early 1980s, first met John in December 1989 when he travelled up to Ayr to hang out with Martyn when he played a gig with Thomson, Bould, Paterson and the former Sensational Alex Harvey Band drummer, Ted McKenna.

Spencer told me of his favourable impressions on starting work with John in February 1990:

> The first day I worked with John I drove all the way up from London across all these moors in freezing weather. We got to his house in Roberton at around 9 p.m. and he lines us all up outside the house to inspect us. Then he said: 'Yeah, you'll do' and takes us into his house and gave us the most incredible food, monkfish and vine leaves in a wonderful sauce – which he had cooked himself. And I just thought 'This is cool, this is a guy who lives life for quality and fun.' I just liked the whole vibe of the band – they had a very real attitude to the music, straight up and honest and very organic.

It was the start of a musical partnership between Spencer and John that lasted to the end of Martyn's career. Though John was always considered to be a solo artist, such collaborations ran throughout his long career. In an interview in December, 2006, Spencer told me how it took him a while to get a handle on what Martyn expected from him.

> Very early on in my career with him I did the *Apprentice* tour and I was thinking: 'Oh, I must do what the record demands and I must play in that one way.' I had a kind of classical point of view on it – he is the leader of the band and he will tell me what he wants. It took me most of that year to realise that actually what he is asking of me is me. He was asking what as a musician and creative person I want to bring to the table. He wants you to be you, he wants to have a laugh and to have fun and for it to be a social thing. When it becomes hard work he doesn't like it and that's not because he is frightened of hard work. He can work all day if he wants to, but it has to be hard work for a purpose. There are times when he will give you

instructions, but he allows you to also make contributions. So, during a live gig, especially early on during a tour when we are all fresh, you will get some moments when someone throws something into the mix, like a different way of playing a chord, and everyone else in the band just goes 'Yes!' It's like a jazz thing really: we take a tune and we just adapt it. There are times when we rehearse a song and he'll just say: 'Oh, that's fine' and you are thinking: 'Bloody hell' . . . but he's happy because we know the shape of it and everyone is tuned into it. Then, when we play it live, that is when things start happening. At the end of our first year together we did a tour of Germany and by then there was such a different attitude – I could do what I wanted to do and our partnership just developed from there.

For the third album in a row, the recording and mixing of *Cooltide* was done at Ca Va Studios – over an eighteen-day stretch. John felt at ease working with studio staff he knew and who in turn knew his quirks. Lyrics for the three songs that came out of the shed jams were improvised in the studio, with John getting wasted to give him the confidence to 'catch a mood and fly away'. Brian Young recalls:

It was great, absolutely stunning, working on that. I remember one night during the recording, he and Annie went in town to see Bonnie Raitt. She came back with us after the show. Bonnie ended up singing the title track – way, way up there – she was just perfect on that song. I wish we had recorded it. But her manager said she couldn't do a recording of it, it would have needed to have been worked out in advance, though she would have loved to. It was a real shame.

Recording coincided with the Glasgow Jazz Festival, and Andy Sheppard and Joe Locke were enlisted when it was found out that they were playing in local pubs near the studio. Andy Sheppard told me how Martyn had been an idol of his for years:

I'd been aware of John's music since I was a teenager. I can remember listening to *Solid Air* in a haze of smoke when it first came out. Around 1987, I was signed to Island Records and John was working for them at the time and I just happened to be around their London studio when he was doing an album. We got introduced and I played on a couple of tracks and we went for a drink, hung out and just got on really well. Subsequently, I played some live gigs with him and got to play on some of his records.

For the making of *Cooltide*, I was playing at the Glasgow Jazz Festival and he asked me to come along to the Ca Va Studios. John asked me to get there for ten in the morning, which was easier for him because he had probably been up all night! I got there for ten and he said, 'We need to go and freshen up, get a drink before we start.' He took me to this bar on Sauchiehall Street, which was full of people who looked like they had not just been there all night, but had been there for several years! Soon as I opened my mouth, everyone looked at me and some old guy at the bar asked me, 'Where are you from?' I said England and he just looked at me and said, 'It's an accident of birth, son.'

It was great to be in the studio with John and to put the headphones on and just hear that voice of his. One of the tunes I later recorded with him, for the album *No Little Boy*, was a version of 'Solid Air'. The way they mixed that track was just fantastic. Instead of being just a thing in the background, the saxophone had a real interaction with John. I just thought, 'Yeah, now you are talking.' I still listen to that track a lot. Unfortunately, something happened with the record company and it never got the exposure it should have. But for me it was just wonderful to work on that song and to work with a guy who had always been one of my heroes. It was a beautiful thing to have done that.

He is quite a contradiction because he sometimes surrounds himself with a kind of dodgy rock 'n' roll entourage and yet his music is so beautiful and gentle. John is a full-on guy, a wild man. He's always been larger than life. One of the first gigs I was with him I saw him drink a bottle of Bacardi in one gulp. Another time, we did this gig in really hot weather in Cambridge and he wore this full-length overcoat. Some time later he said to me, 'Come on the road with me' and I thought, 'Well, if I come on the road with you I might not come back! I'm easily led in all those directions.'

Martyn considered *Cooltide* to be his best work since *Grace and Danger* and paid special praise to Spencer Cozens' work. In Cozens, Martyn found a musical soulmate whose grasp of the very latest computer technology appealed to John – who, though far from being a Luddite, struggled to master some of the new ways of working. Even late on in his life, Martyn 'didn't do computers' and had no e-mail address. In truth, John was not a hands-on producer. He got bored easily and preferred to leave the studio for hours on end and then return to approve or tamper with the work done in his absence. When Spencer had to take time off to sit his final exams, Foster Paterson was drafted back in. The inclusion of tasteful slide guitar and country feel on the record reflected John's fondness for Bonnie Raitt, Hank Williams, Chet Atkins and Willie Nelson. Touring to support the album saw the continuing evolution of the John Martyn band into a true collaborative affair, allowing talented players like John Giblin and Spencer Cozens the opportunity to improvise and get their share of the limelight. For the first time in years, John toured North America in late 1992, with Cozens, Alan Thomson, sax player Jerry Underwood and Gerry Conway on drums.

By 1992, John had clocked up almost quarter of a century toiling away in the music business. The landmark seemed to bring on a rash of intro-spection and a need to re-evaluate his career to date. Reworking some of his old classic songs began in the summer of 1992 in the UK, with Phil Collins and Dave Gilmour helping out. The project initially had John's backing – he wanted to revamp his classic work with the new band sound, feeling that songs like 'Bless The Weather' were hidebound by the original acoustic format. But as was often the case, John was disappointed with the first results and – with the backing of Permanent – he went to the USA in the winter where more work was done on them with producer Jim Tullio at the Chicago Recording Company. But the label then went and released the original re-recordings as *Couldn't Love You More*, which had fifteen Martyn classics given a super-smooth revamp with heavy emphasis on the keyboards and sax. But the release of this album without John's blessing led to much ill feeling and, ultimately, a split from the label. Fans were also unimpressed and critics positively hated it – *The Guitar* magazine called it toothless trash. Even more importantly, John himself hated the very notion of the album, disowning it and making plain that it had been released by his record company while he was in the USA. He called it dull trash which should never have seen the inside of a record store. The upshot was inevitable – John's dislike for the record industry just kept on growing. Now he was talking of starting his own label or releasing future albums through individual licensing deals. The interview with *The Guitar* magazine saw John at his grumpiest, dismissive of many of his contemporaries and of newer artists. There were catty asides about Bert Jansch and John Renbourn and the F-word – folk – got its usual pasting from John. He thought it irrelevant, telling *Mojo* magazine in October 1994 'Who in Santa Barbara in 1994 wants to know about what some geezer said on the gallows in Yorkshire in 1792?' U2 were dismissed as little more than a pub band, Morrissey was branded unmusical, while new age music was described as 'utterly disposable – in ten years' time it will be forgotten'. He also claimed that he now had eleven children to four different women!

The following year saw the release of *No Little Boy*, the original UK re-recordings plus the additional session work in Chicago. John was, as ever, in awe of the high standard of American musicians and talked optimistically about actually moving permanently to the Illinois city. The US sessions also afforded him the opportunity of meeting Levon Helm again – the pair having first met in the halcyon Woodstock days of 1969. This time, Levon flew out from his Woodstock home for two days and the two unique talents combined on a cover of the standard by radical folk singer and poet Bruce 'Utah' Phillips, 'Rock, Salt and Nails', and another track, 'Just Now', which featured Helm on harmony vocals. The journalist Dave Hoekstra recalled the magic moment when the two legends traded vocal blows.

Martyn stood and sang soulful scats with his eyes closed. Helm sat on a stool across from Martyn, and rocked back and forth, tapping his foot and delivering a Delta drawl between long drags from a cigarette.

Helm, who is surely one of the great vocalists himself, told the *Chicago Sun Times* reporter:

I grew up in Arkansas right on the river, so the way John voices music really hits home with me. It reminds me of all my heroes. It sounds like John Martyn, but at the same time I hear everybody from Muddy Waters to Otis Redding. I can even hear Bill Monroe in there.

The album, which Phil Collins subsequently named as one of his all-time favourite records, sold well and got good radio coverage in the USA. In interviews, John said he now actually preferred the new versions to the originals.

Back home in Scotland, John's father died from the effects of wet brain syndrome, aged eighty-four, in the spring of 1994. Up until his death, old Mr McGeachy was – according to his son – still drinking big time. John was keeping up the family tradition, having seemingly turned his back on sobriety for good. Those who knew him during the mid-1990s talk of frequent booze binges and occasional violent outbursts. Spells of sobriety would only last for a handful of days before he ended up in favourite bars in Biggar, downing large Bacardis. At times he was stony broke and – in complete contrast to his early dapper days – looked more like a down and out.

John never liked analysing why he drank so much, but he obviously found it impossible to function in the music business without alcohol. He had long gone past the stage of feeling guilty about it – indeed, he some-times argued that he didn't drink much and that he could and should have been much wilder in the old days. Of course heavy drinking ran in the family: besides his father's alcoholism, his mum was also fond of a tipple. Family history may have provided the predisposition for his alcoholism, but John himself put it down to just wanting to be disconnected and get somewhere else – just like his old blues heroes of the 1920s such as Robert Johnson. John was also a very nervous performer in the early part of his career and relied on a few pre-gig drams for Dutch courage. Over the years of course those drinks became a necessity rather than a preference. But whatever the reason for his boozing, the simple fact was that John Martyn just did not like being straight. In occasional moments of remorse he would tell you that alcohol was the one drug he regretted getting involved with and it's undeniable that alcohol played a major part in negating his talents and ruining the chances to capitalise fully on his genius. Dave Pegg remembers a night that summed up the fine line John seemed to balance between chaotic lifestyle and musical brilliance.

> About ten years ago, I went into Ralph McTell's local, the Half Moon in Putney. My brother and I were having a pint with Ralph and Gerry Conway, the drummer with Fairport Convention. About 9.45 p.m., John burst into the bar in his slippers and pyjamas, obviously in a very relaxed state. He was looking like he was about to die, really in serious pain. He came over and told us he had an accident the night before and had fallen down the fire escape of his hotel. We told the American guy who was with him to get him to the hospital immediately. John had a couple of brandies and a pint and told us he couldn't go to the hospital as he had a gig to play that night in a venue down by the Thames. He said: 'Ah fuck it' and off he went to the gig. He left our names on the door and we went to the gig afterwards. It was just John on his own, playing acoustic. He was absolutely sensational! It was one of the best gigs I've ever seen him do and afterwards we took him to hospital and he was diagnosed with a broken rib!

Exactly how John managed to continue performing and recording when alcohol played such a central part in his day-to-day life continued to amaze those who knew him. Brian Young on witnessing Martyn's behaviour up close in the 1980s said:

> I have no idea how he does it. He has some capacity to be able to do what he does. I've seen him not able to go on stage or be on stage and not be able to do much – but these things did not happen often. Sometimes you can see the band cruising around the same bit of music waiting for John to pick up and follow them. They are all very good at that.

Ralph McTell offers typically incisive views on the way that booze has infected the music business and affected his contemporaries:

I think alcohol is much more insidious than heroin or even cigarettes for that matter. We all drink too much and sometimes it's a relief when you have to give it up. Bert [Jansch] has given it up because he had to. Dick Gaughan too has stopped altogether. Randy Newman said something like it takes a whole lot of medicine to make me feel like I'm somebody else. The alcohol just tells you that you are all right, doesn't it?

Spencer Cozens was John's closest musical partner for over fifteen years and speaking prior to Martyn's death, he had some interesting insights into the cryptic relationship between John Martyn and alcohol, arguing that the public image was not the full story and also revealing that John's liking for the booze was matched only by his appetite for quality food.

John often gives the impression of being a bumbling drunk when actually he is not – underneath it all he is quite clear about what he wants, he's a very driven person. He doesn't care about the things that most people care about. His drinking is just one of those things. He's an alcoholic and that is an illness, that's all there is to it. I've read all those psychological reasons why people drink like that, but the best of people can become alcoholics. John has the constitution of an ox; even fifteen years ago I would look at him drinking and think, 'How do you do that?' But he eats very well too. He hates bad food, in a way his food is just like his music – he wants quality. Say if we are in Ireland, we will have ham and potatoes, but it will be wonderfully done and tastes like nothing else. He loves Indian food and lots of sauces.

The reputation for John being a bit of a 'heavy' character persisted and his choice of company continued to raise eyebrows. Michael Chapman tells of one incident that left a bad taste:

John once played at a club in Carlisle run by Rick Kemp and two other guys. One of the guys that ran it worshipped John and whenever John was in poor condition and couldn't get a gig, this guy would always pay him £750 to play there. For a Tuesday night in Carlisle, that was way over the odds. This guy would give John his last pair of socks when he had buggar-all else to wear. It was just after Hamish Imlach had died, and that scared the shit out of John and he had decided to reform his ways. Alan Thomson did the soundcheck for him, and John turned up four minutes before show time. Someone had rolled him a joint and he got a pint, walked on stage and that was it. But he had turned up with this Glasgow hard man and a rather fat lady. The band had been on stage for about half an hour when these two people walked into the office and said, 'We want the money in cash now – or we pull him off stage.' Well, where do you find £2,000 in cash at 10 p.m. on a Sunday night in Carlisle? Most of the money would have still been in the record shops where the tickets were sold. And this guy who runs the place – who shall have to remain anonymous, but who worships John – had to go around people he knew in the audience and borrow their credit cards to go and empty the cash machines. He paid them all back next week. I'm not sure of John's involvement in all this. Whether it was John's idea, the fat woman's idea or the Glasgow hard man's idea – I couldn't tell you. But it was a very, very shit thing to do to people who were friends of his.

When John Martyn was given the opportunity to read the first draft of this book, the only objection he raised was to this story. He did not ask for it be removed, but he wanted it to be stressed that the events that night in Carlisle were in no way his doing.

21st-century John

I'm an incurable romantic and that can be uncomfortable in these troubled
and cynical times. But I'm proud of it and I'm not going to change now.

John Martyn

He's a tortured artist, but there are bigger artists than John who never went
down that road . . . He could be quite violent but it didn't affect me because
I used to do kickboxing before I met him.

Daisy Flowers

Inevitably the years of alcoholism took their toll on live performing.
Whereas in the early 1970s, the booze and additional relaxing agents added
to the magic of a John Martyn gig, by the 1990s they were beginning to
become an occasional hindrance. Every long-term Martyn fan will tell you
a tale of travelling miles to see their hero and paying good money only for
John to be unable to do his material justice. I witnessed one particularly
embarrassing night when I went to see Bert Jansch perform to a sell-out
crowd at a packed Glasgow club. Jansch was as ever immaculate, but as the
concert progressed he was increasingly the target of drunken hecklers from
the back of the hall. When the lights went up at the intermission it became
apparent that the main hecklers were Hamish Imlach and an exceedingly
inebriated Martyn. Despite Jansch's best efforts, Martyn eventually got
onto the stage and – after some delay – was given a guitar and the two men
agreed on which song they would play. Watching two of the greatest
guitarists/songwriters of our generation should have been an unalloyed
pleasure. Instead, it turned into a dreadful embarrassment with John barely

able to stay on his stool, never mind match the playing of Jansch. Nights like that put many people off seeing John, but they were the exception. As the decade progressed, Martyn continued to tour and to earn rave reviews though promoters who had experienced Martyn at his worst were understandably slow to stage his shows again.

By 1994 his time with Permanent – which had become part of PolyGram – was ending acrimoniously and Martyn was again left without a label. His mood wasn't much enhanced by Island's decision to release a two-CD anthology of his work with the label between 1971 and 1987. John acknowledged the compliment, but said he didn't want to waste time listening to the classic songs on *Sweet Little Mysteries*, an album that strangely featured no songs from his first four LPs. (A four-track CD EP *Snooo*, was given away free to fans during a short UK tour in 1995 and was later released officially.) To add to the feeling of despondency around this time, John's oldest friend, Hamish Imlach died in 1996. After years of carousing and carryouts, John's mentor passed away at the age of just fifty-five. Shortly afterwards, while on tour in Inverness, John got word that his second wife, Annie Furlong, had died. The couple had long since separated, and at the time of her death, John was seriously ill with pancreatitis.

There were many in the music business predicting his demise, but in 1996 he re-emerged through the CD *And* with a fresh sound which defied the critics. The album had its roots in John's trip to Chicago during the recording of *No Little Boy* when he had fallen in love with the energy and new sounds of the local hip hop scene. Though *And* could never be described as genuine hip hop, there's a real vitality and newness to the beats of the album, which was released on the Go! Discs label, which also issued Portishead's work. With the assistance of Chicago producer Stefon Taylor, John came up with some of his best work in years. Songs such as 'Sunshine's Better', 'The Downward Pull Of Human Nature' And 'She's A Lover' harked back to the glory days. John's gravel voice is to the fore – a great improvement from the self-pitying weepy vocals of the 1980s. The album cover was a tribute to one of John's old heroes, Thelonious Monk, with the photo on the sleeve bearing remarkable similarity to the artwork on Monk's *In Italy* album. Much to John's relief, the audiences took to the new sound. He was attracting younger fans to his gigs, alongside the hardy perennials that had stuck by him since the late 1960s. But not everyone was pleased by the mix of new songs and the old favourites, which John called 'lollipops' to keep the audience happy. One woman once burst into his dressing room after a show shouting 'Seven pounds fifty and no "Solid Air"– it's a disgrace!' And occasionally John could find himself in the wrong place – he was given the hardest of times by thousands of drunken fans of The Verve at a 1998 festival in the band's hometown. John found the ordeal disheartening if amusing.

John's partner during the mid-1990s was Daisy Flowers, a five-foot-two South Londoner who helped Martyn get well-paid record deals with both Go! Discs and Independiente and also aided the setting up of his studio and got better wages for the band. The cover for the *And* album pays special thanks to Daisy. John and Daisy had met at a Martyn concert in Blackheath in 1993 and subsequently lived together in Roberton for the best part of five years, but it's not a time that either remembers fondly. The mere mention of her name was enough to upset John and he dismissed his time with her.

With the help of John's doctor, Daisy got the star off the booze eight times, only for John to relapse despite expressing remorse for his behaviour. Daisy memorably described trying to keep John away from the pubs in Biggar as being as easy as 'herding ferrets'. His alcoholism was now so severe that to actually go cold turkey risked withdrawal seizures. On one occasion Daisy found him in seizure, foaming at the mouth and in danger of swallowing his tongue. During the research for the first edition of this book, Daisy told me how Martyn's mood was dependent on his intake of alcohol.

John is a lovely geezer and I actually do still like him very much. But what you have to realise is that with an alcoholic you have two characters. It was very much the Jekyll and Hyde thing. One minute he could be a beautiful human being and then he would turn into something like a monster coming out of the bushes at you in your nightmares. There were still remnants of the real Ian David McGeachy there, but when John had a drink inside him he was a complete pain. You could not be around him as he was completely unbearable. I would go and stay in a local B&B nearby and give him a couple of days to get it out of his system and get Heather, the lady next door, to go in and check on him in case he had fallen down the stairs. I'm sure he paid off the mortgages of most of the publicans in Biggar, the amount he spent in those pubs over the years. He's a tortured artist, but there are bigger artists than John who never went down that road. He did have a quite vicious streak. He could be quite violent, but it didn't affect me because I used to do kick-boxing before I met him. He never landed a punch on me. The drink brought out the violence in him. He used to have things about his mum because she abandoned him as a child. There's a bit of the misogynist in John.

The couple split after Daisy found out that Martyn was having an affair with an heiress.

Following the end of that stormy relationship, John started to redis-cover his interest in Buddhism, which dated back to his teenage years in Glasgow. Back then, it encroached onto the local hippie scene and was seen as an aid for those who had run into trouble through drug-taking. As a fourteen-year-old, Iain McGeachy had read the works of the English barrister Christmas Humphries who had tried to explain the Buddhist way to western society. The teenager had also found traces of Buddhist thought in the writings of Herman Hesse and Aldous Huxley, and many years later he took an interest in Zen Buddhism, telling people that he stayed alongside exiled Tibetan monks at the Samye Ling Monastery retreat in Scotland where residents lived in their own little room on a frugal diet of rice and plums, away from all the madness and temptations of city life. (When I put this claim to one of John's closest friends it was dismissed succinctly as 'bollocks!') John said Buddhism taught him to exercise the power of love whenever possible and to appreciate it greatly whenever it comes to you. 'It all made sense to me and it still does. To me life is one beautiful illusion – it's your own creation.' He found that it helped curb the aggressive side of his nature. In May 2004, sitting under a wall plaque which read 'Soft answer turneth away wrath', he told the *Independent* writer James McNair:

> I still don't suffer fools gladly, but I've learnt to bite my tongue. Buddhism helps me because it gives you freedom of personality. Things are either right or wrong – that sounds dogmatic rather than Buddhist, but it's not. You'll be taught by life if nothing else that what is right is right and what is wrong is wrong. I've always had that touch of superstition, or religion, if you want to call it that, so I can't not believe in a Creator. The birds sing too beautifully and the trout are too speckled. I like gambling with cards, but I could never put that much down to chance.

Above the fireplace of his Roberton home, two Buddhas sat beside a portrait of Robert Burns and a scroll with the Lord's Prayer.

When John reappeared in May 1998 with *The Church With One Bell* it was on the back of a bizarre agreement with his new label, Independiente (formerly Go! Disks). Permanent's founder, Andy Macdonald, had started the new company and John had made the move too. When he became aware that the disused Scots Congregational Kirk in his home village was up for sale he asked the label to lend him the cash to buy it. The tax authorities had been sniffing about his affairs for a while – on one occasion he had to pay the VAT authority £38,000 or they would have taken his home from him. John had coveted the church for years, but didn't have the cash to purchase it. He hoped to transform the church with one bell into a studio and refuge for disadvantaged youngsters. The record company agreed to buy the church if, in return, John recorded his first-ever album of covers. Independiente sent him a tape with their thirty-five preferred choices – most of which Martyn hadn't even heard of. John recorded sixteen tracks, of which ten made the final mix. Rehearsals took three days with John Giblin, Spencer Cozens and drummer Arran Ahmun. Recording and mixing took another eight days.

Among the covers was John's take on the Billie Holiday standard 'Strange Fruit'. John had always adored Holiday and used to say that if he 'had been around when she was around, then she would still be around today.' He confessed that it was one of the most miserable songs ever, but believed that its story of racial lynching in the Deep South, like the Holocaust, had to be told and retold. He felt there was still undeveloped apartheid in the USA. John claimed that espousing such views had led him to be barred from playing in Missouri and Alabama, and led to him carrying a gun for safety while in the USA. Nigel Williamson for *Uncut* magazine admitted that this wasn't Martyn's best album, but argued that – at the age of forty-nine – his voice had never sounded riper. Williamson admired John's boldness in tackling 'Strange Fruit', which many – including Nina Simone – thought was the most difficult song in the world to sing. Williamson thought the choice of Portishead's 'Glory Box' was entirely appropriate given the trip-hop fraternity's debt to the *Solid Air* era. John hadn't heard the Bristol band's music prior to recording the song, but soon saw the link to his early work. Elsewhere there's a nod to John's love of the blues since his teenage years. An ultra-slow version of Elmore James' 'The Sky Is Crying' is included, along with 'Death Don't Have No Mercy' by the Reverend Gary Davis, whom John had seen play in the clubs way back in the 1960s. The eclectic mix also includes songs by Bobby Charles, Ben Harper, Randy Newman and Dead Can Dance. David Hepworth of *Mojo* magazine gave top marks to the Newman cover and John's version of 'Small Town Talk', co-written by The Band's Rick Danko, and also paid tribute to his successful attempts to improve his vocals. Hepworth was especially taken by the gravitas shown on 'Death Don't Have No Mercy' and the grungy vocals on 'Excuse Me Mister'. John actually contacted Ben Harper to say sorry for taking liberties with the tempo of that particular track but in the end he delivered a wonderful version every inch the equal of the original.

As he neared the age of fifty, John's disdain for the 'dishonest' music industry remained as strong as ever. He told the journalist Rob Young: 'There are guys out there putting out records of mine, they don't know a hatchet from a crotchet' (*Wire*, June 1998). He told Young that he felt less need to write than before, and was increasingly uncomfortable in the limelight – spending as little time as possible at a venue before or after a show.

I never sang a love song to anyone in my life, not directly anyway. No, I'm not in the business of that. The reason I write love songs is mostly to expurgate and excise the pain of being involved in the situation. It also keeps certain things in your mind. I've lost a lot of friends, and I have songs about them, so I occasionally sing those, and it brings them back into my mind – I can see them walking, talking, and that's cool.

He thought music was taken too seriously when all it really was a frippery, 'as important as a good game of whist'. But where his own music was concerned he still believed the best was yet to come. The late summer of 1998 saw John in the USA, playing at the Fleadh Festival tour in New York, Chicago and San Francisco alongside Richard Thompson and getting whacked on the side of his head with a baseball bat by a mugger outside his New York hotel. Back in England, in 1999, Beverley Martyn re-emerged after a near thirty-year break from the music scene, with the album *No Frills* on the Mystic Small Productions label.

The general public were given a welcome reminder of John's talents when he appeared on BBC Scotland's excellent TV series *The Transatlantic Sessions*. Under the musical direction of Aly Bain and Jay Ungar, the series of shows in 1995 and 1998 was a bold attempt to bring together the best exponents of traditional and modern acoustic music from both sides of the Atlantic. The likes of Dick Gaughan, Emmylou Harris, Nanci Griffith, Ricky Scaggs, Karen Matheson and Roseanne Cash were filmed at two Georgian mansions – Montgreenan in Ayrshire and Raemoir in Banchory. John's first appearance, looking slightly wasted, saw him perform 'May You Never' along with Danny Thompson, guitarist Kathy Mattea and the excellent Dobro player Jerry Douglas. John ends the immaculate recital with a giggling 'I like that one!' John and Danny's slow-paced version of 'Solid Air' is equally mesmerising, but the real show-stopper is John's take on 'Excuse Me Mister'. With a full band behind him, Martyn gives the audience a real bravura vocal performance, teasing the words out with an impassioned delivery that just leaves you breathless. When you watch him perform like this it makes you realise just why so many people considered Martyn to be a genius. In the words of the song, his performance 'puts the rest to shame'.

One of the artists present for the sessions was the Scots singer-songwriter Eddi Reader, who had shot to fame fronting the band Fairground Attraction before going on to forge a successful solo career in the 1990s. She remembers the sessions as being really relaxed despite the hectic recording schedule.

> We were all coming and going at different times, but there was one night when I met everyone and the feeling was of openness and of people – many of whom were strangers to me – who were willing to collaborate.

Martyn's work was a major influence on Reader and she has covered a number of John's songs during her career. The pair eventually struck up a friendship when they appeared on the same bill during Glasgow's 1990 Year of Culture celebrations. Interviewed in 2007, Eddi recalled:

> John is a phenomenal writer and for years I used to play *London Conversation* constantly. *One World* was also incredibly influential for me; I played it till the grooves were see through! John and Danny at the Transatlantic Sessions were just magical – an amazing experience musically. I got the sense that Danny was very supportive of John and vice versa. Everything was easy and flowed brilliantly. John sat with me later in the lounge and he was really attentive and lovely and when I asked him to play 'Fairytale Lullaby' he obliged. That meant a lot to me because not only is it one of my favourite John Martyn songs, it's also one of the songs I first learnt when I started playing guitar.

The new millennium began with the release of *Glasgow Walker* – the first album in four years to feature original Martyn material. Self-produced in Scotland and mixed in Kilkenny, where his new girlfriend Teresa Walsh, lived, it featured Kathryn Williams, the Mercury-prize winner whose love of Nick Drake's music was part of the reason for her getting the gig. Williams played support when John teamed up with Danny Thompson in the spring of 2001 for a twenty-date tour of the UK, the latter pair going under the improbable billing of the 'Sunshine Boys'. The title alluded to the classic movie where two vaudeville stars – played by George Burns and Walter Matthau – come out of retirement for a TV show. John and Danny may not have had the hate-filled relationship of the movie's characters, but there had certainly been some bad blood between them since the heyday of the 1970s. Still, they agreed to build upon the success of their reunion for BBC Scotland. The subsequent tour was a wonderful reminder of past glories for many fans, but Danny told me how, though he enjoyed the tour, there was a feeling of what might have been.

> I just think it could have been devastatingly better. Beforehand I told him that I didn't want us to just go on the road and for it be like a trip down memory lane. I wanted us to play new stuff and I wanted people to walk out of those concerts and say 'Wow' rather than 'They used to be good, these two old guys'. I think we got away with it, but it could have been a lot better.

Once again, John went through a spell back on the wagon and he revealed for the first time that his boozing had led to his pancreas 'exploding' back in 1996. He said that the incident had reminded him just how much he actually enjoyed living. But as ever with John, total abstinence was out of the question: this time around, he was nursing a dislocated shoulder after taking another tumble. In the years to come, he would break an arm and several toes, before things got much more serious. When the urge took him he liked to drink in Ronnie Scott's in London and the Scotia Bar in Glasgow – one of the few remaining folk clubs in the city where performers played Irish and Scots music. Clubbing was out, though he did still enjoy attending concerts and eating out – La Vigna in Lanark was a favourite restaurant. He was happily in love with Teresa and enjoying his work again.

Financially he was sound, though setting up a studio in his new home had necessitated a five-month spell of hard grind to help balance the books. In addition, he lost a large amount of money when two rogues he knew from his Chelsea Art Club days did a runner with a large amount of cash. The version of the story I've been told is that John, after receiving a big cash sum as part of a record deal, got drunk and gave many thousands of pounds to the men to go down to London to buy cocaine. John never saw them again. That may sound far-fetched but even in the early days, Donnie Barclay recalls that Martyn had no concept of the importance of money. 'It didn't seem to bother him as long as he had his guitar and a place to crash.' Donnie once travelled to Oxford with John for a show. Martyn got paid £15 and then paid £17 for a taxi back to London rather than wait for a train. Daisy Flowers was amazed that, when she first met John, he was unaware that he had been missing out on thousands of pounds of PRS payments.

> When I took over his business affairs he was bankrupt. He wasn't really conscious of PRS; he was living a hand-to-mouth existence. He would get the money from a tour and just go on a complete blow-out, run out of dosh and then try to get someone to organise a tour for him because he had no money. The band told me stories about how they would end up sleeping in cars on European tours because there was no money for hotels.

In interviews, John reflected on how fortunate he had been to escape the drudgery of a 9 to 5 job. Instead, he was travelling the globe and meeting so many good people along the way. It was a lifestyle he had grown to love and found it impossible to live without. He re-emerged promising to be less self-obsessed and to write 'less miserable' songs. But in a promotional interview for the new album he said the subject matter for the majority of his songs would continue to be love. 'I'm an incurable romantic and that can be uncomfortable in these troubled and cynical times. But I'm proud of it and I'm not going to change now.'

For the first time, John had written the songs for the new album on a synthesiser – a Korg Trinity recommended to him by Phil Collins back in 1997. John struggled to master it – he hadn't played piano since he was a child – and actually managed to lose half the tracks after over a year's work on the album. This, added to his illness, led to long delays before – with the help of musician friends – the project saw the light of day. The record contained two covers – 'You Don't Know What Love Is' and the Julie London hit 'Cry Me A River'. The former track was recorded with the Guy Barker International Quintet and its effortlessly languid jazz makes one wish John had tackled similar songs on a more regular basis. The track gained wider appeal when it appeared on the closing credits in Anthony Minghella's movie *The Talented Mr Ripley*. Guy Barker, who describes John, as a 'male Billie Holiday', was the movie's musical arranger. John himself loved the movie, giving it five-star ratings. The film's star, Matt Damon, is a fan of John's music, as was Minghella.

The *Sunday Times* thought *Glasgow Walker* saw John writing his best material since the untroubled days of the early 1970s, giving particular praise to the haunting melody of the anti-war track 'The Field Of Play' and the African-sounding chant 'So Sweet'. The latter's lyric was based on the sweetness felt by one of John's friends on splitting up with her boyfriend. John was once again happy writing gorgeous love songs and selected one such song, the open-hearted 'Wildflower', as his own favourite track from the album. It was the best song he had written in years and remains criminally underrated. The song's lyric is beautiful and painfully honest: 'My resolve is weak – sometimes staggerin' from street to street, but I still love wildflowers . . . Help this helpless heart of mine.' He said the bizarre track 'The Cat Won't Work Tonight' probably wouldn't be understood by anyone and the lyrics came as he mused on what work really meant. Reggie Hastings must be the only musician ever to be credited with playing milk bottles on an album.

Confessions of a one-legged sumo wrestler

So he could have saved the leg, but again in order to do that he would have had to say, 'Right, I mustn't do this and I mustn't do that', which is just not John. So I suppose it was a fait accompli.

Spencer Cozens

Sometimes I get angry about what's happened to me, but anything I had coming was well on its way. I've hammered my body all my life.

John Martyn

In 2001, John made a surprise appearance at a party to mark the actor James MacPherson's departure from the STV detective series *Taggart*. James was leaving the show after appearing in forty-seven episodes, and the cast and crew persuaded John to show up as a leaving present for the actor who names 'The Field Of Play' of *Glasgow Walker* as his favourite song of all time. James had been forced to quit the show after being diagnosed with a collapsed lung. One of Scotland's best-loved actors was seriously ill, but meeting up with his hero for the first time was a wonderful tonic.

I had been a fan since the late 1970s. A girl gave me two albums – *One World* and *Solid Air* – and I hated them! I listened to them and thought, 'Oh Christ, this is dreadful.' But I taped them just in case and started to listen to them more and I just thought they were brilliant. Then, in the early 1980s, I saw him do a floor spot at Paisley Folk Club. I had never met him before the night he appeared on the set, though I passed by him once on the stairs of Henry Afrika's [a fabled Glasgow night club] just before he went on stage.

It was one of those things where I didn't want to meet my hero in case he turned out to be stupid. And of course when I met him it was anything but that.

They incorporated him into my last scene on the show. It was unbelievable; if people have The Beatles or the Stones as their heroes, then it was like turning round and finding them there. He asked me what I wanted to hear and I asked for 'The Apprentice', but he said he couldn't do that. He said, 'I can play you "Solid Air" acoustic,' and I said, 'Yeah just play that,' and he did. I cannot tell you how wonderful that was. He was on his best behaviour and just so nice to everyone. He had come all the way from Ireland and he wasn't well, he had just had an accident. I just thought this is a man who cares totally about his music. He went to the party afterwards, but I didn't want to bug him, because I know what that is like. I just said to him, 'Thank you so much and I'm going to leave you now.'

In January and February 2001, James Yorkston – a young singer-songwriter who had sent John a demo tape on spec under the name 'J Wright presents', supported Martyn on a thirty-date UK tour. John liked the tape and Yorkston gave up his job in a bookshop to do the tour. 'At first it was a sink or swim situation and I think I initially drowned a couple of times' (*Uncut*, February 2003). Martyn's unique vocals found a whole new audience in the spring of 2001 when he recorded with the progressive trance house DJ, Sister Bliss. She was a long-time admirer of John's work and their cover of The Beloved's 'Deliver Me' reached number 31 in the UK singles charts. *The Scotsman* newspaper celebrated the event with a mention in its leader column. Phill Brown, who had worked on the classic album *One World* a quarter of a century before, was also involved on those sessions. He recalls:

Sister Bliss just loved John's voice and always wanted to get him involved on one track. He was just on his best behaviour that day; I was expecting him to come in with a crate of beer. But he turned up looking really well, had one joint and a beer, then did the vocal. He was brilliant, in really good form, and then he left.

With the inspiration of his new girlfriend, Teresa (dubbed Mama T Razor on the *Glasgow Walker* track) powering his work, John seemed to have taken a permanent detour off the road to ruin. He had fallen in love with 'his colleen' after meeting her in Dublin in 1998 and the couple had set up home, with their Jack Russell dog, Gizmo, near Thomastown in County Kilkenny. The dog was bought for £12.50 from local gypsies, and besides being a good rat catcher, has been a fine companion to John. 'The love I have had from that creature . . . well, there's no price on it.' John described his partner Teresa, who was running an antique store when their paths first crossed, as:

> A diamond – down to earth and funky. She is ever so lovely; she has been unbelievable in the last year and a half. This [his leg amputation] is the hardest thing I have ever been through. Without her, I don't think I would have made it through – it was just one of those sticky phases in my life and I am very lucky to have her.

Ireland reminded him of the quiet and quaint Scotland of his youth, living in a remote, trim, white-walled cottage and fishing in the River Nore. Living there also rekindled his childhood love of ornithology.

> I've seen birds here that I've only seen in books. We have long-tailed tits here and they sit up under the eaves and make nests. You have never seen such a bonny thing in your life; it's like being on a tropical island. You get fantastic colours here – for some reason their plumage seems to be brighter for every species of bird. Maybe it's because there are fewer pesticides and the land is wilder.

Thomastown's main pub, Carroll's, with its walls covered in music memorabilia, soon became a favourite haunt. On occasion, John would appear alongside visiting musicians in the pub's beer garden. One memorable gig in July 2004 saw him, decidedly the worse for wear, do an encore alongside The Band's Garth Hudson and his group, Burrito Deluxe. That night, I saw him emerge out of a car sober and walk tall down the main street of

Thomastown, looking incredibly healthy when one considered his past. One hour later, he was holding court in the beer garden of Carroll's, getting steadily merrier. By the time he was called up on stage, Martyn was mortal, but somehow he managed to stay upright and sing a totally undecipherable blues number. At one point, he nearly careered into some rather expensive equipment before miraculously righting himself. The capacity crowd loved every minute of it and cheered their local hero off the stage.

John was upbeat again and back in creative mode, talking up a new album, new label and the prospect of touring again. But in September 2002, on a trip back to Scotland, John's car was involved in a head-on collision with a stray black cow, and the star suffered a broken nose and whiplash injuries. John had to be pulled from the blazing van by Teresa and two family friends. He had to wear a neck brace and a string of dates in Scotland in October were cancelled. As a reporter for *Scotland on Sunday* discovered, the run-in with the cow was just one of a number of hassles assailing the star as he battled to get his life back on an even keel. He was in trouble financially, with the banks moving to repossess, and he put his Roberton home up for sale. The setbacks seemed to have checked his new-found optimism, and he admitted to living a reclusive lifestyle, adding: 'I put on accents; I put on a front, because I'm a very private person. That's what I'm about. I hardly let anyone get close.' The reporter, Adam Lee Potter, had been advised by John's record company to speak to him early in the day in order to catch him sober. When Adam met John at the Chelsea Arts Club around noon, he was onto his third double Bacardi and Coke. Bizarrely, he then went on to say how doctors in rehab had warned him that any alcohol could be fatal. Now he claimed he only drank in moderation and seldom before a concert. He told Potter that Lapsang Souchong tea was now his preferred tipple, before promptly polishing off another double Bacardi. When I met him a couple of years later in the Shawlands pub, Sammy Dow's, he was drinking double vodkas diluted in pints of cider – and addressing bar staff as 'Nurse!' When he emerged through the bat-wing doors, almost 24-stone, wheelchair bound and immaculately dressed, even the local hard men stopped to stare.

When I quizzed him on how he managed to perform so well on stage while drinking so much, he replied: 'I don't drink that much. That's a myth. I drink about three-quarters of a bottle of spirits on an average day plus cider. That's not a lot – a bottle a day would be a lot!' I remember leaving him in his five-star hotel room thinking he would never make it on stage, but a few hours later he was getting a standing ovation from a capacity crowd at the Glasgow Carling Academy.

As for the perennial question of his lack of commercial success, John was as ever refreshingly honest, joking that his career has gone from obscurity to oblivion. 'Why am I not Eric Clapton or Phil Collins? I wouldn't want to be. Don't get me wrong. I wouldn't mind a yacht, a mansion and maidservants. But I don't care enough. I just love to play, to perform and the adulation. Let's be honest – I'm fifty-three years old. What could I spend it all on anyway?' (*Scotland on Sunday*, 8 September 2002). By now, John thought that being a success was when he could look himself in the mirror and not be ashamed by anything. Aspiring musicians were advised to persevere, use their heart not their head, and use the system rather than be used by it. In 2000, he told *Classic Rock*:

> The music industry isn't an intellectual challenge, but it is a moral challenge.
> If you can come through it clean, and live with yourself, then you're cool.
> But most musicians are a bunch of tossers. They think they're God's gift, but
> half of them can't play a damn thing.

The whole debate of why John Martyn was incapable of converting his undoubted talents into commercial success continued to surface in every interview, but really it was a misconceived question. He was born to play music, but his love of music was rivalled by his scorn for the industry and for the formulaic writing that blights the music business. John was not a sweatshop writer but always insisted that if he wanted to he could turn out hit singles for a living. So, he could have released an album of 'May You Never' copies every year and he could have had the Ferrari and the home in LA. But for all his dalliances into jazz, reggae, ambient or conventional riff-based rock, Martyn was always seen by many to be a folkie. And not just Western folk music: many types of ethnic music touched him – he once said his Desert Island Disc would be a record by the Ensemble de la République Bulgare. He was given the album by Sandy Denny and fell in love with the Bulgarian harmonies and rhythm. But the bottom line is that folk music is quite a hard commodity to sell to the public. Even Bob Dylan – the undoubted leader of the folk/acoustic scene from the early 1960s onwards – finds it hard to match record sales to his undoubted artistic reputation. Perhaps only The Beatles can top Dylan in terms of influence, but in terms of shifting records Dylan trails them by miles.

Consider Martyn's contemporaries in the 1960s British folk revival. The only one of that era to achieve lasting worldwide fame and acclaim is of course Billy Connolly. But, by his own admission, Connolly was a journeyman banjo player who made his name by moving away from strumming with groups like The Humblebums and instead capitalised on his remarkable ability to make people laugh. Innovators and mavericks such as Bert Jansch, Davey Graham, Roy Harper, Al Stewart and Nick Drake have always been the critics' favourites, but none of them has ever consistently troubled the charts. Of all the post-Donovan talents to emerge on the British folk scene, only Al Stewart made any major dent on the US top 30 – with his albums *Modern Times* and *Year of The Cat*. Compared to the majority of his contemporaries, John Martyn fared no better or no worse in terms of sales. John himself was unfazed by the lack of fame and fortune. For him, musical integrity always came first. In a promo interview in 2000 for the album *Glasgow Walker*, he said:

> It doesn't annoy me even vaguely because that stuff is a sideshow. I've accomplished my ambitions. I haven't made loads of money, but I've led a very comfortable life, I've had lots of fun and met some beautiful people. I think your spiritual status is far more important than the status of your career. I don't suffer fools gladly. I watch these music biz people talking absolute bollocks and I'll tell them it's nonsense. I don't obey the rules and I don't bow and scrape.

In the spring of 2003, news filtered onto the Martyn websites that John had to have his right leg amputated below the knee. The drastic action was necessary after doctors discovered that for the past seven years he had a cyst growing at the back of his knee. By the time the problem had been diagnosed, the cyst had grown to the size of a cricket ball. The cyst had been caused by a build-up of synovial fluid, thought to have been caused by years of putting weight onto the knee from his large Les Paul guitar. John told the reporter Aidan Smith how the cyst eventually burst and septicaemia ravaged through his leg:

Thinking back, there were lots of times when I fell off the stage. I remember getting booed in Cambridge because the crowd thought I was drunk. It was this motherfucker [his leg] that let me down and it vindicates me for those seven or eight years. All the other nights I fell over was down to pure and shameless over-indulgence!

Anyway, one day I got a jolt from an amp. I've had a few of these shocks in my time and normally I'm quick to recover from them – but six hours later I didn't feel at all cool. The cyst had popped. The leg was infected and the nerves were shot. One toe went in one direction, the one next to it in another, and my heel started climbing up my ankle. Man, it was painful, I couldn't walk.

Doctors told him there was no alternative to amputating the leg, and the grisly deed was done in Waterford Hospital in April 2003. (John told bedside visitors that 'the morphine was wonderful!') The trauma led to a spell where he felt bitter about why this had happened to him. His mood wasn't helped by the constant pain and the bizarre feeling that his toes were still there long after they had departed company from the rest of his body. In the years since the amputation, he went through ten prosthetic limbs. And without being able to exercise properly or go swimming, his weight ballooned up to well over twenty stones. But gradually he came to terms with the change in his life. He sometimes greeted his audience by asking if they needed the services of a one-legged sumo wrestler!

Spencer Cozens believes that John's attitude to life and his drinking probably contributed to the amputation.

> If you are into drink, then that is the centre of your life, you are not going to care about other things. If you need to get to the doctor at 11 a.m. to get your check-up then that is not going to be your priority for that day. I think there was a certain amount of that with John. Things were not getting dealt with, and I think that may have led to the leg amputation. So he could have saved the leg, but again in order to do that he would have had to say, 'Right, I mustn't do this and I mustn't do that' – which is just not John. So I suppose it was a fait accompli.

Dave Pegg of Fairport Convention, who played bass on many of John's classic recordings, told me how the amputation episode was not without its lighter side.

> I tell this story on the proviso that it is in no way meant to be unkind to John. But around that time Dave Swarbrick, our ex-fiddle player, had a double lung transplant. He was really ill in a Coventry hospital in intensive care before the transplant. He had tubes coming out of every part of his body and he couldn't talk. Now, I had heard that John had gone to see a medical expert before having his leg amputated. This doctor had reassured John that it was quite a common thing and patients who get an artificial limb get used to it, adding: 'Prosthetics are coming on in leaps and bounds!' So when I went to see Swarbrick, after talking to him for half an hour without reply, I was running out of things to say. So as a last resort I leant over him and whispered this story to him. Swarb's face just lit up! He gave this huge grin and started mouthing something to me. I couldn't understand what he was saying, so I got closer, till I could just make him out as saying: 'Get me his pedal board!'

In all, the amputation episode and the slow recovery process led to a two-year spell away from the music business. Financial pressures had left him effectively homeless, forcing him to sell his property, including the house in Lanarkshire. He claimed that his penury was because of his expenditure on cocaine; others say that it was because an ex-manager had not been paying income tax on his behalf. With no source of income, John had to rely on Teresa for support, together with the countless goodwill messages from fans on website message boards to see him through. Still struggling from the effect of prescribed painkillers, he didn't feel ready to record. But financial pressures meant he eventually began work on the album *On the Cobbles*. It was eventually released in April 2004: John wasn't entirely pleased with the results, calling it too clean and over-produced, even though it featured Paul Weller, Mavis Staples and The Verve guitarist Nick McCabe. When I interviewed him in a working man's bar near to the Tantallon Road of his youth, I asked him to sign the new CD. With a wink he scrawled the message 'Not under them' beneath the *On the Cobbles* logo. It was his way of saying that no matter how much his enemies wish him dead, he was still defying the odds. The track 'My Creator' was a standout: John called it a work in progress and a Buddhist-Baptist hymn. The track 'One For The Road' dated back to the 1970s and was 'his Val Doonican song'. Throughout his illness, John never lost the urge to perform and was determined to get back on the road – eventually achieving his aim, aged fifty-five, with a series of comeback gigs in Ireland. Sometimes he was wheeled on stage, sometimes he managed to waddle on, waving his walking stick to adoring crowds, before settling into his seat to play.

Talking to Aidan Smith, he reflected on the years of excess.

Aye well, sometimes I get angry about what's happened to me, but anything I had coming was well on its way. I've hammered my body all my life. If I wasn't playing rugby I was rock-climbing or deep-sea diving or fighting. Then I was flying round the world, doing drugs, staying out too late and drinking far too much. But anger is cool, you know, because I've always thrived on being aggressive and I can channel it into a positive vibe. The angrier I get the hipper and sweeter I seem to become. My excesses weren't like lollipops handed over at the school gates – I knew what I was doing with those drugs, man, and I went for it. Heroin and the rest, I loved every single piece of mince I took. It was a great feeling waking up in the morning and thinking 'Well, I tried that and I'm still alive.' But I know I'm a lucky bastard. I'm very lucky to have met Teresa. I used to be hopeless with women – I fell in love too easy or not at all. If your own family unit is bust, you can end up doubting love, and I made mistakes with both my marriages. Teresa is the only woman I've wanted to marry, and the only one I've asked. She's turned me down twice, and now I'm such a fat git after what's happened to my leg that I've broke her sofa. I've put on three-and-a-half stone because I haven't been able to go swimming. Basically, I go round in circles now. But I'm going to get a pair of flippers and lose some weight. Then maybe I'll ask her again.

The year 2004 also saw John get the tribute he has long deserved on TV with the airing of a documentary, *Johnny Too Bad* – first on the fledgling BBC4 and then to a much bigger audience on BBC 2. The one-hour special didn't pull any punches, and when John's contemporary Ralph McTell asserted that most men would be dead having done what John has done, it's hard not to disagree. The show spanned his whole fifty-five years, with rare home movies of the young Iain David McGeachy playing on holidays to the recording of *On the Cobbles* and John's first tentative comeback gigs. Teresa is seen pushing the wheelchair-bound star through the countryside. Two years later, Island Records finally succumbed to fans' demands and released *John Martyn at the BBC*, a stunning 154-minute retrospective of some of the great man's many shows at the Beeb. Watching them back to back – from the early *Old Grey Whistle Test* shows with Danny Thompson through to the solid jazz-funk workouts of the 1980s – is a welcome reminder of just why so many people love John Martyn and his music.

As he neared the age of sixty, John was realistic about the mistakes of the past. So many of his friends had paid the price for living on the edge – now he was more laidback about his own life and making friends more easily. John joked that his own survival against the odds had been down to his strong heart and strong will, allied to a plate of porridge and salt, whisky and five Woodbine cigarettes for breakfast every morning. He realised that too much time could be spent worrying about what could have been. On a visit to Martyn's home, the writer James McNair was given tea and cake while the mellow man puffed on a joint and played his Gibson SG superbly on two unreleased tracks, 'Took All My Colours' and 'Paddy Ronan'. When Teresa asked if James would like a glass of wine, Martyn gently scolded her saying: 'Darling, he is a Scotsman. That is a rhetorical question.' McNair asked about the lyrics for the song 'Ghosts', wondering if they alluded to long-gone friends like Drake and Kossoff. The reply showed a man increasingly aware of his own mortality.

Yeah . . . Some ghosts are more important than others. I'm not going to see Lord Johnson the 23rd walking around with his head under his arm, clanking chains – I'm going to see friends. Sometimes, I even see my own ghost in dreams. He says nothing at all – he just stares at me blankly. I mean, how rude can you get? Watching the BBC film was weird, there's footage of me as a little boy and as I am now, and because I've put on three stone since all this nonsense happened, I thought, 'What the fuck happened to me?' When I could still play guitar standing up, I'd sweat out eleven pounds a night, but that's not going to happen any more. You can't mess with Father Time, can you? He's going to catch you, whether you run fast or slow.

Willing to work

Someone who can write 'You curl around me like a fern in the spring' – that's the man that is going to be missed, not the guy who is chucking beer all over you and poking you in the chest.

Danny Thompson

Over the years I would say John has become more open and more approachable, a demonstrably more tender person. Actually, I believe that is the person that he has always been.

Bridget St John

John Martyn's final years were a strange mix of frustration and long-overdue recognition of the brilliance of his musical heritage. The frustration came through his inability to produce fresh material. With each new tour came a round of interviews where he promised a new album – but *Willing to Work* remains unreleased. His self-deprecating comment to me in 2006 that he did not know 'when or why it will see the light of day' was sadly prophetic. On a personal level though, he seemed a more content man. He said latterly that he honestly believed 'no man who has ever lived has had more fun than I have'.

The freak accidents and drunken rages became fewer although alcohol and hashish remained constants in his life. When I asked him once if he had ever tried the newer designer drugs like ecstasy he whispered in my ear 'Nah, the doctors tell me I need to take care of my heart'. The fact that he was puffing away on the largest joint I have ever seen in my life and had just ransacked the mini-bar in his Glasgow hotel room sent out a contradictory message! He continued to tour though his health made that very problematic. In the autumn of 2007, a short tour of Ireland had to be cancelled when John took ill and was rushed to hospital. A lack of accurate updates on his official website led to worrying rumours, and I was told by more than one Martyn fan that the star's condition was 'extremely serious'. So, his eventual re-emergence into public life came as a great relief, even though he must have known that the final curtain would fall soon. At one comeback concert he told the audience: 'Last night I prayed for death!'

Ironically for an artist never too keen to dwell on past glories, there was an upsurge of interest in John's classic recordings of the 1970s. Every hip young artist seemed eager to doff their cap to John. (Paolo Nutini has called Martyn one of the great soul singers.) On John's birthday, 11 September 2006, he gave in to the nostalgia freaks and performed the whole of his timeless masterpiece *Solid Air* album in front of a sell-out crowd at London's Barbican Theatre. The gig was part of the *Don't Look Back* series, where artists recreate classic albums. Other concerts included Iggy and the Stooges performing *Fun House* and Teenage Fanclub revisiting their finest hour with *Bandwagonesque*. Reaction to Martyn's show was generally favourable though there were reports of some fans leaving early, complaining that John was incoherent and that he hadn't played the songs in the correct sequence. John told the audience that to do so would have meant a lengthy change-over of instruments between songs. The critics, though, were as always wholly positive. Nick Coleman in *The Independent* loved the gig and told readers:

> Whether you're drunk or sober, in love or out, alone at night or entertaining by day, struggling with tax returns or sitting in a bath, *Solid Air* never fails to work. Which is a plain way of saying that its emotional, structural and technical integrity is of such a high order that there isn't a context in which it doesn't make life beautiful.

Inspired by such praise, John agreed to take the show on the road in January 2007, playing at selected venues throughout the UK. The following year he did a similar tour based around *Grace and Danger*.

On the eve of that tour, Spencer Cozens explained to me why John favoured reinterpreting his old favourites and why he much preferred the fun and companionship of playing with a band to going on the road solo.

People often say to him 'Oh why don't you play a song like "Solid Air" exactly like it sounds on the album?' The answer is that he recorded it that way over thirty years ago and now his voice doesn't sound the same as it did back then and he's not the same person. He has moved on, and if he doesn't want to do it the old way then he just will not do it that way. I have asked him why he doesn't play solo any more and he says that he just gets lonely. He likes the vibe of playing with a band. He likes the way that we all have to read each other when we are playing a gig. It's a communal thing, really. Life on the road with John is great fun, full of very pleasant memories. When we are all on the road we play this game 'Norman', where we are all in a restaurant and at the end of the meal each person has to say 'Norman' louder than the last person. The person who chickens out has to pay the bill. You get these mad nights on tours that are really off the wall. One night when we were on tour in Holland, we were playing 'John Wayne', and during that song there is a silence; and Alan just shouted out 'Norman' during the silence. It was just so funny, everyone just collapsed laughing. I think Arran almost fell off his drum stool. My best memories are of just hanging out and gigging with John. In the early years it was just a total buzz and then in the mid-1990s it went through a bit of a dip when he was changing record companies a lot. Around then it seemed like hard work, but over the past four or five years it's been real fun. For me, the gigs are now better than they ever were. There have been a few bad times, but if it ever gets nasty I just tell him that I don't want to be in his space and I leave the room.

The general consensus is that there were fewer and fewer in the way of nasty outbursts and that John grew more genial in his final years. Spencer Cozens saw many friends and partners come and go in over seventeen years with Martyn and he paid special tribute to Teresa's role in helping to rein in the excesses.

I suppose when you are in a wheelchair with only one leg and weigh twenty-four stone, you are going to have a different attitude to life. Teresa is an angel, a total star. She's very understanding and has a lot of energy. She keeps him in his place and gives up her life for him, but she is also honest with him. There's no bullshit with her: she doesn't see him as John Martyn, she sees him simply as an ordinary guy. She has helped facilitate certain things for him and has helped him an awful lot. She can also put him in his place when it's needed!

Right to the bitter end, Martyn remained at best indifferent to the music industry, but Cozens believed much of that is down to the 'men in suits' who failed to treat the singer in the right way.

Whenever we talk business it's very short and abrupt – it's just something we have to discuss to make the wheels go round. John's attitude is that people get too involved in percentages and contracts and he thinks that when people are like that they are not being themselves. The whole thing about his attitude to the men in suits is that in a way he sees the suit as a cover and a way of making everything uniform. John hates that – he sees through all the falsehoods and he wants to know the real person. If he doesn't see the real person, then you can forget it. There are plenty of people in the business who he gets on with and they are always the people who are straight up with him. His attitude is 'OK, we have to do business, but that is not really what life is all about.' It's the same with his playing, if he doesn't feel it is real, he is not going to do it. We have been in situations where record companies ask for an album, say, by Christmas, and that kind of way of doing things just puts him off. He has got to be chilled out and relaxed and in the right head space.

He is very much a now person – he doesn't really think about tomorrow or next week. Managers have come to him in the past and just talked business all day long and his attitude to them is 'just fuck off'. It's as absurd as someone like a grocer telling him how to play his music and how to run his life – he just thinks it's irrelevant. He also likes to keep things close to his chest all the time. That's why he has a disdain for the men in suits, though ironically that attitude has seen him shoot himself in the foot a couple of times. He has pissed people off who could actually have been very helpful to him. But then he has never lived his life in what people would consider to be 'the best way' for him. He has to tune into people's emotional soul one way or another.

When I was working on the first edition of this book I asked a number of John's friends how he would be remembered. Their answers then are still relevant today. His detractors sometimes argue that John somehow wasted his natural ability as a guitarist, singer and songwriter. But Ralph McTell gave short shrift to any question that Martyn was in some way a wasted talent.

No, he's not. I am a great admirer of John Martyn: he made three of the most masterful albums of his generation – *Solid Air*, *One World* and *Grace and Danger* are peerless works. If those were the only three albums he ever made, he should still be immensely proud. They are head and shoulders above most of the stuff that gets raved about. My thoughts on him come from an admiration and an attempt to understand him along with compassion for his condition.

Around the time of *Grace and Danger* he had the best manager in my brother, [Bruce May] he had the best producer in Martin Levan and he had the best record company. He was at the top of his powers; people like Eric Clapton and Phil Collins were queuing up to work with him. Maybe after those years he began to believe that he was as good as everyone was saying he was, and that is always a danger. I don't think he should have wandered into jazz; I love his mystical meandering on songs like 'Small Hours' and 'Solid Air'. If these songs don't move you, then there is something wrong with you. They are absolutely exquisite. Until John gets rid of the anger within him and gets back into the love thing, you will never hear those classic songs again. He needs to kick those machines he uses into touch and get back to acoustic guitar – it'll come around again.

Another survivor from the Cousins days, Steve Tilston, reflected on the friendship he had and lost with Martyn:

I don't know whether our paths will ever cross again. I suppose part of me would like it. I've mixed memories, but a lot of them still bring a smile to my face. I still remember him as a good-looking, curly-haired, baby-faced, young bloke. I am still one of those people who love his acoustic stuff. To tell you the truth, I haven't really heard much of his stuff over the last twenty-odd years. It seems almost formulaic now and has little relevance to my life –

maybe that does him a disservice, because other people love it. He was a great guitar player – very strong player, very strident. Great volume would come out of the guitar. Some people would play hunched over the guitar, playing pristine stuff – myself included – but John was right out there – in your face! He was a real one-off; *Bless the Weather* was a beautiful album.[1]

Wizz Jones is another who has very strong memories of Martyn at his peak.

When I think back to all the driving I did all over Europe during those years, the two artists I would listen to most on the van stereo were John Martyn and JJ Cale. I must have played *Solid Air* and *One World* for thousands and thousands of hours. I did buy some of his subsequent records, but for me they never reached those heights, and that is not to belittle his musical journey. A musician has got to go all the way and investigate everything there is, but obviously the drugs and booze did not help him physically. I know that John still maintains his devil-may-care attitude – in a way, he has the George Best syndrome. That is a danger for all artists. I'm very weak-willed and I know that if I had been a bigger success I would have been an alcoholic. You are up there on stage playing away and afterwards you are forever looking for a reward. I shall always think of John, like Bert Jansch and Robin Williamson, as a true Scottish original.

Though John seldom saw his old friend and favourite musical collaborator, Danny Thompson in the final years, the pair still had a strong emotional bond. Danny, who fretted a good deal over John's drinking habits, told me how special his time with John had been.

I think meeting him was God-sent and that these things happen for a reason. The duo we had was unlike anything else – I don't mean that it was better or worse, it was just different. And people really took to it. I always say that

1. Just prior to John's death, Steve Tilston wrote a lovely song 'The Devil May Care' about Martyn where he mused on their relationship and the chances of their paths crossing again. The song can be found on Steve's album *Ziggurat* and contains the lyric 'Oh, I want you to know that I wish you well, before you go. Before it's undone by the devil may care. From this land of the living to god knows where.'

the media does not give the public enough credit for being as open-minded as they are. If it is great and exciting music they will love it, whether it is jazz, folk or world music. I think John was a really innovative artist in what he was doing electronically alongside some great songwriting. John is a person who is passionate about his music. John swings! He writes good songs – and he swings. I said to him once: 'Why is a big soft teddy bear like you trying to build himself into this kind of belligerent, stroppy arrogant geezer?' Because he is really not like that. Someone who can write 'You curl around me like a fern in the spring' – that's the man that is going to be missed, not the guy who is chucking beer all over you and poking you in the chest. John is just a lovely, cuddly boy – he's an angel inside.

People talk about the wild days too much when really the most important thing for me is to have been with him and to have had this musical experience. It was a phenomenal experience to be on the stage with him doing that music, which was unlike anything else that other people were doing. We blew a lot of people away. The most important story is of John Martyn, the songwriter and great musical innovator.

Those who know John best are convinced that he mellowed over the final years. Bridget St John, who first met John back in the hazy days of 1967, lives in New York now and saw her old friend infrequently prior to his death. But she did visit him in Ireland once and was heartened by what she saw.

Over the years I would say John has become more open and more approachable, a demonstrably more tender person. Actually, I believe that is the person that he has always been. In the past, he let this tender side of his character show through the very beautiful music he has created; now I think it is coming through more in him as a person. John and I have a relationship that can be picked up wherever we last left. My feelings for him were set in motion in those early days and I choose not to judge him from what I read or hear about him because that is not my experience of him. Yes, I have experienced him high and strung-out, and worried about him and feared for him, but I know we all choose our paths and I accept him for everything he is – or at least everything I have experienced him to be – whenever our paths intersect.

The saxophonist Andy Sheppard also had great affection for Martyn and gave me a timely reminder of just what an important figure John is in the history of rock music.

John is really highly respected by so many musicians. He is an institution. When I played with him at the Island anniversary party at Pinewood, it was just incredible. I had been playing with the great American bandleader George Russell, the guy who discovered Bill Evans and actually introduced him to Miles Davis. I finished playing a festival in Bracknell with George around midnight and I had to get a car to Pinewood Studios. When I arrived, John said, 'Great to see you, come and meet the band.' He took me through security and into the dressing room and it was like walking into Madame Tussauds. There was Eric Clapton, Ringo Starr, Andy Summers and Lee 'Scratch' Perry – and we all played for an hour or so. And all these guys were doing it because they all have a great respect for John, but that has never come across to the wider public. But in a way, that is why his music is so great.

I rate John really highly. He just writes fantastic tunes and his music is so beautiful. I haven't seen him for a few years – every now and then he asks me to do something, but it always seems to be when I'm tied up in another country or doing other gigs. John has a fantastic guitar technique, especially his acoustic stuff. And his voice is just fantastic. Apart from all that he has always had a really strong concept of sound, creating a whole sound world while also writing fantastic songs. The really hard thing to do is write songs that stick around, and he can do it. I'm a fan. If more people listened to John's music, the world would be a better place.

In the end, maybe that's all that really matters about John Martyn and that is what will endure. For all his faults and frailties, his beautiful music really has made the world a better place. When you listen to a song like 'Small Hours' it's really a unique, wonderful sound he produces – with the Echoplex and his strange concussed vocals – it sounds like nothing that came before or indeed has been recorded since. You could argue – and many critics do – that John's musical reputation rests on a handful of records from over thirty years ago and that over the years of excess his song writing and guitar playing abilities were blunted. But if that is the case, then John is in good company. Just about every major recording artist of the 1970s has seen their creative output tail away in the subsequent years. It's an accusation that is often levelled at the likes of The Who, David Bowie, Paul McCartney and even Bob Dylan. John never did find a sympathetic producer and record company to help resurrect his career in much the same way as Johnny Cash did in his later years but given Martyn's predilection for pressing the self-destruct button maybe even that wouldn't have worked.

*

Near the end of his life, it would appear that John Martyn had finally admitted defeat in his war with the bottle. With some degree of irony, he was sober when he died; he had been dry for a number of weeks. He had completed a tour of the UK and played his last gig on 25 November 2008 and had already pencilled dates in Scotland for early 2009. I understand that he spoke to record company bosses three days before his death and sounded in good humour and optimistic about the future. He had received a new prosthetic limb which helped to ease the physical pain he was in. John was also extremely enthusiastic about the prospect of recording with one of his heroes, Pharaoh Sanders. But in the end the years of abuse caught up with John. His old friend Davie MacFarlane, told me 'One of the last times I saw him was backstage at a concert in Glasgow. I nearly started crying when I saw the way he had ended up. He was just so overweight and when he turned around to see people you could see that he was wincing in pain.'

In February 2008, John won a lifetime achievement award at the BBC Radio Two Folk Awards, held rather appropriately at a London venue called The Brewery. The award was presented to John by his old friend Phil Collins. Martyn performed refreshingly good versions of 'May You Never' and 'Over The Hill', accompanied on the latter by John Paul Jones of Led Zeppelin, on mandolin. Eric Clapton couldn't attend but sent a video message, telling the audience that, in his heyday, John was 'so far ahead of everything, it's almost inconceivable'. Later that year Martyn won the Les Paul award at the *Mojo* honours list. And at the start of his final month on this earth, it was announced that John was to become an OBE. It's just a crying shame that he didn't live to collect the award in person – a photo of John with Her Majesty would have been a wonder to behold!

John passed away on 29 January 2009. As he once predicted, his obituaries were stunning. Within hours of his death, websites were overflowing with heartfelt tributes from fans. Over sixty news organisations from South Korea to Canada paid tributes or noted his passing. He even got a mention on the BBC's leading current affairs programme *Newsnight*. Phil Collins issued an emotional tribute which spoke for many: 'He was uncompromising, which made him infuriating to some people, but he was unique and we'll never see the likes of him again. I loved him dearly and will miss him very much.' Chris Blackwell commented that John had probably done more for British folk and jazz than any other individual over the past fifty years.[2]

A memorial service was held in St Mary's Church in Kells, Kilkenny, and John's remains were later cremated at Newlands Cross in Dublin. His dearest friend Danny Thompson cut one of Martyn's curls to keep and gave his old partner a kiss and a hug. Danny recently told the BBC presenter Edi Stark, 'I miss him every day. If I could bring back one person of all the people I worked with it would be my John.' Just over a year after his death, it was reported that John had left a net estate of £82,000, quite an impressive amount considering the financial problems he had back in the 1990s and the fact that he had no lucrative recording contract at the time of his death. The *Mail on Sunday* reported that three-quarters of the estate went to Teresa with the rest going to John's daughter Mhairi. There was nothing left to his sons.

When I first spoke to John, he agreed to help with this book, but only if I went to stay with him in Ireland for a couple of days. To my eternal

---

2. Despite all the accolades, not everyone has been won over to the cause. A recent edition of BBC's *Mastermind* included the following exchange:

> Q: Which singer-songwriter who died in January 2009 wrote 'May You Never', which was covered by Eric Clapton on the *Slowhand* album?
> A: (after a long pause). . . . Reg Presley?

I think John would have enjoyed that!

regret that never happened – instead I met him on a half dozen occasions in hotels, backstage rooms and, of course, crowded bars. On every occasion he was charming company; witty, courteous and eager to help in my research, and fiercely intelligent. But inevitably the drink would get the better of him, he would grow melancholy and the interviews would end rather abruptly. It would have been wonderful to just sit and ask him in much more detail about things like his relationship with his mother and father, about Hamish Imlach and Nick Drake and about why he kicked every hard drug into touch and yet couldn't beat the booze.

I was lucky in that I only saw the angelic side of John's character, but as this book has shown he had a less attractive and boorish side. Violent behaviour – especially against women – is of course inexcusable but much of that behaviour can be attributed to his alcoholism (Linda Dunning told me that during their time together, before the heavy drinking set in, John never as much as raised a finger against her). Much of the antipathy towards John no doubt stems from his behaviour in his heyday, and while drug addiction will lead the most decent of men to do bad things, I'm certain that John did feel genuine remorse about the way his marriages ended. Hopefully through time the bad memories will fade and people will focus on his wonderful musical legacy. John was a flawed genius but a genius nonetheless. Bless the weather that brought him to us and curse the storm that took him away.

The Cousins Era

This gig list is taken from the pages of *Melody Maker*, which at that time focused mainly on the London scene. As a result, it is far from being a complete list of all the gigs John played between 1967 and 1971. John was certainly playing numerous gigs in the provinces and his native Scotland around this time, but they were seldom advertised in the national music press and are therefore almost certainly lost in time. I have transcribed the gig adverts as they appeared in the paper.

After 1971, John had graduated from the club scene into the universities and then into the main city halls. He did long tours sometimes two or three times a year and detailing every gig would take up too much space and be repetitive. Those who want to find out more about post-1971 gigs are advised to look at the excellent John Martyn website 'Big Muff', run by the redoubtable Hans van den Berk.

1967

April 13   Kingston Folk Barge – Steve Spurling, John Martin (sic).

April 27   Kingston Folk Barge – Jack Sheppard, John Martyn, Roger Hill.

May 11   Kingston Folk Barge – Jack Sheppard, John Martyn, Classic Washboard Band.

May 18   Kingston Folk Barge – Jack Sheppard, John Martyn and introducing Come All Ye.

May 25   Kingston Folk Barge – Jack Sheppard, John Martyn, Chris Mills, Steve Bridges.

June 9   Ewell Folk Club – John Martyn, Roger Hill.

July 5   Crawley Civic Hall – Alex Campbell, The Flint Hill Three (local blues group), Roger Evans, John Martyn, Roger Hill.

November 18   Cousins – all-nighter – 'Beverley', admission 5 shillings.

1968

February 9   Les Cousins, 7.30–11 p.m. – John Martyn (contemporary Scottish base (sic) songwriter). 5 shillings.

February 17	Les Cousins – all-nighter Gerry Lockram, John Martyn plus guests.
February 19	Putney, Folksville, Half-Moon – Gerry Lockram, special guest John Martyn, welcomed by Lisa Turner, Boyd Rivers, Fingers Lewis and guitarist Horace.
March 3	London – The Horseshoe – Tottenham Court Road – The Pentangle with guest John Martyn, 7.30 p.m.
March 17	The Horseshoe – Stefan Grossman, The Compendium, John Martyn.
March 24	London Troubadour – John Martyn, 9.30 p.m.
March 30	Cousins – 7.30–11 p.m. – an evening with three fine blue artists, Beverley, Wizz Jones, Dave Deighton (fine electric blues guitarist). All-night session, 12–7 an evening of organised chaos John Martyn, Ron Geesin, Ralph McTell. (*Author's note*: According to Ralph, John Martyn never played this gig, Roy Harper stood in for him.)
April 1	Richmond – The Vineyard Hanging Lamp Club – Scoopy (first UK appearance with special guest John Martyn plus Frank McConnell and Verity Stephens) 8.15 p.m.
April 6	Teddington, New Anglers – Steve Baker, John Martyn.
April 7	The Horseshoe, Tottenham Court Road – Stefan Grossman, John Martyn, 7.30 p.m.
April 13	Cousins – all-night session – John Martin (sic) and Mike Cooper. 12–7 a.m.
April 14	The Horseshoe – Stefan Grossman, John Martyn, Panama Ltd. Jug Band. 7.30 p.m.
May 5	Horseshoe – Mike Cooper, John Martyn. 7.30 p.m.
May 10	Cousins – John Martyn, Paul Wheeler.
May 11	The Horseshoe – Sandy Denny, John Martyn. 7.30 p.m.
May 13	Richmond – The Hanging Lamp – John Martyn plus residents and guests. 8.15 p.m.
May 15	Cousins – 7.30–11 p.m. – John Martyn, Paul Wheeler – admission 5 shillings.
May 29	Cousins – 7.30–11 p.m. – Paul Wheeler, John Martyn – admission 5 shillings.
June 2	Troubadour – John Martyn – 9.30 p.m.
June 5	Cousins – John Martyn, Paul Wheeler (two new contemporary artists) – 5 shillings.

June 8	Cousins June Ball 'Dress formal – rucksacks and Norwegian pullovers, well maybe' – all-night session 12–7 a.m. – Mike Cooper, John Martyn, bed socks and cocoa.
June 13	Sheffield Highcliffe Folk Club Festival – Ron Geesin, Stefan Grossman, John Martyn.
June 15	Sheffield Highcliffe Folk Club Festival – Hamish Imlach, The Jugular Vein, John Martyn (again).
June 19	Cousins – John Martyn and Paul Wheeler alternating with Clive Palmer and Wizz Jones, plus guests, 7.30–11 p.m. come early to obtain seats! – 5 shillings.
June 26	Cousins – 7.30–11 p.m. – John Martyn and Paul Wheeler, plus guests.
July 10	Cousins – 7.30–11 p.m. – Clive Palmer, Paul Wheeler, Wizz Jones, John Martyn.
July 17	Cousins – 7.30–11 p.m. – John Martyn, Clive Palmer.
July 22	Richmond, The Vineyard, at the Hanging Lamp – the Monday night club in the crypt of St Elizabeth's – John Martyn.
July 19	Westminster Central Hall – Folk concert in aid of Human Rights Year – 7 p.m. – Julie Felix, Al Stewart, The Fairport Convention, John Martyn, Shirley Bland, Doris Henderson, Theo Johnson, Stephen Delft, Mouse Proof, David Campbell.
July 24	Cousins – 7.30–11 p.m. – Paul Wheeler, John Martyn, Stephen Delft.
July 27	Cousins – 7.30–11 p.m. Davey Graham. All-night session – 12–7 a.m. – 'A magnificent guitarist from Hull' Mike Chapman, and a fine contemporary artist John Martyn, plus guests.
August 6	The Dungeon Club, The Copper, Tower Bridge Road – Cliff Aungier presents John Martyn, Shelagh MacDonald.
August 7	Cousins, London's folk and blues centre – 7.30–11 p.m. – John Martyn, Paul Wheeler – 5 shillings.
August 14	Cousins – John Martyn, Claire – 5 shillings.
August 21	Cousins 7.30–11 p.m. – John Martyn, Ian Anderson – 5 shillings.
August 27	Cousins – 7.30–11 p.m. – Clive Palmer, John Martyn.
August 29	Chelsea, La Fiesta – 168 Fulham Road – London's top late night folk and blues club – 10 p.m.–2 a.m. – John Martyn, a very fine contemporary guitarist and songwriter plus many guests.
August 30	Richmond Community Centre – 7.45 p.m. Al Stewart, John Martyn, Frank McConnell.

August 31	Cousins – 12–7 a.m. – Ralph McTell, John Martyn, two fine contemporary songwriters.
September 4	Cousins – 7.30–11 p.m. – John Martyn plus many guests – 5 shillings.
September 11	Cousins – 7.30–11 p.m. – John Martyn, Clive Palmer – Come early for seats. 5 shillings.
September 18	Cousins – John Martyn, Clive Palmer – 5 shillings.
September 25	Cousins – 7.30–11 p.m. – LP out soon – John Martyn.
September 28 and 29	Battersea Park Folk Festival at the open-air concert pavilion in aid of a Social Services Centre for Battersea – John Martyn, Shelagh MacDonald and Mike Absalom plus many others. 5 shillings admission to each concert.
September 30	The Phoenix, Cavendish Square – John Martyn, Helen Kennedy and Frank Taylor.
October 2	Cousins – 7.30–11 p.m. – John Martyn – 5 shillings.
October 6	Slough, Dolphin Folk Club – John Martyn – 5 shillings – with bar!
October 9	Cousins – 7.30–11 p.m. – John Martyn – 5 shillings.
October 19	Cousins all-nighter 12–7 a.m. – John Martyn, Peter Starstedt.
November 6	Cousins 7.30–11 p.m. – John Martyn, Gordon Giltrap – 5 shillings.
November 10	Bounds Green – Folk Club – John Martyn, Stuart Emms.
November 13	Cousins – John Martyn, Gordon Giltrap 7.30–11 p.m. – 5 shillings.
November 23	Greenwich Theatre Folk Club – John Martyn, Four Square Circle – 7.30 p.m.
November 25	Enfield, The Hop-pole – John Martyn, Stuart Emms.
December 7	Cousins – 7.30–11 p.m. – Marc Brierley, John Martyn (Jackson C. Frank doing the all-nighter).
December 16	Richmond, The Hanging Lamp – John Martyn, plus residents. 8 p.m.
December 27	Cousins – 7.30–11 p.m. John Martyn.

1969

| January 4 | Cousins – 7.30–11 p.m. – John Martyn, Dr Strangely Strange. |
| January 18 | Cousins – all-night session 12–7 a.m. – John Martyn, Beverley, Al Jones. |

February 4	Three Horseshoes Folk Club – John Martyn, plus your residents The Exiles.
February 14	Cousins – 7.30–11 p.m. – John Martyn, Beverley. 5 shillings.
February 24	Richmond, Hanging Lamp – John Martyn.
March 7	Cousins – John Martyn – 5 shillings.
March 21	Ilford – General Haverlock – John Martyn.
March 22	Cousins – 7.30–11 p.m. – John Martyn, Mike Chapman.
March 28	Cousins – 7.30–11 p.m. – Jackson C. Frank, John Martyn – 5 shillings.
March 29	Greenwich Theatre Folk Club – John Martyn, Jenni and Mary. 7.30 p.m.
April 7	Cousins – 7.30–11 p.m. – John Martyn – 5 shillings.
May 2	Cousins – 7.30–11 p.m. – John Martyn – 5 shillings.
May 5	Enfield Folk Club, the Hop-poles – John Martyn, The Folk Couriers.
May 12	Richmond, Hanging Lamp – John Martyn plus residents.
May 21	Rochford Folkus – John Martyn, 8 p.m.
May 24	Chalk Farm Roundhouse – benefit following death of Fairport Convention drummer Martin Lamble in M1 motorway crash – featuring Family, Pink Floyd, John Martin (sic) and Beverley amongst others.
May 29	Roehampton Digby Stuart College – John Martyn, floor singers welcome.
May 31	Cousins – all-nighter – John Martyn, Victor Brox, Keith Christmas.
August 22	Cousins – 7.30–11 p.m. John Martyn – 5 shillings.
August 30	Cousins – all-night session – John Martyn, Sam Mitchell.
September 9	Birmingham Mothers – weekly folk session – John Martyn, Ron Geesin.
September 12	Same day as festival below – Rugby Rag Festival – blues day— Alexis Korner, Groundhogs, John Martyn and others.
September 12	Farnham Folk and Blues Festival – first concert features The Johnstons, John Martyn, and Allen 'Spud' Taylor – 9 shillings (second concert was for blues acts).
September 20	Cousins – 7.30–11 p.m. – John Martyn, Keith Christmas.
October 2	Kingston College of Technology – Students Union – John Martyn, Johnny Silvo – 8 p.m.
October 19	Norwich Folk Club – John Martyn.

November 18	Barking College – John Martyn.
November 21	Ilford, General Havelock – John Martyn.
November 26	London College of the Distributive Trades – John Martyn, Rick Davey, Barry Youldon.
November 27	Mile End, Queen Mary College – John Martyn, 8 p.m.
December 2	Hayes Folk Club – John Martyn plus guests.
December 2	(Same date as above) – Watford College of technology – John Martyn.
December 19	Cousins – 7.30–11 p.m. John Martyn.

1970

January 8	Kingston Polytechnic Student Union – John Martyn 8 p.m.
January 16	Dorking Congregational Hall – Shelter with Bridget St John, John Martin (sic). 6 shillings, 7.30 p.m.
January 17	Cousins – 7.30–11 p.m. – John Martyn, Mike Cooper, Nick Drake.
January 21	London College for the Distributive Trades – John Martyn, Rick Davey, Barry Youldon.
January 23	Walthamstow Technical College – Concert in aid of Shelter. – John Martyn, Richard Digance, Gasworks, Terry Hutchings. 5 shillings, 7/6.
January 24	Greenwich Theatre Folk Club – John Martyn.
February 7	Cousins – 7.30–11 p.m. – John Martyn, Dr Strangely Strange.
February 7	Bristol Troubadour – John Martyn.
February 9	Putney Half-Moon – John Martyn, Cliff Aungier, Royd River, Gerry Lockran.
February 21	London Queen Elizabeth Hall – John and Beverley Martin (sic) and their musicians – a concert of contemporary songs, plus Nick Drake, tickets 20, 16, 12, and 8 shillings. A NEMS presentation.
March 5	Bedford College – John Martyn.
March 6	Hull University Folk Club – John Martyn.
March 14	Cousins – 7.30–11 p.m. – John Martyn, Dando Shaft (very good sensitive band of minstrels).
March 18	Holloway Northern Polytechnic – John Martyn.
April 18	Cousins – 7.30–11 p.m. – John Martyn.
May 8	Bedford College all-nighter – Nick Drake, John Martyn, Spencer Davis, Graham Bond etc.

May 22	East Ham – Denmark Arms – John Martyn, Chris Davies, Richard Digance.
May 23	Sheffield University – Principal Edwards Magic Theatre, Strawbs, and John Martyn.
May 29	Ware College – John Martyn, John James, John Foot – 8 p.m.
June 5	London City University – John Martyn, 8 p.m.
June 21	London Westfield College – Elton John, Stefan Grossman, John Martyn, and The Humblebums will take part in what is loosely termed as a 'folk event'. Starts after end of World Cup Final.
June 22	London Phonograph – John Martyn, Mythica – 7.30–11 p.m.
July 11	Cousins – John Martyn.
July 27	Richmond Hanging Lamp – John Martyn.
August 15	Cousins – 7.30–11 p.m. – John Martyn, Ceilidh at the House.
October 1	Kingston Polytechnic Folk Club – John Martyn – 8 p.m.
November 17 ·	Redruth Room at the Top – John Martyn.
December 7	London South Bank Students Union – John Martyn.

1971

January 2	Cousins – 7.30–11 p.m. – John Martyn.
January 11	Richmond Hanging Lamp – John Martyn – 8 p.m.
January 12	Hayes Folk Club – John Martyn, John Coverdale, Richard Bartram.
February 13	Cousins – 7.30–11 p.m. – John Martyn.
March 11	Guildford Civic Halls – John Fahey, Gordon Giltrap, John Martyn, Nick Grey, Bernie Roy.
March 18	Bradford University – Michael Chapman, John Martyn, and Dr Strangely Strange.
March 20	Cousins – 7.30–11 p.m. – John Martyn.
April 5	Richmond Hanging Lamp – John Martyn.
April 24	Cousins – 7.30–11 p.m. – John Martyn.
May 11	Kingston Get Stuffed – John Martyn – 8 p.m.
June 18	Sheffield University – Principal Edwards Magic Theatre, John Martyn.
June 19	Reading Town Hall – Michael Chapman, John Martyn, Wizz Jones, Pete Berryman. 7.30 p.m., tickets at door.
July 10	Cousins – 7.30–11 p.m. – John Martyn.
July 31	Cousins – 7.30–11 p.m. – John Martyn.
August 16	Richmond Hanging Lamp – John Martyn, 8 p.m., please come early!

September 4	Cousins – 7.30–11 p.m. John Martyn.
September 10	London Queen Elizabeth Hall – Sandy Denny, John Martyn, Duncan Browne (part of the Festival of Progressive Music at the QEH).
October 3	Chalk Farm Roundhouse – IMPLOSION! 3.30 p.m. – 11.30 p.m. – Fresh from Frisco – Stoneground, Brinsley Schwartz, John Martyn, Help Yourself, Derrick and Armstrong, Jeff Dexter.
October 23	Cousins – 7.30–11 p.m. – John Martyn.
October 30	London Festival Theatre – 7.30 p.m. – Loudon Wainwright III, John Martyn, Mr Fox, Ian Campbell Group, Jeremy Taylor.
November 4	Kingston Polytechnic – John Martyn, Roger Ruskin Spear, 8 p.m. – 35p (members).
November 9	London University College – Bridget St John, John Martyn.
November 12	Lancaster University – Amazing Blondel, Bronco, John Martyn. 60p.
November 18	London Queen Mary College – John Martyn, 7.45 p.m. – 30p.
November 25	Croydon Fairfield Halls – Amazing Blondel, John Martyn – 7.45 p.m.
December 19	Chalk Farm Roundhouse – IMPLOSION! – Mott the Hoople, John Martyn, England Dan and John Ford Coley, Brett Marvin and the Thunderbolts, Max Merritt and the Meteors. 3.30 p.m.– 11 p.m. – 50p.

Selected discography

The following is a list of John's official album releases. Anyone wanting more information on the many re-releases on CD along with compilations, remastered and expanded versions, etc., is best advised to check the websites (see page 252) which are crammed with every detail on Martyn's recording career. The same goes for single releases, memorably dismissed by John as 'cheap, disposable, nasty and tasteless'.

LONDON CONVERSATION (Released October 1967 ISLAND ILP 952)
Fairy Tale Lullaby/ Sandy Grey/ London Conversation/ Ballad Of An Elder Woman/ Cocaine Blues/ Run Honey Run/ Back To Stay/ Rolling Home/ Who's Grown Up Now?/ Golden Girl/ This Time/ Don't Think Twice.

The impressive title track was co-written by John Sundell, a New Yorker who was friendly with Martyn back in 1967.

THE TUMBLER (December 1968, ISLAND ILPS 9091)
Sing A Song of Summer/ The River/ Goin' Down To Memphis/ The Gardeners/ A Day At The Sea/ Fishin' Blues/ Dusty/ Hello Train/ Winding Boy/ Fly On Home/ Knuckledy Crunch And Slipp Ledee Slee Song/ Seven Black Roses.

Some critics argued that the track 'Fishin' Blues', which John is credited with, bears remarkable similarity to a song recorded by Henry 'Ragtime Texas' Thomas.

STORMBRINGER (February 1970, ISLAND ILPS 9113 with Beverley Martyn)
Go Out And Get It/ Can't Get the One I Want/ Stormbringer/ Sweet Honesty/ Woodstock/ John The Baptist/ The Ocean/ Traffic Light Lady/ Tomorrow Time/ Would You Believe Me?

Around this time John seemed to have a strong interest in the tale of John the Baptist. Visitors to his London home told me how the Martyns had a print hanging on their toilet door showing Salome holding John the Baptist's head.

THE ROAD TO RUIN (November 1970, ISLAND ILPS 9133 with Beverley Martyn)
Primrose Hill/ Parcels/ Auntie Aviator/ New Day/ Give Us A Ring/ Sorry To Be
So Long/ Tree Green/ Say What You Can/ The Road To Ruin.

The front cover engraving is taken from the surreal collage novel Une Semaine de
Bonte *by the German writer Max Ernst.*

BLESS THE WEATHER (November 1971, ISLAND ILPS 9167)
Go Easy/ Bless The Weather/ Sugar Lump/ Walk On The Water/ Just Now/ Head
And Heart/ Let The Good Times Come/ Back Down The River/ Glistening
Glyndebourne/ Singing In The Rain.

*The title track was selected by the award-winning English actor Colin Firth as one
of his all-time favourite songs when he was a guest on Steve Earle's American radio show.*

SOLID AIR (February 1973, ISLAND ILPS 9226)
Solid Air/ Over The Hill/ Don't Want to Know/ I'd Rather Be The Devil/ Go
Down Easy/ Dreams By The Sea/ May You Never/ The Man In The Station/ The
Easy Blues.

Five songs from the album would feature in the 1998 BBC film Titanic Town, *set
in Belfast and starring Julie Walters.*

INSIDE OUT (October 1973, ISLAND ILPS 9253)
Fine Lines/ Eibhi Ghail Ghiuin Ni Chearbhaill/ Ain't No Saint/ Outside In/ The
Glory Of Love/ Look In/ Beverley/ Make No Mistake/ Ways To Cry/ So Much In
Love With You.

*The album's second track translates from Irish as 'The Fair and Charming Eileen
O'Carroll'.*

SUNDAY'S CHILD (January 1975, ISLAND ILPS 9296)
One Day Without You/ Lay It All Down/ Root Love/ My Baby Girl/ Sunday's
Child/ Spencer The Rover/ Clutches/ The Message/ Satisfied Mind/ You Can
Discover/ Call Me Crazy.

*'Satisfied Mind' has also been recorded by Johnny Cash, Jeff Buckley and Daniel
O' Donnell, though sadly not at the same time.*

LIVE AT LEEDS (September 1975, ISLAND ILPS 9343)
Outside In/ Solid Air/ Make No Mistake/ Bless The Weather/ The Man In The
Station/ I'd Rather Be The Devil.

*Although originally only on a mail-order basis, the album was subsequently also sold
to fans on a 1975 UK tour and at Virgin record shops.*

SO FAR SO GOOD (March 1977, ISLAND ILPS 9484 compilation)
May You Never/ Bless The Weather/ Head And Heart/ Over The Hill/ Spencer
The Rover/ Glistening Glyndebourne/ Solid Air/ One Day Without You/ I'd
Rather Be The Devil.

'Spencer the Rover' was selected by the actress Kristin Scott Thomas as one of her Desert Island Discs.

ONE WORLD (November 1977, ISLAND ILPS/ZCI 9492)
Couldn't Love You More/ Certain Surprise/ Dancing/ Small Hours/ Dealer/ One
World/ Smiling Stranger/ Big Muff.

The song 'Certain Surprise' had originally been titled 'Sweet Day' during demos recorded in November 1976.

GRACE AND DANGER (October 1980, ISLAND ILPS/ICT 9560)
Some People Are Crazy/ Grace And Danger/ Lookin' On/ Johnny Too Bad/ Sweet
Little Mystery/ Hurt In Your Heart/ Baby Please Come Home/ Save Some For
Me/ Our Love.

It's agreed now that Chris Blackwell delayed the album's release because he found the subject matter too upsetting. But, an alternative, less plausible reason given for the delay was that the album sat uneasily in a music scene dominated by punk rock.

GLORIOUS FOOL (September 1981, WEA K/K4 99178)
Couldn't Love You More/ Amsterdam/ Hold On My Heart/ Perfect Hustler/
Hearts And Keys/ Glorious Fool/ Never Say Never/ Pascanel (Get Back Home)/
Didn't Do That/ Please Fall In Love with Me/ Don't You Go.

The front cover shot is by German photojournalist Eberhard Grames.

WELL KEPT SECRET (August 1982, WEA K/K4 99255)
Could've Been Me/ You Might Need A Man/ Hung Up/ Gun Money/ Never Let
Me Go/ Love Up/ Changes Her Mind/ Hiss On The Tape/ Back With A
Vengeance/ Livin' Alone.

The album reached number 20 in the UK charts, John's best show to date, yet it has been voted his worst album by fans. Go figure.

PHILENTROPY (November 1983, BODY SWERVE JMLP 001 live album)
Sunday's Child/ Don't Want To Know/ Johnny Too Bad/ Make No Mistake/ Root
Love/ Lookin' On/ Hung Up/ Smiling Stranger.

Featured keyboard player Ronnie Leahy is best known for his work with Scots band Stone the Crows.

SAPPHIRE (November 1984, ISLAND ILPS/ICT 9779)
Sapphire/ Over The Rainbow/ You Know/ Watching Her Eyes/ Fisherman's
Dream/ Acid Rain/ Mad Dog Days/ Climb The Walls/ Coming In On Time/
Rope Soul'd.
   *Though John produced the album, six different engineers are credited on the
sleevenotes.*

PIECE BY PIECE (February 1986, ISLAND ILPS/ICTCID 9807)
Nightline/ Lonely Love/ Angeline/ One Step Too Far/ Piece By Piece/ Serendipity/
Who Believes In Angels?/ Love of Mine/ John Wayne.
   *Keyboard player Foster Paterson previously worked with Any Trouble and David
Knopfler.*

FOUNDATIONS (October 1987, ISLAND ILPS/ICT/CID 9884 live album)
Mad Dog Days/ Angeline/ The Apprentice/ May You Never/ Deny This Love/
Send Me One Line/ John Wayne/ Johnny Too Bad/ Over The Rainbow.
   Recorded on 13 November 1986, live at the Town and Country Club, London.

THE APPRENTICE (March 1990, PERMANENT PERM CD/MC/LP 1)
Live On Love/ Look At The Girl/ Send Me One Line/ Hold Me/ The Apprentice/
The River/ Income Town/ Deny This Love/ UPO/ Patterns In The Rain.
   'Income Town' was recorded live at the Green Banana club in Toronto.

COOLTIDE (November 1991, PERMANENT PERM CD/MC/LP 4)
Hole In The Rain/ Annie Says/ Jack the Lad/ Number Nine/ The Cure/ Same
Difference/ Father Time/ Call Me/ Cooltide.
   *John likened his guitar playing on 'Jack the Lad' to the style of his early hero Bukka
White.*

COULDN'T LOVE YOU MORE (October 1992, PERMANENT PERM CD/MC/LP 9)
Lonely Love/ Couldn't Love You More/ Sweet Little Mystery/ Head And Heart/
Could've Been Me/ One Day Without You/ Over The Hill/ Fine Lines/ May You
Never/ One World/ Ways To Cry/ Angeline/ Man In The Station/ Solid Air/
Never Let Me Go.
   Mojo magazine selected this compilation as the Martyn album to avoid at all costs.

NO LITTLE BOY (July 1993, PERMANENT PERM CD/MC 14 old songs reworked)
Solid Air/ Ways To Cry/ Could've Been Me/ I Don't Wanna Know/ Just Now/
One Day Without You/ Sweet Little Mystery/ Pascanel/ Sunday's Child/ Head

And Heart/ Fine Lines/ Bless The Weather/ Man In The Station/ One World/ Rock Salt And Nails/ Hole In The Rain.

Anton Corbijn, who took the wonderful cover shot for this album, selected 'One World' when The Word *magazine asked celebrities to pick the most underrated album of all time.*

AND (August 1996, GO! DISCS 828798–2/-4)
Sunshine's Better/ Suzanne/ The Downward Pull Of Human Nature/ All In Your Favour/ A Little Strange/ Who Are They?/ Step It Up/ Carmine/ She's A Lover.

'A Little Strange' was co-written by Detroit soul singer Leon Ware who carries business cards introducing him as 'The Sensual Minister'. 'Sunshine's Better' is a favourite track of the actor Michael Caine, who selected it as one of his 'chill-out' tracks on the 2007 album Cained.

THE CHURCH WITH ONE BELL (March 1998, INDEPENDIENTE ISOM 3CD)
He's Got All The Whiskey/ God's Song/ How Fortunate The Man With None/ Small Town Talk/ Excuse Me Mister/ Strange Fruit/ The Sky Is Crying/ Glory Box/ Feel So Bad/ Death Don't Have No Mercy.

During the recording sessions the lyrics of some songs had to be faxed up from London to John.

GLASGOW WALKER (May 2000, INDEPENDIENTE ISOM 15CD)
So Sweet/ Wildflower/ The Field Of Play/ Cool In This Life/ Feel So Good/ Cry Me A River/ Mama T/ Can't Live Without/ The Cat Won't Work Tonight/ You Don't Know What Love Is.

John's son, Spenser McGeachy, is one of the engineers credited on the sleevenotes.

ON THE COBBLES (April 2004, INDEPENDIENTE ISOM 43CD)
Baby Come Home/ Under My Wing/ Ghosts/ Back To Marseilles/ Cobbles/ My Creator/ One For The Road/ Go Down Easy/ Walking Home/ Goodnight Irene.

'Baby Come Home' was originally recorded by John as part of a tribute album to Frankie Miller, the gutsy Glasgow singer who was recovering from a brain haemorrhage.

In the last few years there has been a rush of live recordings, mostly released on the One World record label. Most are of excellent quality. Two live recordings with Danny Thompson, *Live in Germany 1986* and *Live at the Brewery Arts Centre 1986*, are especially worth listening to – links to buying the CDs are available on the Martyn websites. *Mad Dog Days* (Shakedown Records, 2004) is a good quality box set which mixes live and studio recordings, and it has the added bonus of a DVD interview with John.

For DVDs look no further than *John Martyn at the BBC*, a splendid 154-minute showcase of John's finest work at the Beeb, from 1973 to 1982.

Bibliography and sources

Magazine articles

Melody Maker – 11 November 1967 – 'The future's beginning again for Beverley' by Tony Wilson

Melody Maker – 28 February 1970 – 'Is John Martyn still a folk singer or not?' by Jeremy Gilbert

Melody Maker – 26 December 1970 – 'John and Beverley – on the road to Scotland' anonymous

Melody Maker – 18 December 1971 – 'Martyn – between head and heart' by Andrew Means

Melody Maker – 27 January 1973 – 'Music speaks for Martyn' by Andrew Means

Melody Maker – 10 February 1973 – 'American music scene' by Todd Tolces

NME – 21 July 1973 – 'The Stormbringer comes into the sun' by Ian Macdonald

Sounds – 18 August 1973 – 'Music on impulse from John Martyn' by Jerry Gilbert

Supersnazz – October 1973 – 'A happy man talking with John Martyn' by Andy Childs and Les Ord

Melody Maker – 13 October 1973 – 'John Martyn inside out' by Geoff Brown

Let It rock – December 1973 – 'Fire and water. The elemental, avant-garde John Martyn' by Dave Laing

Melody Maker – 16 February 1974 – 'John Martyn with love' by Geoff Brown

Zigzag – April/May 1974 – 'Talking with John Martyn' by Andy Childs

NME – 25 January 1975 – 'Mister Martyn makes whoopee' by Neil Spencer

Sounds – 1 February 1975 – 'Life after dark' by Jerry Gilbert

NME – 15 February 1975 – 'Out of the wishing well': Paul Kossoff interview by Steve Clarke

Guitar Player – May 1975 – 'John Martyn: A fingerpicking Brityn' by Dan Hedges

Street Life – 1–14 November 1975 – 'Martyn and Garfunkel: eyeballs and a cocoon' by Angus Mackinnon

NME – 29 November 1975 – 'The bitterest beard in Britain' by Rod McShane

Liquorice # 4 – January/February 1976 – 'Singing in the rain' by Malcolm Heyhoe and Paul Hunter

Zigzag – March 1977 – 'Up to date with John Martyn' by Andy Childs

Sounds – 5 March 1977 – 'Blood, sweat and cheers' by Vivien Goldman

Gongster – 24 January 1978 – 'John Martyn – talking through *Solid Air*' by Dave Beblin

Atem – number 12 – March 1978 – interview with Gerard Nguyen and Xavier Beal

NME – 25 October 1980 – 'Johnny so good' by Angus Mackinnon

NME – 29 November 1980 – 'John Martyn: the exorcism' by Nick Kent

NME – 10 October 1981 – 'Johnny done badly' – by Chris Salewicz

NME – 4 September 1982 – ' 'Ello John, got a new album?' by Danny Baker

History of Rock – March 1983, Number 29, 'The great musicians: John Martyn' by Tony Bacon

Moondogs – April 1983 – Dutch Radio 3 – interview with Bram van Splunteren and Wim Bloendaal

Music UK – June 1983 – 'John Martyn' by Max Kay

Musin' Music – 12 November 1984 – *Sapphire* interview by Rob O'Dempsey

BBC Radio One – *Saturday Live* – 25 May 1985 – interview about Nick Drake by Richard Skinner

Piece by Piece promo box set – February 1986 – interview with Trevor Dann

Musin' Music – 1 May 1986 – interview by Rob O'Dempsey

International Musician and Recording World – March 1989 – interview with John Perry on fretwork

Q – September 1989 – Danny Thompson interview on playing bass

Zip Code – March 1990 – 'John Martyn – living on love' by Kevin Ring

BBC *Radio One* – April 1990 – interview with Nicky Campbell

Q – May 1990 – 'Same again' by Mark Cooper

Guitarist – June 1990 – 'The acoustic-electric John Martyn' by Rick Batey

Record collector – April 1991 – John Martyn by Chas Keep

Sunday Times – 28 September 1991 – 'Down that lonesome road' by Jonathan Futrell

International Musician – December 1991 – interview by Keith Grant

Dirty Linen – October–November 1992 – 'The triumphant return of John Martyn' by Lahri Bond

Chicago Sun-Times – 17 December 1992 – 'Martyn's moments make the music' by Dave Hoekstra

The Guitar magazine – 7 August 1994 – 'Grace and danger' by Paul Tingen

Mojo – October 1994 – 'The boy can't help it' by Nick Coleman

Record Collector – September 1996 – 'Frog to Prog' by Stuart Penney and Chris Savage

Discoveries – November 1996 – 'John Martyn' by Chris Nickson

Mojo – March 1998 – 'The bell! The bell' by David Hepworth

The Daily Telegraph – 21 March 1998 – 'The two-minute interview' by Casper Llewellyn Smith

Uncut – April 1998 – Solid Airs – 'The church with one bell': review by Nigel Williamson

The Wire – June 1998 – 'Feeling gravity's pull' by Rob Young

Magnet – September 1998 – interview with Mitch Myers

The Sunday Times – 7 May 2000 – 'Going quietly now' by Mark Edwards

London Live – 31 May 2000 – radio interview with Robert Elms

iCast website – May 2000 – 'From art school to recording artist' interview by Mike Conway

Classic Rock – June 2000 – 'The talented Mr Martyn' by Andy Robson

The Scotsman – 27 June 2000 – Q & A interview

Solid Air deluxe liner notes – 21 July 2000 – by John Wood

Mojo – August 2000 – 'John's karmic journey' by James McNair

Uncut – December 2000 – 'Emotional rescue' – *Solid Air* in Classic Albums revisited by David Stubbs

Mojo – May 2001 – 'Been gone so long': interview with Beverley Martyn by Bob Stanley

Newsprint – March 2002 – 'Live in your living room' by John Hillarby

Scotland on Sunday – 8 September 2002 – 'Battered and bruised . . . but still standing' by Adam Lee Potter

The Guardian – 15 November 2002 – Phil Collins feature in Home Entertainment

Scotland on Sunday – 25 April 2004 – 'I'm still standing' by Aidan Smith

The Independent – 5 May 2004 – 'Heaven can wait' by James McNair

Daily Telegraph – 15 May 2004 – 'Cultural baggage' by Hedge Seel

Uncut – June 2004 – 'A record that changed my life': interview by Rob Hughes

Uncut – July 2004 – 'John Martyn/Leeds February 1975' by Allan Jones

The Sunday Herald – 22 May 2005 – 'The thinking man's drinking man' by Alan Taylor

The Herald – 26 November 2005 – 'I've had a wonderful time' by Graeme Thomson

Mojo – August 2006 – 'Wading through hell . . .' interview with Mat Snow

The Independent – 17 September 2006 – 'Who killed my echo machine?' by Nick Coleman

Uncut – November 2006 – 'John Martyn: album by album' by Paul Moody

Books

Cod Liver Oil and The Orange Juice, Ewan McVicar and Hamish Imlach, Mainstream, 1992

Blue Suede Brogans: Scenes from the Secret Life of Scottish Rock Music, Jim Wilkie, Mainstream, 1992

All That Ever Mattered: The History of Scottish Rock and Pop, Brian Hogg, Guinness Publishing, 1993

Love Is the Drug, John Aizlewood (ed.), Penguin, 1994; the final chapter – *Johnny Too Bad* by Mark Cooper – is about John Martyn

Streets of London: The Official Biography of Ralph McTell, Chris Hackenhull, Bordon, Northdown, 1997

Phil Collins: The Definitive Biography, Ray Coleman, Simon Schuster, 1997

Nick Drake: The Biography, Patrick Humphries, Bloomsbury, 1998

Heavy Load: Free, David Clayton and Todd K Smith, Moonshine Publishing, 2000

Stoned, Andrew Loog Oldham, Secker & Warburg, 2000

Dazzling Stranger: Bert Jansch and the British Folk and Blues Revival, Colin Harper, Bloomsbury, 2000

Al Stewart: The True Life Adventures of a Folk Rock Troubadour, Neville Judd, Helter Skelter, 2002

Be Glad: An Incredible String Band Compendium, Adrian Whittaker (ed.), Helter Skelter Publishing, 2003

White Bicycles – Making Music in the 1960s, Joe Boyd, Serpent's Tail, 2006

John Martyn: Grace & Danger, Lee Barry, Lulu, 2006

Websites

Martyn fans are lucky to have the choice of two superb websites. *www.johnmartyn.com* is the link to a fine official site with extensive information on the man and his music. *www.johnmartyn.nl* is a Dutch site with a fantastic variety of detail. Many of the articles mentioned above can be read in full at this site.

Index

About the author

John Neil Munro lives in Laxdale on the Isle of Lewis. He is a former student of the University of Glasgow, New College, Florida, and the Centre for Journalism Studies in Cardiff. His other books are *The Sensational Alex Harvey* (Polygon 2008) and *When George Came to Edinburgh* (Birlinn 2010).